W9-AXH-453

FIGHTING DISEASE WITH FOOD

FIGHTING DISEASE WITH THE AMAZING POWER OF FOOD

FAMILY HOME
CHRISTIAN BOOKS

FIGHTING DISEASE WITH FOOD
Copyright © 2019 by Remnant Publications

All Rights Reserved
Printed in the USA

Published by
Remnant Publications
649 East Chicago Road
Coldwater, MI 49036
(800) 423-1319
www.remnantpublications.com

Compiled by: Colleen Louw
Cover Designer: David Berthiaume
Text Designer: Nicole Warren
ISBN: 978-1-5136-0570-8

10 9 8 7 6 5 4 3 19 20 21 22 23 24

DISCLAIMER

The medical information contained in this book is provided for informational purposes only, to inform the reader of the nutritional, preventative and curative value of foods and recipes. While the information provided is appropriate, it is of a generalized nature and not specific to any individual set of health circumstances. It is not intended to be a substitute for professional medical advice, diagnosis or treatment. Always seek the advice of your physician or qualified health care provider regarding your medical condition or treatment before undertaking a new health care program. Some foods can cause allergic reactions in sensitive individuals, and some foods can have negative reactions when combined with medications. Dietary supplements are not to be used in place of dietary nutrients found in food, or to replace medications unless indicated by your health care provider. The publisher and compiler cannot assume responsibility for problems that arise from the inappropriate use of foods or recipes by the reader.

Contents

Introduction

"You are what you eat!" If you pause for a moment to seriously think about it, this saying is often true! Good nutrition is the key to building healthy cells. Healthy cells build healthy bodies, leading to recovery from disease and good health. Fruits, vegetables, legumes, grains, nuts and seeds provide your body with a vast array of nutrients that are needed for health recovery and the prevention of disease.

This volume is designed to serve as an introduction to some of the dietary nutrients that may be helpful in dealing with the health concerns reviewed in this book.

Regularly eating the nutrients or foods suggested will not bring about a miracle cure or guarantee to heal you in a short space of time. Rather, regular intake of the nutrients your body needs will help to restore nutritional balance and aid in the healing of disease.

We have suggested only a few nutrients and foods for each health condition. With careful research you will find there are multiple foods that provide the same dietary nutrients. Eating a wide variety of fruits, vegetables, legumes, grains, nuts and seeds in sensible quantities is encouraged. This will eliminate boredom and help keep you motivated about improving your health naturally.

We have suggested a few simple ways to use the various foods we have highlighted. This is only to get you started. There are multiple ways these foods can be prepared, within the guidelines given for good health.

There is an index of recipes for each fruit, vegetable, cereal, grain, nut or seed recommended. It is not an exhaustive index, but provides ideas to get you started on your journey to healthier eating for better health. Recipes that contain ingredients marked with an asterisk(*), indicate that the recipe for this item is available elsewhere in this book. Please consult the recipe index to find it.

Most ingredients used in this volume are available from local supermarkets. There are, however, a few instances in which you may need to purchase ingredients from a health food store or online.

No specialized kitchen equipment is needed to prepare the recipes in this volume except for a blender and a simple food processor. Investing in your health may mean you need to make a small investment in your kitchen, too.

Nutrition plays a vital role in health recovery, but, embracing all Ten Guidelines for Good Health is essential for health recovery. Faithfully take one step at a time to incorporate the health principles and nutrients suggested into your lifestyle, and you will soon be on your way to better health.

Foods That Optimize Health

The Original Diet

Athletes know that for peak performance optimal nutrition is essential, and that the foods they consume have a direct effect on their bodies. The laws of life and health that winning athletes follow are closely linked to the original laws of life and diet that God gave to mankind. God said, "See, I have given you every herb that yields seed which is on the face of all the earth, and every tree whose fruit yields seed; to you it shall be for food" (Genesis 1:29, NKJV). The ideal diet given in the Garden of Eden was fruit, nuts, seeds and grains. Later, when sin began, we find in Genesis 3:18 that vegetables ("herbs") were added. Much later God gave permission for man to eat the flesh of animals, but with that their lifespan was greatly diminished. God designed humanity to thrive on a whole food, plant-based diet, and modern science is starting to prove this is true.

God is as truly the author of physical laws as He is the author of the moral law. His law is written with His own finger upon every nerve, every muscle, every faculty, which has been entrusted to man. And every misuse of any part of our organism is a violation of that law. All should have an intelligent knowledge of the human frame that they may keep their bodies in the condition necessary to do the work of the Lord.[10]

Fresh Fruit and Vegetables

Nutrition and health status can be dramatically improved by adding more fruit and vegetables to the diet. The nutrition derived from fresh fruit and vegetables is perfectly designed to benefit the human body. Packed with vitamins, minerals, antioxidants, phytochemicals, bioactive compounds and fiber, fruits and vegetables are the ideal foods for regaining and maintaining health. The risk of developing chronic disease, such as heart disease, decreases with the regular consumption of a wide variety of fruit and vegetables.[1] All types of fruit are highly beneficial to health, however, dark orange citrus fruits have been found to be effective in reducing the risk of disease. Cruciferous, dark-green leafy, and deep yellow and orange vegetables also play an important role in the prevention of disease.[2] The majority of individuals do not consume adequate quantities of fruit and vegetables daily. The USDA's dietary guidelines suggest that half of the plate should be made up of fruit and vegetables,[3] and the Loma Linda School of Public Health suggests that individuals should consume three to four servings of fruit and five to nine servings of vegetables each day.[4]

VEGETABLES: 6–9 servings per day.
1 serving = 1 cup leafy vegetables, or ½ cup fresh chopped vegetables, or ½ cup cooked vegetables.

FRUITS: 3–4 servings per day.
1 serving = 1 medium sized fruit, or 1 cup berries, or 1 cup chopped fruit or ¾ cup fruit juice or ¼ cup dried fruit.

Whole Grains

Grains such as brown rice, corn, barley, quinoa, millet and oat groats are always best used as unrefined as possible. They provide a good supply of nutrients including B vitamins (folate, riboflavin, niacin and thiamin), minerals (magnesium, iron, selenium) and dietary fiber. The B vitamins play a vital role in metabolism and are essential for a healthy nervous system. Iron carries oxygen in the blood, and helps to prevent iron-deficiency anemia. Magnesium is used to build bones, and selenium has a protective effect on the cells, preventing oxidation. The dietary fiber contained in grains helps to lower cholesterol, and works to reduce the risk of type 2 diabetes, heart disease and obesity. Dietary fiber is essential for maintaining good bowel function.[5]

GRAINS: 5–12 servings per day.
1 serving = ½ cup cooked grains, rice or pasta, or 1 slice bread, or ½ bagel, or 3-4 crackers.

Legumes and Soy

Legumes are an inexpensive source of good quality protein. There are many varieties of beans available such as black beans, pinto beans, soy beans, navy beans, lentils, garbanzo beans, lima beans, and broad beans, to mention only a few. Beans are low in fat, high in protein, and provide many vitamins, minerals and essential nutrients. High in fiber, they help to lower cholesterol, normalize bowel movements, stabilize blood sugars, and reduce obesity.[6] To reduce any gaseous after effect, soak legumes for 12 to 24 hours before cooking, pour off the soaking water, rinse thoroughly, and then cook them in new clean water.

LEGUMES AND SOY: 3 servings per day.
1 serving = ½ cup cooked beans, peas, lentils, soy, or ½ cup tofu, or 1 cup soy beverage.

Nuts and Seeds

Nuts are high in protein and unsaturated fatty acids, which help to lower bad cholesterol levels. They are one of the best plant-based sources of omega-3 fatty acids, which contribute to heart health. The fiber found in nuts not only helps to lower cholesterol, but also helps to satisfy the appetite, thus reducing the desire to overeat. Nuts also contain valuable nutrients such as vitamin E, plant sterols and L-arginine, which help to keep arteries healthy.[7] Regular consumption of seeds in modest amounts helps to lower obesity, normalize triglycerides, reduce inflammation, and decrease the risk of cardiovascular disease.[8]

NUTS AND SEEDS: 2 servings per day.
1 serving = 1 ounce nuts and seeds or 2 tablespoons nut butter or tahini, or ¼ cup nuts.

Healthy Fats

Not all fats need to be eliminated from the diet, but choosing healthy fats is important. Fats are needed in small quantities and are essential for a providing energy and for the healthy functioning of the body. The best way to consume fats is in the whole form such as eating avocados, nuts, seeds, or olives. If refined oil is going to be consumed, cold pressed olive oil is often preferred. Cold pressed oils are preferable as less vitamins and phytosterols are destroyed through this method of refining. Oils provide the body with simple fats, as well as vitamin E. Liposoluble vitamins A, D, E and K require healthy fats to assist and transport them in the body, and to improve their absorption. Healthy fats help to promote heart health, healthy liver function, control cholesterol and prevent constipation.[9]

VEGETABLE OILS: 1–2 servings per day.
1 serving = 1 tablespoon olive oil, or ¼ avocado, or 23 olives, or 1 tablespoon salad dressing.

Healthy Sweets

Fresh fruits are high in natural sugars, however they will not put stress on the body if they are eaten whole and with their natural fiber intact. The fiber in fruit aids in slowing down the absorption of the sugar into the blood stream.[11] Occasional simple desserts made from whole grains, dried or fresh fruits, nuts and seeds will not damage the health. Refined sugars should be avoided as they deplete the body of valuable nutrients and contribute toward disease.[12]

SWEETS: Optional
1 serving = ⅛ naturally sweetened fruit pie, or 1 tablespoon naturally sweetened fruit preserve.

Ten Guidelines for Good Health

Pure air, sunlight, abstemiousness, rest, exercise, proper diet, the use of water, trust in divine power – these are the true remedies. Every person should have a knowledge of nature's remedial agencies and how to apply them.[1]

Nutrition

- Eat a simple, whole food, plant–based diet consisting of a wide variety of fruit, vegetables, unrefined grains, nuts and seeds.
- For optimal health avoid all animal products, processed foods, excessive salt, saturated fat, refined sugar, artificial sweeteners, colors, flavors and preservatives.
- Eliminate hot spices, caffeine and alcohol. These substances irritate the stomach, have a negative impact on healthy cells and often lead to disease.
- Eat a large breakfast, moderate–sized lunch and if you do eat supper, make it very light. Supper should be eaten three hours before bedtime so that digestion does not interfere with sleep quality.
- Plan to have your meals at regular times, at least five hours apart, as the stomach functions best on a regular schedule.
- Eliminate snacking between meals. Snacking delays stomach emptying and can lead to fermentation of partially digested food, which ultimately negatively affects health.
- It is preferable not to drink much with your meals as this dilutes digestive enzymes.
- Avoid overeating as this causes disease and clouds the mind.
- Enjoy mealtimes, eat slowly and chew food well for optimum digestion.

Grains, fruits, nuts, and vegetables constitute the diet chosen for us by our Creator. These foods, prepared in as simple and natural a manner as possible, are the most healthful and nourishing. They impart a strength, a power of endurance, and a vigor of intellect that are not afforded by a more complex and stimulating diet.[1]

Exercise

- Plan ahead and schedule time each day to exercise.
- Plan to complete 30 minutes of aerobic exercise 3 times a week. Brisk walking in the open air is one of the best and safest exercises. Aim to walk at least two miles a day.
- Plan to complete 30 minutes of flexibility and strength training alternate days, 3 times a week.
- If you don't have a 30–minute block of time to exercise, break it down into two blocks of 15 minutes.

- Vary your exercise to make use of all your muscles.
- Let your body rest one day a week from training and do gentle walking instead.
- Choose a good attitude and make exercise fun.

Walking - where it is possible, is the best remedy for diseased bodies, because in this exercise all the organs of the body are brought into use - By it the circulation of the blood is greatly improved.[2]

Water

- Drink a minimum of six to eight, eight-ounce glasses of water daily, enough to ensure the urine is pale. Drink two glasses of water on rising, three glasses during the morning, and three glasses during the afternoon. Water may be drunk in the evening if needed.
- Drink your water and liquids more than fifteen minutes before meals, or at least an hour after meals.
- Limit drinking with meals to five ounces or less as the additional liquid dilutes the digestive juices and slows down digestion.
- Bathing or showering daily helps to eliminate toxins and improve circulation. Good circulation is essential for optimum health.

Pure water is one of heaven's choicest blessings. Its proper use promotes health…Drunk freely, it helps to supply the necessities of the system and assists nature to resist disease.[1]

Sunlight

- Open the curtains, windows, and doors and let the sunshine into your home. Sunlight helps to destroy disease–causing germs.
- Spend a minimum of ten to twenty minutes in the sunshine each day. Sunlight improves circulation, stimulates the metabolism, promotes healing, lessens stress and improves mental health.
- Avoid sunburn by not sleeping in the sun or sunbathing around noon, and by wearing protective clothing as needed.

Sunlight…is one of nature's most healing agents…the precious sunlight may fade your carpets, but it will give a healthful color to the cheeks of your children.[2]

Temperance

- Be mindful of when you eat, what you eat, how much you eat. Don't overeat.
- Choose to eliminate all substances such as caffeine, alcohol, tobacco and drugs, which damage cells and compromise your health.
- Avoid overwork. Learn to relax and spend time with family and friends.

Abstemiousness in diet and control of the passions, will preserve the intellect and give mental and moral vigor, enabling men to...discern between right and wrong, the sacred and the common.[2]

Air

- Improve your lung function by learning to breathe deeply. Breathing deeply oxygenates the blood, helps eliminate toxins, soothes the nerves and helps to relieve stress.
- Open the windows and let the fresh air in. Breathing fresh air improves circulation and helps you to sleep better.
- Flood your body with oxygen by exercising.
- Quit smoking.

Exercise, and a free, abundant use of the air and sunlight,—blessings which Heaven has bestowed upon all,—would in many cases give life and strength to the emaciated invalid.[2]

Rest

- Have your last meal at least three hours before going to bed.
- Walking for half an hour after supper may help you sleep better.
- Go to bed at a regular time and plan on seven to eight hours sleep in a 24-hour period. For best sleep, bedtime should be no later than 10 p.m.
- Slow down and change pace: take a walk, work in the garden, or pursue a hobby.
- Take one day a week to rest: go to church, fellowship with friends or go out in nature.

The stomach, when we lie down to rest, should have its work done, that it may enjoy rest...The work of digestion should not be carried on through any period of the sleeping hours.[3]

Trust in Divine Power

- Invite God into your day and talk to Him about everything.
- Take time for spiritual development. Spend time studying the Bible and praying.

- Enjoy worship and fellowship with other believers at least once a week.
- Give your worries and anxieties to God.

The religion of the Bible is not detrimental to the health of the body or of the mind. The influence of the Spirit of God is the very best medicine that can be received by a sick man or woman.[4]

Gratitude

- Count your blessings; be grateful for all you have today! Keep a gratitude journal.
- Express your gratitude to your family and friends for the things they do—be specific.
- Look for opportunities throughout the day to give thanks to God for the little things.

Nothing tends more to promote health of body and of soul than does a spirit of gratitude and praise.[1]

Service

- Take time to listen to a family member. Help them with something that matters to them.
- Reach out to your neighbors and do something to encourage or surprise them.
- Volunteer for a few hours a week and make someone's life better.
- Regularly find a way to express gratitude to those who serve in the community.

Every kind and sympathizing word spoken to the sorrowful, every act to relieve the oppressed, and every gift to supply the necessities of the destitute, given or done with an eye single to God's glory, will result in blessings to the giver.[5]

"I beseech you therefore, brethren...that ye present your bodies a living sacrifice, holy, acceptable unto God....be not conformed to this world: but be ye transformed by the renewing of your mind, that ye may prove what is that good, and acceptable, and perfect, will of God."

Romans 12:1–2 KJV

ACNE

The local inflammation of the skin when hair follicles become blocked by dead skin cells. Sebum accumulates in the sebaceous glands, making them swollen and inflamed, and causing eruptions on the skin. Acne commonly occurs on the face, neck, chest, shoulders and back.

Food	Health Benefits	How To Use	Composition (based on Cup)
Papayas	Papaya promotes elimination of waste products through the urine, reducing the accumulation of impurities on the skin. High in vitamin A, it helps to build healthy skin.[1,2]	Tropical Fruit Salad: combine chopped papaya, pineapple, kiwi, banana, and mango, and the juice of 1-2 freshly squeezed oranges.	Fresh Papayas Carbohydrate: 14 g Fat: 0 g Protein: 1 g Sodium: 4 mg Vitamin A: 1,531 IU Vitamin C: 86.5 mg Calcium: 33.6 mg
Butternut Squash	Butternut, like all vegetables, promotes efficient elimination of waste, and is particularly high in vitamin A. It also contains vitamin C, calcium and a small amount of iron.[1,2]	Baked Butternut: Cut a triangle out of the flesh on the wider end of the butternut. Place the whole butternut in a baking dish. Roast in the oven at 400°F until tender.	Baked Butternut Carbohydrate: 16 g Fat: 0 g Protein: 1 g Sodium: 6 mg Vitamin A: 14,883 IU Vitamin C: 29.4 mg Calcium: 67.2 mg
Peas	Peas are high in niacin and contain vitamins A and C, calcium and iron, which are essential for healthy skin and hair. High in fiber, they assist in the elimination of toxins from the body.[1,2]	Green Pea Guacamole: Process 1 peeled, chopped avocado, 3 chopped green onions, 2 cloves garlic, 16 ounces thawed frozen peas, 4 tablespoons lime juice, and a pinch of salt, until smooth. Enjoy with vegetable sticks or crackers at mealtime.	Fresh Green Peas Carbohydrate: 21 g Fat: 1 g Protein: 8 g Sodium: 7 mg Niacin: 3.0 mg Vitamin A: 1,109 IU Vitamin C: 58 mg
Avocados	Vitamin E found in avocado works with vitamin A to build healthy skin cells.[1] Avocados are a source of fiber which helps detoxify the body and contain calcium which promotes a clear skin.[2]	Creamy Avocado Pasta: process 1 avocado, 1 clove garlic, ¼ cup fresh basil leaves, 1 tablespoon olive oil, 1 tablespoon fresh lemon juice, a little water as needed and salt to taste, until creamy. Stir into hot cooked pasta.	Fresh Avocados Carbohydrate: 13 g Fat: 22 g Protein: 3 g Sodium: 11 mg Vitamin C: 15 mg Calcium: 18 mg Iron: 0.8 mg
Pumpkin Seeds	Pumpkin seeds are an excellent source of zinc and calcium. Zinc helps to suppress bacteria and promotes the efficiency of the glands. Calcium assists in maintaining the PH balance of the skin.[1]	Tropical Fruit and Seed Oatmeal: Top a bowl of cooked oatmeal with finely chopped pineapple and papaya, sliced banana, coconut flakes and green pumpkin seeds.	Dried Green Pepitas Carbohydrate: 25 g Fat: 63 g Protein: 34 g Sodium: 25 mg Calcium: 59.3 mg Iron: 20.7 mg Zinc: 10.3 mg
Soybeans	Soybeans, as well as the foods made from them, such as soymilk and tofu, contain phytoestrogens that help to balance the hormones, which reduces the risk of acne.[2]	Mixed Berry Smoothie: Blend 2 cups fresh or frozen mixed berries, 1 sliced banana, 1 cup plain unsweetened soy milk and one tablespoon honey until smooth and creamy.	Plain soy milk Carbohydrate: 8 g Fat: 4 g Protein: 7 g Sodium: 119 mg Calcium: 299 mg Iron:1.1 mg Zinc: 0.6 mg

HEALTH TIP: Breathing fresh air, daily exercise and adequate rest will assist in eliminating acne.

ADHD

Attention deficit hyperactivity disorder is a chronic condition which begins in childhood and may last into adulthood. This brain disorder manifests itself persistently though symptoms such as difficulty in concentrating and paying attention, impulsive behavior and hyperactivity.

Food	Health Benefits	How To Use	Composition (based on Cup)
Bananas	Vitamin B6 found in bananas is an essential nutrient needed for producing brain chemicals such as dopamine, serotonin and norepinephrine, which play a role in maintaining normal behavior.[1]	Banana Peanut Butter Smoothie: Blend 1 sliced fresh or frozen banana, 2 tablespoons of unsweetened peanut butter, 1 date, and 1 cup unsweetened non-dairy milk.	Fresh Bananas Carbohydrate: 34 g Fat: 0 g Protein: 2 g Sodium: 2 mg Vitamin B6: 0.6 mg Magnesium: 40.5 mg Iron: 0.4 mg
Apricots	Apricots are a good source of iron, a key nutrient for the healthy development of the central nervous system. Iron deficiency may lead to decreased attention span and behavioral disorders.[2]	Apricot Date Balls: Process 1 ½ cups dried apricots, ¾ cup pitted dates, 1 cup chopped almonds, 1 cup unsweetened desiccated coconut. Add just enough water to be able to form small balls. Roll in coconut and refrigerate.	Dried Apricots Carbohydrate: 81 g Fat: 1 g Protein: 4 g Sodium: 13 mg Vitamin B6 0.2 mg Iron: 3.5 mg Zinc: 0.5 mg
Chia Seeds	Chia seeds contain omega-3 fatty acids which assist brain cell communication, and facilitate the normal transmission of the neurotransmitters serotonin and dopamine in the brain.[3]	Banana Chia Pudding: Blend 1 ½ cups non-dairy milk, ½ cup unsweetened peanut butter, and 2 ripe bananas. Pour into a bowl. Stir in three tablespoons of chia seeds. Cover. Refrigerate for at least 5 hours before serving.	Chia Seed Carbohydrate: 72 g Fat: 51 g Protein: 26 g Sodium: 31 g Calcium: 1,029 mg Zinc: 5.71 g Omega-3: 28,610 mg
Peanuts	Zinc found in peanuts is a cofactor for enzymes which play a role in the metabolism of neurotransmitters. Zinc deficiency slows mental development, leads to impaired concentration and contributes to hyperactivity.[2]	Peanut Apricot Trail Mix: Combine ½ cup peanuts, ½ cup cashews, ½ cup almonds, ½ cup sunflower seed, ½ cup pumpkin seed, ½ cup unsweetened dried banana slices, ½ cup raisins and ½ cup dried apricot chunks. Store in a glass jar.	Dry Roasted Peanuts Carbohydrate: 31 g Fat: 73 g Protein: 35g Sodium: 9 mg Vitamin B6: 0.4 mg Magnesium: 257 mg Selenium: 11 mcg
Soybeans	Tofu, which is made from soybeans, contains the minerals zinc, phosphorous, selenium, and calcium, as well as protein and riboflavin which work together to decrease the risk of ADHD.[4]	Scrambled Tofu: Sauté one chopped onion in a little olive oil. Add one package crumbled tofu, ½ teaspoon cumin, ½ teaspoon turmeric, ½ teaspoon onion powder, ½ teaspoon garlic powder, salt to taste. Stir-fry until slightly browned.	Regular Tofu Carbohydrate: 4 g Fat: 12 g Protein: 20 g Sodium: 18 mg Phosphorus: 240 mg Selenium: 22 mcg Zinc: 2 mg
Navy Beans	Navy beans contain magnesium which helps to activate approximately 300 enzymes and controls some of the processes of the central nervous system. Magnesium deficiency can cause neuromuscular hyperactivity.[2]	Navy Bean Hummus: Process 1 ½ cups cooked navy beans, 2 tablespoons tahini, ½ teaspoon garlic powder, ½ teaspoon onion powder, ¼ teaspoon cumin, 2 tablespoons lemon juice, 2 tablespoons olive oil, and salt to taste.	Cooked Navy Beans Carbohydrate: 48 g Fat: 1 g Protein: 15 g Sodium: 0 mg Magnesium: 96.4 mg Phosphorus: 262 mg Zinc: 1.9 mg

ENCOURAGEMENT: Put your trust in the Lord, and do not be afraid.[5]

ALZHEIMER'S DISEASE

A progressive disease which causes degeneration and death of brain cells, and results in a steady decline in memory and mental function. It begins with mild memory loss, progressing to mental confusion, apathy, and in many cases depression. It is the most common cause of dementia, and results in the loss of intellectual and social skills..

Foods	Health Benefits	How To Use	Composition (based on Cup)
Blueberries	Blueberries contain many antioxidants including vitamins A, C and E, which are absorbed into the cells to protect them against oxidization by free radicals.[1]	Blueberry Pecan Oatmeal: Top a bowl of cooked oatmeal with fresh, ripe blueberries, a tablespoon of chopped pecans, and a drizzle of honey.	Fresh Blueberries Carbohydrate: 21 g Fat: 0 g Protein: 1 g Sodium: 1 mg Vitamin A: 79.9 IU Vitamin C: 14.4 mg Vitamin E: 0.8 mg
Collard Greens	Silicon, found in green leafy vegetables such as collard greens, helps prevent absorption of aluminum.[2] They also contain folic acid, which helps to keep homocysteine levels from going too high.[3]	Sautéed Collard Greens: Shred collard greens finely. Sauté lightly with chopped garlic and a little olive oil. Squeeze a little lime juice over sautéed collard greens when ready to serve.	Cooked Collards Carbohydrate: 9 g Fat: 1 g Protein: 4 g Sodium: 30 mg Folate: 177 mcg Vitamin A: 15,416 IU Vitamin C: 34.6 mg
Black-Eyed Peas	Tryptophan, found in black-eyed peas, cannot be produced by the body. The body needs an adequate amount of this amino acid to prevent and deal with neurological disorders.[4]	Black-Eyed Pea Soup: In a large pot combine 2 cups shredded collard greens, 6 cups vegetable broth, ½ cup each chopped carrots, celery, and onion, and minced garlic until tender. Add cooked black-eyed peas and salt to taste.	Boiled Black-Eyed Peas Carbohydrate: 36 g Fat: 1 g Protein: 13 g Sodium: 7 mg Vitamin A: 25.8 IU Calcium: 41.3 mg Magnesium: 91.9 mg
Flaxseeds	Vitamin E, an antioxidant found in flaxseeds, not only protects neurons from free radicals, but also helps to repair the neurons in the areas that the neurotransmitters enter them.[5]	A tablespoon of ground flaxseeds can be blended into fruit smoothies or sprinkled on cereal. It can also be mixed into yogurt and applesauce, or sprinkled over a vegetable salad.	Ground Flaxseeds Carbohydrate: 32 g Fat: 48 g Protein: 16g Sodium: 32 mg Calcium: 286.4 mg Magnesium: 438.4 mg Folate: 97.6 mg
Carob	Carob contains calcium, which helps to prevent the absorption of aluminum into the body.[5] It also contains magnesium, which supports adequate biochemical reactions necessary for brain health.[6]	Hot Carob Drink: Whisk 1 cup non-dairy milk and 1 tablespoon carob flour in a saucepan on medium heat. Add 1 tablespoon honey and 1 teaspoon vanilla extract.	Carob Powder Carbohydrate: 92 g Fat: 1 g Protein: 5 g Sodium: 36 mg Calcium: 358 mg Magnesium: 55.6 mg Vitamin A: 14.4 IU
Buckwheat	Magnesium found in buckwheat contributes to building a healthy nervous system, and plays an important role in maintaining health of the brain and preventing Alzheimers.[6]	Buckwheat Salad: Combine cooked buckwheat with red onion, broccoli florets, yellow pepper, green olives, chopped walnuts, dill, mint, lime juice, and a little olive oil and salt.	Buckwheat Carbohydrate: 122 g Fat: 6 g Protein: 23 g Sodium: 2 mg Calcium: 30.6 mg Magnesium: 393 mg Folate: 51 mcg

DID YOU KNOW? 30 to 60 minutes of exercise, several times a week, helps to keep your brain sharp.[7]

ANEMIA

A condition in which the body does not have an adequate supply of red blood cells or hemoglobin. Hemoglobin assists in carrying oxygen to the cells in the body. Fatigue results when the organs don't get the oxygen they need to function properly. Anemia can also cause symptoms such as shortness of breath, palpitations and a paler than normal skin color.

Foods	Health Benefits	How To Use	Composition (based on Cup)
Molasses	Blackstrap molasses is a rich and safe source of iron supplementation and preferable to iron supplements, which sometimes carry health risks.[1]	Pumpkin Pie Smoothie: Blend 1 cup non-dairy milk, ½ cup cooked pumpkin, 1 teaspoon blackstrap molasses, 1 teaspoon pumpkin pie spice, and one fresh or frozen banana.	Molasses Carbohydrate: 252 g Fat: 0 g Protein: 0 g Sodium: 125 mg Iron: 15.9 mg Calcium: 691 mg Magnesium: 816 mg
Soybeans	Soybeans are good source of iron and folate, nutrients the body needs in order to be able to create new red blood cells.[2]	Soybean Hummus: Process 2 cups cooked soybeans, ½ cup water, 3 teaspoons lemon juice, 2 medium cloves garlic, and 1 teaspoon of salt. Enjoy with carrot and celery sticks, or on dried crackers.	Cooked Soybeans Carbohydrate: 17 g Fat: 15 g Protein: 29 g Sodium: 2 mg Iron: 8.8 mg Folate: 92.9 mcg Vitamin C: 2.9 mg
Asparagus	The folic acid found in asparagus helps to optimize the cellular processes of the body, enabling it to produce sufficient red blood cells.[3] It also contains iron, which helps prevent deficiency.	Steamed Asparagus: Place asparagus in a steamer basket over boiling water for two to six minutes. Cover. Steam until soft enough to pierce. Drizzle with a little olive oil and lemon juice. Add salt to taste.	Cooked Asparagus Carbohydrate: 8 g Fat: 0 g Protein: 4 g Sodium: 26 mg Vitamin C: 13.8 mg Folate: 268 mcg Iron: 1.6 mg
Beets	Beets provide a good supply of folic acid, a nutrient essential to the manufacture of red blood cells.[3] They also provide vitamin C, which helps with the absorption of iron.[1]	Beet Veggie Salad: On individual plates layer baby spinach, shredded beets, shredded carrots, cooked quinoa, edamame, slivered almonds, cubed avocado and cilantro. Drizzle with a little lime juice and olive oil.	Fresh Beets Carbohydrate: 13 g Fat: 0 g Protein: 2 g Sodium: 106 mg Folate: 148 mcg Iron: 1.1 mg Vitamin C: 6.7 mg
Turmeric	Turmeric provides the body with some of the iron required to make red blood cells. A deficiency in iron has been linked with deficiency anemias, often found in the ailing or elderly.[3]	Mix one tablespoon of powdered turmeric very thoroughly into the non-dairy milk of your choice. Drink one to three times a day with meals.	Turmeric Powder Carbohydrate: 65 g Fat: 16 g Protein: 16 g Sodium: 48 mg Folate: 41.6 mcg Iron: 44.8 mg Vitamin C: 27.2 g
Oranges	Vitamin C as well as the folic acid found in citrus fruit such as oranges helps with iron absorption.[1, 3] The folic acid also optimizes cellular processes supporting the production of red blood cells.[3]	Orange Salad Dressing: Blend 3 tablespoons orange juice, 1 teaspoon honey, 3 teaspoons lime juice, ½ ripe avocado, 3 tablespoons olive oil, ¼ teaspoon cumin, and salt to taste.	Fresh Orange Juice Carbohydrate: 26 g Fat: 0 g Protein: 2 g Sodium: 2 mg Folate: 74.4 mcg Iron: 0.5 mg Vitamin C: 124 mg

ENCOURAGEMENT: Strength and grace can be found in prayer.[4]

ANXIETY

A recurring feeling of nervousness, fear and apprehension because of a perceived danger, a feeling that is difficult to control and may be out of proportion to the actual danger. Anxiety can cause physiological changes in the body such as sweating, trembling, dizziness and a rapid heartbeat.

Foods	Health Benefits	How To Use	Composition (based on Cup)
Walnuts	Walnuts are a rich source of omega-3 fatty acids, which may help to lower the level of cytokines resulting from nervousness and this may help to reduce anxiety.[1,2]	Walnut Pesto: Process ½ cup walnuts, 2 cups fresh basil, 1-2 cloves garlic, ¼ cup olive oil, and salt to taste. Use on pasta or sandwiches or mix with grains.	English Walnuts Carbohydrate: 16 g Fat: 76 g Protein: 18 g Sodium: 2 mg Magnesium: 185 mg Potassium: 516 mg Omega-3: 10,623 mg
Bananas	Bananas contain carbohydrates, vitamin B6, magnesium and potassium. A deficiency in any of these nutrients has been found to contribute toward anxiety.[3]	Banana Sunflower Seed Oatmeal: Top a bowl of oatmeal with sliced banana, chopped strawberries, 2 teaspoons sunflower seeds and a drizzle of honey.	Sliced Bananas Carbohydrate: 34 g Fats: 0 g Protein: 2 g Sodium: 2 mg Magnesium: 40.5 mg Potassium: 537 mg Choline: 14.7 mg
Millet	Millet is a good source of phosphorous, which is required for the efficient functioning of the brain. A deficiency in phosphorous is a factor contributing to anxiety.[4]	Millet Veggie Salad: Combine cooked millet with chopped cucumber and tomato, yellow bell pepper slices, sliced green onions, a little fresh parsley and mint, olive oil, lemon juice and a little salt.	Cooked Millet Carbohydrate: 41 g Fat: 2 g Protein: 6 g Sodium: 3 mg Magnesium: 76.6 mg Potassium: 108 mg Phosphorous: 174 mg
Barley	The complex carbohydrates found in barley may help to increase the serotonin levels in the brain. Having adequate serotonin has a calming effect on the body.[5]	Barley Burgers: Mash 2 cups cooked barley and 2 cups cooked pinto beans. Add ½ cup finely chopped onion, ½ teaspoon sage, ¼ cup flour, 1 tablespoon olive oil and 1 teaspoon salt. Form into burgers. Bake at 360˚F for 40 minutes, turning over after 20 minutes.	Cooked Pearl Barley Carbohydrate: 44 g Fat: 1 g Protein: 4 g Sodium: 5 mg Phosphorous: 84.8 mg Choline: 21 mg Zinc: 1.3 mg
Mung Beans	The choline found in mung beans helps to maintain the central nervous system and prevent choline deficiency, which contributes toward causing anxiety.[6]	Mung Bean Sprouts: Rinse and then soak two tablespoons mung beans in water; cover for 8 hours. Drain. Rinse. Place in jar and cover top with cheesecloth and hold cloth on with an elastic band. Keep in cool dark place. Rinse and drain every 12 hours for 2-5 days until sprouted.	Sprouted Mung Beans Carbohydrates: 6 g Fat: 0 g Protein: 3 g Sodium: 6 mg Potassium: 155 mg Choline: 15 mg Zinc: 0.4 mg
Sunflower Seeds	Sunflower seeds contain zinc, an important trace element. Zinc helps alleviate the symptoms of anxiety that can be caused by a zinc deficiency.[7]	Sunflower Seed Smoothie: Blend 1 ¼ cups non-dairy milk, 1 sliced banana, 1 slice fresh pineapple, 2 tablespoons sunflower seeds and 1 teaspoon honey	Sunflower Seeds Carbohydrate: 28 g Fat: 72 g Protein: 29 g Sodium: 13 mg Magnesium: 455 mg Potassium: 903 mg Zinc: 7 mg

DID YOU KNOW? A contented mind, a cheerful spirit, is health to the body and strength to the soul.[8]

ARTERIOSCLEROSIS

A condition in which the arteries become thicker and start to harden, which occurs in the heart as well as elsewhere in the body. When arteries harden they restrict the flow of nutrient-laden, oxygen rich blood to organs, muscle and tissues. This can lead to stroke, heart attack or eventual organ failure.

Foods	Health Benefits	How To Use	Composition (based on Cup)
Kiwifruit	Kiwifruit is high in vitamin C, an antioxidant which may reduce the risk of and slow down hardening of the arteries. It may also be helpful in maintaining flexibility of the arteries.[1]	Kiwifruit can be peeled and sliced up or cut in half and scooped out with a spoon. Diced kiwifruit fruit can be sprinkled on hot or cold cereal, waffles or pancakes, or blended into a fruit smoothie.	Fresh Kiwifruit Carbohydrate: 28g Fat: 0 g Protein: 2 g Sodium: 10 mg Vitamin A: 318 IU Vitamin C: 136.4 mg Magnesium: 54.7
Pomegranates	The antioxidants in pomegranate juice, including vitamin C, may help to keep the arteries flexible and slow down the accumulation of plaque on them.[2]	Daily consumption of 50 ml of pomegranate juice is recommended.[2] Pomegranate seeds add color, taste and texture to fruit salads and green vegetable salads.	Pomegranate Juice Carbohydrate: 33 g Fat: 1 g Protein: 0 g Sodium: 22 mg Vitamin C: 0.2 mg Folate: 59.8 mcg Magnesium: 17.4 mg
Almonds	The vitamins, minerals and nutrients in almonds help to lower the levels of LDL cholesterol, work against the formation of plaque and keep the artery walls flexible.[3]	Chopped, sliced or slivered almonds make a good topping for hot or cold cereal. They can also be sprinkled as a topping on pancakes and waffles, or used in baking.	Almonds Carbohydrate: 27 g Fat: 73 g Protein: 30 g Sodium: 1 mg Vitamin E: 35.9 g Folate: 45. mcg Magnesium: 395 mg
Spinach	Adequate levels of magnesium may reduce the risk of developing atherosclerotic plaque.[4] Spinach provides a good source of dietary magnesium.	Sautéed Spinach: Sauté onions and garlic with a little water or olive oil in a saucepan. Add a generous amount of spinach as it will wilt fast and cooks quickly. Season with a little salt.	Cooked Spinach Carbohydrate: 7 g Fat: 0 g Protein: 5 g Sodium:126 mg Vitamin A: 18867 IU Vitamin C: 17.6 mg Magnesium: 157 mg
Garlic	Garlic is a source of antioxidants and other dietary nutrients which have been found to help slow down the progression of the hardening of arteries.[5]	Oil-Free Garlic Butter: Blend ½ cup cashews with 1 cup water until smooth. Add ¾ cup warm cooked cornmeal, 2 large cloves garlic, 4 teaspoons lemon juice, 1 tablespoon nutritional yeast flakes, 1 teaspoon each of onion powder, dried dill and salt. Blend until smooth	Raw Garlic Carbohydrate: 45 g Fat: 1 g Protein: 9 g Sodium: 23 mg Vitamin A: 12.2 IU Vitamin C: 42.4 mg Magnesium: 34 mg
Pinto Beans	Pinto beans contain folic acid, which helps to decrease the levels of homocysteine in the body, which has been associated with damage to artery walls.[6]	Breakfast Pinto Beans: Sauté chopped garlic, onions, tomato and green bell pepper in a little water or olive oil until soft. Add cooked pinto beans, tomato purée, dried sweet basil, cumin and salt to taste. Serve warm on toast.	Cooked Pinto Beans Carbohydrate: 45 g Fat: 1 g Protein: 15 g Sodium: 2 mg Vitamin C: 1.4 mg Magnesium: 85.5 mg Folate: 294 mcg

DID YOU KNOW: A good way to avoid artery problems is to adhere to a strict vegan diet.

ARTHRITIS

Arthritis is inflammation of one or more joints. While there are many kinds of arthritis, rheumatoid arthritis and osteoarthritis are the most common. Rheumatoid arthritis is an autoimmune disease that targets the joint linings. Osteoarthritis occurs when the cartilage that covers the end of the bones starts to wear away. Symptoms of arthritis include redness, swelling, stiffness and pain.

Foods	Health Benefits	How To Use	Composition (based on Cup)
Pineapples	Bromelain is a natural anti-inflammatory enzyme, found in fresh pineapples, that helps to alleviate pain and decrease swelling.[1]	Pineapple Carrot Smoothie: Blend 1 cup chopped fresh pineapple, ½ cup ice, ¼ cup fresh orange juice, ¼ cup chopped carrot, ½ banana until smooth.	Fresh Pineapples Carbohydrate: 22g Fat: 0 g Protein: 1 g Sodium: 2 mg Vitamin A: 95.7 IU Vitamin C: 78.9 mg Omega-3: 28.1 mg
Plums	Plums contain vitamins A, C and E. These antioxidants may prevent tissue damage, and can significantly decrease pain and swelling in the joints.[2]	Spinach Plum Salad: On each plate place a layer of salad greens, a layer of thinly sliced plums and a few whole pecans. For salad dressing combine equal parts orange juice, lemon juice and olive oil.	Fresh Plums Carbohydrate: 19 g Fat: 0 g Protein: 1 g Sodium: 0 mg Vitamin A: 569 IU Vitamin C: 15.7 mg Omega 6: 72.6 mg
Kale	Omega-3 and omega-6 fatty acids found in green leafy vegetables help to reduce morning stiffness, as well as tenderness and swelling of the joints.[3]	Kale Prune Sauté: Sauté 1 bunch shredded kale in 1 tablespoon olive oil, with ½ cup diced pitted prunes, 1 teaspoon grated ginger, and 1 teaspoon cumin until wilted, but still bright green. Add salt to taste.	Fresh Kale Carbohydrate: 7 g Fat: 0 g Protein: 2 g Sodium: 29 mg Vitamin A: 10,302 IU Omega-3: 121 mg Omega-6: 92.4 mg
Brazil Nuts	Brazil nuts are one of the best sources of the antioxidant selenium, the deficiency of which contributes to reducing morning stiffness, tenderness, and swelling of the joints.[2]	Brazil Nut Arugula Pesto: Process 1 ½ cups brazil nuts, ¼ cup water, 1 cup fresh arugula, ½ cup fresh basil leaves, juice of 2 limes, 2 tablespoons olive oil, 1 tablespoon nutritional yeast and a little salt. Enjoy on pasta or on crackers.	Brazil Nuts Carbohydrate: 16 g Fat: 88 g Protein: 19 g Sodium: 4 mg Selenium: 2,550 mcg Omega-3: 23.9 mg Omega-6: 27350 mg
Sweet Red Peppers	Sweet red peppers contain vitamin B5, which helps the body to produce and repair cartilage. Healthy cartilage in the joints helps to facilitate pain-free movement.[2]	Sweet Red Pepper Salad: Combine 1 ripe diced avocado, 1 large diced bell pepper, ½ cup sliced cherry tomatoes, 2 sliced green onions, 2 tablespoons chopped cilantro, lemon juice and a little salt.	Fresh Red Peppers Carbohydrate: 9 g Fat: 0 g Protein: 1 g Sodium: 6 mg Vitamin A: 4,666 IU Vitamin C: 190 mg Vitamin E: 2.4 mg
Ginger	Ginger has the ability to suppress inflammatory molecules as well as to switch off some inflammatory genes. It has been found to reduce arthritis pain and inflammation.[4]	Fresh grated ginger brings flavor to creamy soups. It will also spice up most vegetable stir-fry dishes, and can be added to vegetable curries.	Fresh Ginger Root Carbohydrate: 16 g Fat: 0 g Protein: 0 g Sodium: 12 mg Calcium: 15.2 mg Omega-3: 32.8 mg Omega-6: 115.2 mg

HEALTH TIP: Avoid sugar–consumption of added sugar increases inflammation in the human body.[5]

ASTHMA

A condition that makes breathing difficult as a result of the airways narrowing, swelling and producing extra mucus. This can trigger shortness of breath, wheezing and coughing. For some individuals an asthma attack can be life threatening, while for others it is just a minor issue.

Foods	Health Benefits	How To Use	Composition (based on Cup)
Strawberries	Strawberries contain vitamin C, which may help to keep the airways in the lungs open, and may reduce the amount of irritation in the lungs and the wheezing experienced.[2]	Strawberry Fruit Salad: Combine 2 cups fresh sliced strawberries, ½ cup fresh blueberries, 1 sliced banana, 1 chopped orange, ½ cup chopped pineapple and ½ cup orange juice.	Fresh Strawberries Carbohydrate: 12 g Fat: 0 g Protein: 1 g Sodium: 2 mg Vitamin C: 89.4 mg Choline: 8.7 mg Magnesium: 19.8 mg
Apples	The antioxidant quercetin, found in apples has anti-allergic properties and is well known for its ability to inhibit the release of histamine and decrease inflammation.[3]	Apple Celery Walnut Salad: In a large bowl combine 2 sliced apples dipped in lemon juice, lettuce leaves, 1 cup cooked garbanzos, 1 cup mandarin segments, 1 cup sliced celery, ½ cup walnuts. Serve with Orange Salad Dressing.*	Fresh Apples Carbohydrate: 17 g Fat: 0 g Protein: 0 g Sodium: 1 mg Vitamin C: 5.7 mg Choline: 4.2 mg Magnesium: 6.3 mg
Sweet Potatoes	Beta-carotene and, vitamins C and E are antioxidants found in sweet potatoes. These antioxidants may help to reduce inflammation in the lungs caused by free radicals.[1]	Baked Sweet Potatoes: Wash and pierce skin with a fork five or six times. Place on a foil-lined baking sheet. Bake at 400°F for 45 to 60 minutes until soft.	Sweet Potatoes Carbohydrate: 41 g Fat: 0 g Protein: 4 g Sodium: 72 mg Vitamin C: 39.2 mg Choline: 26.2 mg Magnesium: 54 mg
Onions	Onions contain quercetin, which reduces the production of histamine, which triggers allergy symptoms. They also supply other helpful nutrients like choline and magnesium.[2]	Roasted Onions: Peel and cut onions in half, place them in a baking dish. Brush lightly with a little olive oil. Sprinkle with a little salt. Bake on lowest rack of oven for 25 to 30 minutes until soft.	Cooked Onions Carbohydrate: 21 g Fat: 0 g Protein: 3 g Sodium: 6 mg Vitamin C: 10.9 mg Choline: 14.3 mg Magnesium: 23.1 mg
Lentils	Lentils contain choline, an essential micronutrient, which may be helpful in reducing both the frequency and severity of asthmatic attacks.[2]	Easy Savory Lentils: Simmer chopped onion, garlic and tomato in a little water or olive oil until soft. Add cooked lentils. Season to taste with sage or thyme, parsley and salt. Serve on brown rice or whole-grain toast.	Cooked Lentils Carbohydrate: 40 g Fat: 1 g Protein: 18 g Sodium: 4 mg Vitamin C: 3 mg Choline: 64.7 mg Magnesium: 71.3 mg
Parsley	Parsley is a good source of magnesium. Asthmatics often have a low level of magnesium,[2] which has been correlated with lower levels of airflow, as well as lower levels of capacity in the lungs.[4]	Fresh chopped parsley is a good way to add extra nutrition to green salads, vegetable stews, soups and burger patties. Parsley can also be sprinkled on top of baked potatoes and gravy.	Fresh Parsley Carbohydrate: 4 g Fat: 0 g Protein: 2 g Sodium: 34 mg Vitamin C: 79.8 mg Choline: 7.7 mg Magnesium: 30 mg

ENCOURAGEMENT: Keep your mind from dwelling upon yourself. Cultivate a contented, cheerful spirit.[5]

BRONCHITIS

Inflammation of the air passages in the lungs. Acute bronchitis is usually caused by a viral infection and starts as a cold and sinus infection which spreads to the airways in the lungs. Chronic bronchitis usually occurs in people who smoke, and manifests with inflamed airways and a persistent wet cough. Eventually scar tissue forms in the lungs and breathing becomes difficult.

Foods	Health Benefits	How To Use	Composition (based on Cup)
Onions	Onions contain an essential oil that works to dissolve mucus, acts as an expectorant, and also has antibiotic properties.[1]	Carrot Onion Salad: Combine 3 cups thinly sliced lightly cooked carrots, ½ small onion thinly sliced, ½ cup chopped cilantro. Dressing: mix 2 tablespoons olive oil, 2 teaspoons lemon juice, ½ teaspoon honey and salt to taste. Sprinkle with sliced almonds.	Fresh Onions Carbohydrate: 15 g Fat: 0 g Protein: 2 g Sodium: 6 mg Vitamin A: 3.2 IU Vitamin C: 11.8 mg Selenium: 0.8 mcg
Leeks	Leeks, like onions, also contain an essential oil that helps to dissolve the mucous associated with bronchitis.[1]	Leek Soup: Sauté 6 cubed potatoes and 2 large sliced leeks. Add 2 sliced carrots, thyme, dill and a little salt. Sauté another 5 minutes. Add 6 cups vegetable stock. Simmer 45 minutes. Blend before serving.	Cooked Leeks Carbohydrate: 9 g Fat: 0 g Protein: 1 g Sodium: 12 mg Vitamin A: 1,007 IU Vitamin C: 5.2 mg Vitamin E: 0.6 mg
Carrots	Carrots provide a good source of vitamin A, which is essential for a healthy respiratory system. Deficiency in vitamin A leads to an impaired immune system and susceptibility to infection.[2]	Carrot Orange Smoothie: Blend 1 banana, ¾ cup shredded carrot, ½ cup fresh orange juice, ¾ cup fresh pineapple and ¼ cup ice until creamy.	Fresh Carrots Carbohydrate: 12 g Fat: 0 g Protein: 1 g Sodium: 88 mg Vitamin A: 21,383 IU Vitamin C: 7.6 mg Vitamin E: 0.8 mg
Radishes	Radishes contain a sharp-tasting, sulfurated essence which helps to remove excess bronchial mucus from the body.[1]	Radish Dip: Process 4 raw radishes, 1 garlic clove, 1 cup soaked cashews and ½ teaspoon salt. Can be eaten in lettuce leaves topped with fresh vegetables.	Fresh Radishes Carbohydrate: 4 g Fat: 0 g Protein: 1 g Sodium: 45 mg Vitamin A: 8.1 IU Vitamin C: 17.2 mg Selenium: 0.7 mcg
Cherries	Cherries are high in antioxidants and nutrients that help to strengthen the immune system and assist in reducing inflammation.[3]	Cherry Citrus Smoothie: Blend 1 cup frozen cherries, 1 banana, and 1 cup freshly squeezed orange juice until smooth and creamy.	Fresh Cherries Carbohydrate: 22 g Fat: 0 g Protein: 1 g Sodium: 0 g Vitamin A: 88.3 IU Vitamin C: 9.7 mg Magnesium: 15.2 mg
Honey	Honey works to prevent or relieve coughing, is mildly sedative, and has a soothing effect on the respiratory system.[1]	Add two teaspoons of honey and some fresh lemon juice to a cup of hot water. Drink during the day when needed to suppress cough and reduce mucus.	Honey Carbohydrate: 279 g Fat: 0 g Protein: 1 g Sodium: 14 mg Vitamin C: 1.7 mg Magnesium: 6.8 mg Selenium: 2.7 mcg

HEALTH TIP: Full, deep inspirations of pure air, which fill the lungs with oxygen, purify the blood.[4]

CANCER

A condition that results from abnormal cell growth and can start in any place and spread through the tissues of the body. Some cancers form tumors or masses of tissue, while others may not. This disease interferes with the normal functioning of the body, and if not controlled may result in death. There are almost 100 different kinds of cancer.

Foods	Health Benefits	How To Use	Composition (based on Cup)
Blueberries	Blueberries contain nutrients that slow down the formation of carcinogens, decrease damage by free radicals, decrease growth of cancer cells and even cause certain cancer cells to self-destruct.[1]	Blueberry Oatmeal: Add 1 cup of rolled oats to 2 cups boiling water. Reduce heat. Simmer 5 minutes. Add ½ cup blueberries, ½ cup nondairy milk. Simmer a few minutes until thick and creamy. Add salt to taste.	Fresh Blueberries Carbohydrate: 21 g Fat: 0 g Protein: 1 g Sodium: 1 mg Vitamin A: 79.9 IU Vitamin C: 14.4 mg Vitamin E: 0.8 mg
Broccoli	The nutrients in broccoli stimulate enzymes that deactivate carcinogens, and activate genes which inhibit tumor and cancer cell growth, and stimulate cancer cell death.[2]	Broccoli Apple Salad: Combine finely chopped broccoli, chopped apple, slivered almonds, sunflower seeds, shredded carrot, and a little minced red onion. Dressing: ¼ cup Tahini,* 2 tablespoons lemon juice, 1 clove minced garlic, a little water to thin as needed. Salt to taste.	Fresh Broccoli Carbohydrate: 6 g Fat: 0 g Protein: 3 g Sodium: 30 mg Vitamin A: 567 IU Vitamin C: 81.2 mg Vitamin E: 0.7 mg
Carrots	Beta-carotene, lycopene and lutein are carotenoids found in carrots, which all act as cancer fighting antioxidants, protecting cells from free radicals.[3]	Carrot Pineapple Salad: Combine 4 cups of grated carrots and 2 cups of fresh shredded pineapple. Refrigerate for ½ hour before serving.	Fresh Carrots Carbohydrate: 12 g Fat: 0 g Protein: 1 g Sodium: 88 mg Vitamin A: 21,383 IU Vitamin C: 7.6 mg Vitamin E: 0.8 mg
Kale	Kale contains nutrients which help to neutralize the formation of cancer-causing chemicals in the body, and which block the conversion of nitrates to cancer-causing nitrosamines.[4]	Kale Pesto: Process ¾ cup soaked brazil nuts, 2 ounces fresh basil, 2 ounces fresh destemmed kale, 2 cloves garlic, the flesh of 1 avocado, juice of ½ lemon and salt to taste.	Fresh Kale Carbohydrate: 7 g Fat: 0 g Protein: 2 g Sodium: 29 mg Vitamin A: 10,302 IU Vitamin C: 80.4 mg Omega-3: 121 mcg
Garlic	Garlic consumption may protect against cancer by stimulating the immune system, and may help to inhibit tumor cell growth.[5]	Finely chopped fresh garlic can easily be swallowed down with fresh vegetable juice, vegetable soup or unsweetened non-dairy milk. Parsley can help to neutralize garlic odor.	Fresh Garlic Carbohydrate: 45 g Fat: 1 g Protein: 9 g Sodium: 23 mg Vitamin A: 12.2 IU Vitamin C: 42.4 mg Selenium: 19.3 mcg
Turmeric	Curcumin, an active ingredient in turmeric, may be able halt pre-cancerous changes in the body, and may be able to kill or prevent the growth of certain kinds of cancer cells.[6,7]	Turmeric Fruit Smoothie: Blend ½ cup water, 1 orange, ½ grapefruit, ½ banana, ½ mango, ½″ fresh peeled ginger, ¼ cup baby carrots, 1 teaspoon ground turmeric. Serve cold.	Turmeric Powder Carbohydrate: 65 g Fat: 16 g Protein: 16 g Sodium: 48 mg Vitamin C: 27.2 g Phytosterols: 88 mg Folate: 41.6 mcg

ENCOURAGEMENT: Whatever your anxieties and trials, spread out your case before the Lord. Your spirit will be braced for endurance.[8]

CANDIDIASIS

An opportunistic disease caused by the Candida fungus which results in infection, particularly in individuals with reduced immune function or those taking antibiotics. This infection most commonly affects the skin, the oral mucosa, the respiratory tract and genital tract.

Foods	Health Benefits	How To Use	Composition (based on Cup)
Lemons	Lemons contain Vitamin C which helps to strengthen the immune system by boosting the function of the leukocytes.[1] Vitamin C also helps to reduce inflammation.[2]	Lemon Water: Combine the juice of one freshly squeezed lemon with ¼ cup boiling water, and then fill the glass with cold water. Drink lemon water with a straw, first thing each morning.	Fresh Lemon Juice Carbohydrate: 21 g Fat: 0 g Protein: 1 g Sodium: 2 mg Vitamin A: 48.8 IU Vitamin C: 112 mg Folate: 31.7 mcg
Sweet Red Peppers	Sweet red peppers are high in antioxidants that neutralize free radicals, which strengthen the resistance of the immune system. Antioxidants such as provitamin A, vitamins C and E, and flavonoids enhance immune system health.[1]	Roasted Red Pepper Hummus: Process 2 cups garbanzos, 1 cup roasted red peppers, ⅓ cup lemon juice, ¼ cup tahini,* 2 tablespoons water, and 1 teaspoon salt until smooth	Cooked Red Peppers Carbohydrate: 9 g Fat: 0 g Protein: 1 g Sodium: 3 mg Vitamin A: 3,971 IU Vitamin C: 231 mg Vitamin E: 2.2 mg
Tomatoes	Tomatoes provide a good source of antioxidant carotenoids, such as provitamin A, as well as minerals that help to maintain the defense systems of the body.[1]	Roasted Tomato Sauce: Combine 4 cups chopped tomato, 3 cloves chopped garlic, 3 teaspoons olive oil, ¼ teaspoon marjoram, ¼ teaspoon thyme, ¼ teaspoon salt. Roast on a baking sheet 20 minutes. Place in saucepan with ¾ cup vegetable broth. Simmer 8 minutes. Blend.	Cooked Tomatoes Carbohydrate: 10 g Fat: 0 g Protein: 2 g Sodium: 26 mg Vitamin A: 1174 IU Vitamin C: 54.7 mg Vitamin E: 1.3 mg
Beet Greens	A deficiency in folate encourages candidiasis. Greens, such as beet greens, help to provide dietary folate which helps to lower the risk of candidiasis.[1]	Warm Beet Green Salad: Combine 1 cup warm cooked beet greens, 1 cup warm cooked quinoa, ½ cup warm cooked garbanzos, ½ cup chopped cooked beets, and ½ cup cherry tomatoes. Drizzle with olive oil and add seasoning and salt to taste.	Cooked Beet Greens Carbohydrate: 8 g Fat: 0 g Protein: 4 g Sodium: 347 mg Vitamin A: 11,021 IU Folate: 20.2 mcg Iron: 2.7 mg
Black Beans	Legumes, including black beans, supply the body with iron. Inadequate levels of iron may promote candidiasis. Black beans also provide the body with dietary folate, lowering the risk of candidiasis.[1]	Black Bean Stew: Sauté 2 chopped onions, ½ cup each chopped celery, carrot, and sweet red pepper, 2 tablespoons minced garlic in a little olive oil. Add 2 cups vegetable broth, 1 cup diced tomato and 5 cups cooked black beans, 2 teaspoons cumin. Reduce heat. Simmer 35 minutes.	Cooked Black Beans Carbohydrate: 41 g Fat: 1 g Protein: 15 g Sodium: 2 mg Folate: 256 mcg Iron: 3.6 mg Zinc: 1.9 mg
Garlic	Garlic acts as an antibacterial and antifungal antibiotic.[3] The sulfurated essence in garlic inhibits the multiplication of the fungus that causes candidiasis. It also helps in balancing intestinal flora.[1]	Garlic Mashed Potatoes: Cook four large cubed potatoes in 6 cups water until soft. Drain. Combine cooked potato with 4 large cloves roasted garlic, 2 teaspoons olive oil, 1 cup warm unsweetened non-diary milk and 1 teaspoon salt. Mash to desired consistency.	Fresh Garlic Carbohydrate: 45 g Fat: 1 g Protein: 9 g Sodium: 23 mg Vitamin A: 12.2 IU Vitamin C: 42.4 mg Folate: 4.1 mcg

HEALTH TIP: Letting the sunshine in will lift spirits, increase energy and improve sleep.[4]

CANKER SORES

These are the most common open mouth sores, usually found inside the lip or cheek, and are also known as aphthous ulcers. They are often painful, yellow or white in color and the soft tissue around them is usually red and inflamed. Canker sores will usually heal in one to three weeks, with the pain diminishing after seven to ten days.

Foods	Health Benefits	How To Use	Composition (based on Cup)
Kiwifruit	Kiwifruit are high in vitamin C, which in some cases has been found to reduce the frequency of outbreaks of canker sores, as well as decrease the pain that they cause.[1]	Kiwifruit Strawberry Jam: Blend 1 cup kiwifruit with 1 cup strawberries and 2 tablespoons honey. Warm slightly and stir in 2 tablespoons chia seeds. Leave to thicken for 15 minutes.	Fresh Kiwifruit Carbohydrate: 28g Fat: 0 g Protein: 2 g Sodium: 10 mg Vitamin C: 136.4 mg Iron: 0.8 mg Magnesium: 54.7 mg
Oats	Deficiency in B vitamins is a contributing factor to the development of recurrent canker sores.[2] Oats are a good source of many of the B vitamins which help to prevent this condition.	Hot Oatmeal Cereal: Boil 1 cup of water in a saucepan, then add a pinch of salt. Stir ½ cup of oatmeal into the water. Cook on medium heat, stirring occasionally, for five minutes until thick. Top with chopped fruit and seeds.	Raw Oats Carbohydrate: 103 g Fat: 11 g Protein: 26 g Sodium: 3 mg Thiamin: 1.2 mg Niacin: 1.5 mg Folate: 87.4 mcg
Sesame Seeds	Sesame seeds are high in iron. Iron deficiency has been found to be a contributing factor to the development of canker sores.[3]	Tahini Paste: Toast 1 cup of sesame seeds in a dry skillet, on medium heat. Cool. Process in a food processer until creamy by gradually adding 2 tablespoons olive oil. Add salt to taste. Store in airtight jar in refrigerator	Sesame Seeds Carbohydrate: 34 g Fat: 72 g Protein: 26 g Sodium: 16 mg Folate: 140 mcg Iron: 20.9 mg Zinc: 11.2 mg
Pumpkin Seed	Zinc deficiency has been associated with oral mucosal diseases such as canker sores.[4] Pumpkin seed is one of the best nutritional sources of zinc.	Pumpkin Seed Energy Mix: Combine 1 cup of pepitas, 1 cup walnuts, 1 cup sunflower seeds, ½ cup raisins, ½ cup cranberries, 1 cup flaked coconut. Store in glass jar.	Dried Green Pepitas Carbohydrate: 25 g Fat: 63 g Protein: 34 g Sodium: 25 mg Folate: 80 mcg Iron: 20.7 mg Zinc: 10.3 mg
Lentils	Individuals who suffer with canker sores often do not have an adequate dietary intake of folate. Lentils provide a good source of folate for the body.[5]	Lentil Hummus: Process 2 cups cooked lentils, 2 cloves garlic, ¼ cup tahini,* 2 tablespoons olive oil, 2 tablespoons lemon juice, 1 teaspoon ground cumin, and ½ teaspoon salt.	Cooked Lentils Carbohydrate: 40 g Fat: 1 g Protein: 18 g Sodium: 4 mg Vitamin C: 3 mg Choline: 64.7 mg Magnesium: 71.3 mg
Soybeans	Soymilk enriched with vitamin B12 may help to reduce the frequency of outbreaks of canker sores, as well as the length of duration and level of pain associated with them.[6]	Strawberry Oatmeal Smoothie: Blend ¼ cup rolled oats, 15 fresh or frozen strawberries, 1 banana, 1 cup unsweetened soy milk.	Plain Soy milk Carbohydrate: 8 g Fat: 4 g Protein: 7 g Sodium: 119 g Calcium: 299 mg Iron: 1.1 mg Zinc: 0.6 mg

DID YOU KNOW? Consumption of processed foods and sugar increases the risk of canker sores in some individuals.[7]

CARDIOVASCULAR DISEASE

The term cardiovascular disease refers to diseases which affect the blood vessels and the heart, and is also sometimes known as heart disease. It includes diseases such as atherosclerosis where plaques build up and narrow the arteries, increasing the risk of heart attack or stroke resulting from a blood clot. Also included are heart conditions such as heart failure, arrhythmias and heart valve problems.

Foods	Health Benefits	How To Use	Composition (based on Cup)
Grapes 	The polyphenol compounds found in grapes help to reduce the risk of cardiovascular disease by working to maintain blood vessel health, decreasing inflammation in the arteries and preventing blood clots.[1]	Grape Broccoli Salad: Combine 2 cups broccoli florets, ¾ cup red grapes halved, ¼ chopped almonds, ¼ cup dried raisins, ¼ cup diced onion. Dressing: blend ½ cup soaked cashews, 1 tablespoon each of honey, water and lemon juice, ¼ teaspoon minced garlic and ¼ teaspoon salt.	Fresh Grapes Carbohydrate: 16 g Fat: 0 g Protein: 1 g Sodium: 2 mg Arginine: 42.3 mg Omega-3: 22.1 mg Dietary Fiber: 0.8 mg
Strawberries 	The powerful antioxidants in strawberries neutralize free radicals, thus improving the health of the arteries and coronary arteries. This may stop the progression of angina and reduce the risk of heart attack.[2]	Strawberry Yogurt: Process 1 cup Silken tofu, 1 cup fresh chopped strawberries and 1-2 tablespoons honey until smooth. Refrigerate for at least two or three hours before serving.	Fresh Strawberries Carbohydrate: 12 g Fat: 0 g Protein: 1 g Sodium: 2 mg Vitamin C: 89.4 mg Arginine: 42.6 mg Dietary Fiber: 3 g
Walnuts 	Nuts, in particular walnuts, help to lower LDL cholesterol, one of the main causes of cardiovascular disease. Moderate nut consumption also improves the health of artery linings and reduces the risk of blood clots and heart attacks.[3]	Walnut Taco Meat: Briefly process 1 cup walnuts, 1 tablespoon olive oil, 1 tablespoon soy sauce, 1 teaspoon cumin, 1 teaspoon oregano, ½ teaspoon garlic powder, ¼ teaspoon salt and 1 teaspoon paprika (optional). May be served warmed.	English Walnuts Carbohydrate: 16 g Fat: 76 g Protein: 18 g Sodium: 2 mg Arginine: 2,666 mcg Omega-3: 10,623 mg Dietary Fiber: 7.8 g
Flaxseed 	Flaxseed is high in healthy omega-3 fatty acids, which are beneficial to the heart. Omega-3 fatty acids may help to prevent dangerous heart rhythms which can result in heart attacks.[3]	Flaxseed Crackers: Combine 2 cups ground flaxseeds, 1 cup water, 1 teaspoon oregano, ½ teaspoon salt and ½ teaspoon onion powder. Spread dough ¼″ thick on lined baking sheet. Cut into squares. Bake 25 minutes at 400˚F until browned.	Ground Flaxseed Carbohydrate: 32 g Fat: 48 g Protein: 16g Sodium: 32 mg Arginine: 2,160 Omega-3: 25,552 mg Dietary Fiber: 30.4 g
Soybeans 	Tofu, made from soybeans, is a good source of L-arginine which may help to increase the flexibility of artery walls, reducing the risk of blockage by blood clots. Soy milk is enriched with vitamin E that helps to arrest plaque formation in the arteries.[3]	Strawberry Smoothie: Blend 12 ounces tofu, 1 cup soymilk, 2 cups organic strawberries, 1-2 tablespoons honey, and ½ to 1 cup ice cubes until smooth.	Silken Tofu Carbohydrate: 5 g Fat: 7.4 g Protein: 17.4 g Sodium: 89 mg Arginine: 1,282 mg Calcium: 79.4 mg Magnesium: 67 mg
Barley 	Barley is high in fiber which reduces the risk of cardiovascular disease. Fiber helps to lower blood sugar and cholesterol levels, and helps individuals feel full longer, contributing to reduced weight gain.[4]	Southwestern Barley Salad: Combine 2 cups cooked barley, 1 cup sweet corn kernels, 1 cup sliced grape tomatoes, ¼ cup chopped cilantro, 4 chopped green onions, 2 tablespoons lime juice, 1 tablespoon olive oil, ½ teaspoon garlic powder and salt to taste.	Cooked Pearl Barley Carbohydrate: 44 g Fat: 1 g Protein: 4 g Sodium: 5 mg Arginine: 177 mg Omega-3: 33 mg Dietary Fiber: 6 g

HEALTH TIP: Eating a vegetarian diet will help you live longer and reduces your risk of cardiovascular disease.[5]

CELIAC DISEASE

This is a digestive and autoimmune disorder also known as gluten-sensitivity, sprue or coeliac. For individuals with this condition, eating foods containing gluten causes damage to the small intestine and leads to inadequate absorption of nutrients. Common symptoms include digestive problems, skin rashes, iron deficiency anemia, tingling in legs, musculoskeletal problems and mouth ulcers.

Foods	Health Benefits	How To Use	Composition (based on Cup)
Mangos	Mangos provide a good source of vitamin A which is a common deficiency associated with celiac disease.[1] This deficiency results from inadequate absorption of nutrients.[2]	Mango Banana Ice Cream: Process 1 ½ cups frozen mangos, 1 sliced frozen banana with 2 to 3 tablespoons of non-dairy milk until smooth and creamy. Serve immediately.	Fresh Mangos Carbohydrate: 28 g Fat: 0 g Protein: 1 g Sodium: 3 mg Vitamin A: 1,262 IU Vitamin B6: 0.2 mg Calcium: 16.5 mg
Prunes	Consumption of vitamin B6, found in prunes, prevents deficiency and helps to lower homocysteine levels.[3] It also aids in relieving depression associated with celiac disease.[4]	Prune Preserve: Soak 2 cups of pitted prunes in 1 cup fresh orange juice for 5 hours. Process until slightly chunky. Add a pinch of salt. Serve as a topping for oatmeal, or as a spread for gluten free bread or pancakes.	Dried Prunes Carbohydrate: 111g Fat: 1 g Protein: 4 g Sodium: 3 mg Vitamin A: 1,359 IU Vitamin B6: 0.4 mg Calcium: 78.4 mg
Beet Greens	Beet greens provide calcium, which prevents a deficiency which can lead to osteoporosis. Due to inadequate absorption in the intestine, individuals with celiac disease may be calcium deficient.[5]	Cooked Beet Greens: Wash thoroughly and remove stems. Blanch for 2 minutes until tender, plunge in ice water, drain. Slice into smaller pieces, sauté in a little olive oil, with a little minced garlic for a few minutes. Add salt to taste.	Cooked Beet Greens Carbohydrate: 8 g Fat: 0 g Protein: 4 g Sodium: 347 mg Vitamin A: 11,021 IU Calcium: 164 mg Iron: 2.7 mg
Millet	Malabsorption due to celiac disease frequently results in folate deficiency. Adequate daily folate intake may assist in preventing some types of anemia, and also regulates the metabolic processes of homocysteine.[6]	Millet Breakfast Bowl: Cook ½ cup millet in 1 ½ cups water with ¼ teaspoons salt for 15 minutes on medium heat. Reduce heat to low, add ½ cup coconut milk and simmer for 5 minutes. Place in bowl, top with chopped banana, mango, sunflower seeds and non-dairy milk.	Cooked Millet Carbohydrate: 41 g Fat: 2 g Protein: 6 g Sodium: 3 mg Folate: 33.1 mcg Calcium: 5.2 mg Zinc: 1.6 mg
Sunflower Seeds	Sunflower seeds provide a large portion of the daily allowance of dietary zinc required. Zinc deficiency is very prevalent in individuals with celiac disease.[1]	Sunflower Seed Dressing: Blend 1 cup soaked sunflower seeds, ½ cup water, ¼ cup lemon juice, ¼ cup olive oil, 1 small clove garlic, ½ teaspoon salt, 1 teaspoon dried basil, and ½ teaspoon dried dill, until smooth.	Sunflower Seeds Carbohydrate: 28 g Fat: 72 g Protein: 29 g Sodium: 13 mg Folate: 318 mcg Iron: 7.3 mg Zinc: 7 mg
Pinto Beans	Anemia often occurs as a result of iron deficiency caused by celiac disease.[1] Daily consumption of beans such as pinto beans assists in building up iron levels and fighting anemia.	Pinto Bean Hummus: Process 2 cups cooked pinto beans, 2 tablespoons tahini,* 1 tablespoon olive oil, ¼ teaspoon cumin and salt to taste. Serve with chopped vegetable sticks.	Cooked Pinto Beans Carbohydrate: 45 g Fat: 1 g Protein: 15 g Sodium: 2 mg Folate: 294 mcg Calcium: 78.6 mg Iron: 3.6 mg

DID YOU KNOW? The Lord is gracious, and full of compassion; slow to anger, and of great mercy (Psalm 145:8).

CELLULITIS

A common, yet potentially serious, bacterial infection of the skin which can spread rapidly from one area of the body to another. Cellulitis will appear red and swollen and may feel hot and tender to the touch. Symptoms may include red spots, blisters and skin dimpling. Left untreated infection can spread to the lymph nodes and bloodstream.

Foods	Health Benefits	How To Use	Composition (based on Cup)
Pears	The consumption of fruit, including pears, promotes the elimination of waste and helps to rid the body of the fluid that accumulates under the skin. Eating fruit helps to prevent and cure cellulitis.[1]	Pear Raspberry Smoothie: Blend 2 chopped pears, 1 cup whole raspberries, 1 sliced banana and ¼ cup non-dairy milk until creamy. Enjoy immediately	Fresh Pears Carbohydrate: 25 g Fat: 0 g Protein: 1 g Sodium: 2 mg Beta-Carotene: 20.9 mcg Vitamin C: 6.8 mg Dietary Fiber: 5 g
Raspberries	Raspberries are high in flavonoids which seem to help reduce lymphedema and the associated risk of cellulitis.[2] They also contain dietary fiber, which helps to eliminate waste and cure cellulitis.[1]	Raspberry Chia Seed Jam: In a medium pot bring 3 cups of raspberries and 2 tablespoons of honey to boil. Simmer 5 minutes. Slightly mash raspberries. Stir in 2 tablespoons chia seeds and cook 1 more minute. Cool for a couple of hours. Serve once thickened. Keep refrigerated.	Fresh Raspberries Carbohydrate: 15 g Fat: 1 g Protein: 1 g Sodium: 1 mg Beta-Carotene: 14.8 mcg Vitamin C: 32.2 mg Dietary Fiber: 8 g
Kale	Green leafy vegetables such as kale provide a good source of beta-carotene, contributing to healthy skin cells. They also contain vitamin C, which promotes skin healing.[1]	Baked Kale Chips: Destem, wash and dry 10 ounces of kale. Tear into large pieces. Massage leaves with 2 tablespoons olive oil. Place a single layer on baking trays. Sprinkle with 5 tablespoons nutritional yeast and 1 teaspoon garlic salt. Bake at 300°F for 15 to 20 minutes.	Fresh Kale Carbohydrate: 7 g Fat: 0 g Protein: 2 g Sodium: 29 mg Beta-Carotene: 6,182 mcg Vitamin C: 80.4 mg Dietary Fiber: 1.3 g
Peas	Peas are high in fiber, which aids in elimination of toxic substances from the intestine before they enter the bloodstream and are deposited in the tissues.[1]	Italian Peas: Sauté 1 small chopped onion with 1 clove minced garlic in a little olive oil until soft. Add 1 lb frozen green peas and 2 tablespoons vegetable stock. Cover and cook until tender.	Frozen Green Peas Carbohydrate: 18 g Fat: 1 g Protein: 7 g Sodium: 145 mg Beta-Carotene: 1,641 mcg Vitamin C: 24.1 mg Dietary Fiber: 6 g
Quinoa	The nutrients in whole grains, such as quinoa, play an important role in helping to maintain the health of the cells under the skin, and keep it free from cellulitis.[1]	Baked Quinoa Breakfast: In a baking dish combine 2 cups uncooked quinoa, 2 cups non-dairy milk, 2 peeled, diced apples, ⅓ cup ground flaxseed, 1 teaspoon cinnamon, and a pinch of salt. Bake 45 minutes, sprinkle with chopped walnuts before serving.	Cooked Quinoa Carbohydrate: 39 g Fat: 4 g Protein: 8 g Sodium: 13 mg Magnesium: 118 mg Riboflavin: 0.2 mg Dietary Fiber: 5.2 g
Soybeans	Legumes such as soybeans provide phytoestrogens which help to correct the hormonal imbalances that contribute to cellulitis.[1]	Edamame Pesto: Process 2 cups shelled, thawed edamame, 1 cup fresh basil leaves, ¼ cup fresh cilantro, 1 clove garlic, 2 tablespoons fresh lemon juice, 1 teaspoon olive oil, 1 clove garlic, and 1 teaspoon salt. Serve with hot wholegrain pasta.	Green Soybeans Carbohydrate: 28 g Fat: 17 g Protein: 33 g Sodium: 38 mg Vitamin C: 74.2 mg Magnesium: 108 mg Dietary Fiber: 11 g

HEALTH TIP: Avoid sugary and caffeinated beverages, which are detrimental to your health.[3]

CHRONIC FATIGUE

A debilitating medical condition, the cause of which is unknown. Common symptoms might include extreme fatigue which does not go away with rest, weakness, muscular aching, insomnia, poor concentration and depression. These symptoms inhibit the ability of an individual to function normally on a daily basis.

Foods	Health Benefits	How To Use	Composition (based on Cup)
Tomatoes	Tomatoes contain the carotenoid lycopene, a powerful antioxidant which helps to fight harmful free radicals, and decreases inflammation in the body.[1]	Tomato Avocado Salad: Combine chopped tomatoes, cucumber, and avocado with chopped cilantro or sliced green onion, and a little lime or lemon juice. Add salt to taste.	Fresh Tomatoes Carbohydrate: 6 g Fat: 0 g Protein: 1 g Sodium: 7 mg Vitamin A: 1,241 IU Vitamin C: 18.9 mg Magnesium: 16.4 mg
Apples	Polyphenols, such as the flavonoid quercetin in apples, help to decrease inflammation, regulate the immune system, and stimulate healthy cell functioning.[1]	Apple Almond Smoothie: 1 sliced banana, ¼ cup soymilk, 6 almonds, 1 peeled, chopped apple, and ½ cup orange juice. Blend until completely smooth. Enjoy with breakfast.	Fresh Apples Carbohydrate: 17 g Fat: 0 g Protein: 0 g Sodium: 1 mg Vitamin A: 67.5 IU Vitamin C: 5.7 mg Magnesium: 6.3 mg
Brazil Nuts	Brazil nuts are high in magnesium, which may be helpful in increasing energy levels, promoting a better mental state, and reducing pain.[2]	Brazil Nut Pâté: Soak 1 cup brazil nuts for 20 minutes. Rinse. Drain. Process with ½ cup raw almonds, ½ cup onion, 2 cloves garlic, 4 teaspoons lemon juice, and a pinch of salt, until spreadable. Enjoy with fresh vegetables or on crackers.	Brazil Nuts Carbohydrate: 16 g Fat: 88 g Protein: 19 g Sodium: 4 mg Magnesium 500 mg Selenium: 2,550 mcg Omega-3: 23.9 mg
Sunflower Seeds	Thiamine, also known as vitamin B1, may be able to help reduce fatigue as well as other symptoms. Regular consumption of sunflower seeds may help to avoid deficiency of this vitamin.[3]	Sunflower Seed Trail Mix: Combine ½ cup sunflower seeds, ½ cup chopped almonds, ¼ cup unsweetened dried cranberries, ¼ cup unsweetened coconut flakes. Store in glass jar.	Sunflower Seeds Carbohydrate: 28 g Fat: 72 g Protein: 29 g Sodium: 13 mg Thiamine: 0.7 mg Magnesium: 455 mg Omega-3: 104 mg
Barley	Barley is a complex carbohydrate containing polyphenols, which help in the process of reducing inflammation, normalizing the immune system, and assisting with healthy cell function.[1]	Warm Barley Cereal: Add 1 cup barley to 4 cups boiling water. Bring to the boil, reduce heat and simmer for 45 to 55 minutes until cooked. Enjoy topped with with nuts, raisins, chopped fresh fruit and non-dairy milk.	Cooked Pearl Barley Carbohydrate: 44 g Fat: 1 g Protein: 4 g Sodium: 5 mg Thiamine: 0.1 mg Magnesium 34.5 mg Omega-3: 33 mg Zinc: 1.3 mg
Collard Greens	The nutrients in collard greens, including vitamin A and magnesium, help to build a healthy immune system and may help to reduce inflammation and fatigue.[4]	Creamed Collard Soup: Steam collards in a little water. Blend with 1 boiled potato. Sauté 1 diced onion with 2 cloves minced garlic. Stir in 2 teaspoons flour. While stirring add ½ cup vegetable broth and 1 cup non-dairy milk. Add collard potato mixture. Simmer briefly. Season to taste.	Cooked Collards Carbohydrate: 9 g Fat: 1 g Protein: 4 g Sodium: 30 mg Vitamin A: 15,416 IU Vitamin C: 34.6 mg Thiamine: 0.1 mg

ENCOURAGEMENT: The person whose mind is quiet and satisfied in God is on the pathway to health.[5]

CIRRHOSIS

A chronic liver disease that causes inflammation and permanently destroys liver cells. When damage occurs in the liver it works to repair itself, and fibrous scar tissue is formed, decreasing normal liver function. Symptoms include increased pressure in the portal venous system, abdominal fluid retention, and loss of the normal detoxification function of the liver.

Foods	Health Benefits	How To Use	Composition (based on Cup)
Grapes	Eating grapes helps improve the flow of blood from the digestive system to the liver, helping to take the pressure off the portal system as a result of cirrhosis, and decreasing fluid build-up in the abdominal cavity.[1]	Sprinkle washed, seeded, sliced grapes on hot or cold cereal or stir them into non-dairy yogurt. Grapes can be used in fruit salad or added to green leafy salads.	Fresh Grapes Carbohydrate: 16 g Fat: 0 g Protein: 1 g Sodium: 2 mg Vitamin A: 92 IU Vitamin K: 13.4 mcg Folate: 3.7 mcg
Strawberries	The consumption of the nutrients found in strawberries improves the circulation in the veins of the liver's portal system. As a result, there may be less buildup of fluid in the abdominal cavity.[1]	Strawberry Topping: Process or blend fresh or defrosted frozen strawberries to the thickness desired. Makes a great topping for oatmeal, crepes, pancakes or non-dairy ice cream.	Fresh Strawberries Carbohydrate: 12 g Fat: 0 g Protein: 1 g Sodium: 2 mg Vitamin C: 89.4 mg Folate: 36.5 mcg Zinc: 0.2 mg
Beets	Beets contain a nutrient called betaine which helps to lower homocystein levels in those with liver disease. The betaine in beets may help to improve liver function.[2]	Roasted Beets: Wash beets, slice off tops, wrap loosely in foil, and place on baking sheet. Roast for about 60 minutes at 375°F until soft. Cool. Peel, slice, and store in the refrigerator.	Cooked Beets Carbohydrate: 16 g Fat: 0 g Protein: 4 g Sodium: 130 mg Vitamin C: 6.2 mg Folate: 136 mcg Zinc: 0.6 mg
Cashews	The zinc found in cashews promotes normal function of the immune system, contributes to better metabolism of amino acids, and may improve brain function for individuals with liver disease.[3]	Cashew Cheese Spread: Soak 1 ½ cup raw cashews for 1 hour. Rinse. Drain. Process with 1 clove garlic, ¼ cup water, 2 ¼ teaspoons lemon juice and ½ teaspoon salt. Enjoy on crackers, sandwiches, or as a dip for vegetables.	Cashews Carbohydrate: 47 g Fat: 63 g Protein: 26 g Sodium: 17 g Vitamin K: 48.7 mcg Folate: 35.7 mcg Zinc: 8.3 mg
Garbanzos	Garbanzos are rich in folate, which helps to prevent liver disease. Folate deficiency may result in creation of defective and less stable DNA, leading to an increased risk of liver cancer.[4]	Pimento Hummus: Process 2 cups cooked garbanzos, 1 clove of garlic, 2 teaspoons ground cumin and 2 ounces diced bottled pimento until smooth.	Cooked Garbanzos Carbohydrate: 45 g Fat: 4 g Protein: 15 g Sodium: 11 mg Vitamin K: 6.6 mcg Folate: 282 mcg Zinc: 2.5 mg
Onions	Raw onions help to detoxify the liver and help it to function more effectively by activating the liver detoxification enzymes systems.[5]	Greens, Grapes, and Sweet Onion Salad: Combine 6 ounces mixed greens 1 cup sliced, seedless grapes, ½ sliced sweet onion, ½ cup toasted sliced almonds, 2 teaspoons fresh lemon juice, and ¼ teaspoon salt.	Fresh Onions Carbohydrate: 15 g Fat: 0 g Protein: 2 g Sodium: 6 mg Vitamin K: 0.6 mcg Folate: 30.4 mcg Zinc: 0.3 mg

DID YOU KNOW? Overeating weakens and debilitates the digestive organs, often resulting in disease.[6]

COMMON COLD

A viral infectious disease of the upper respiratory system, which includes the nose, sinuses, Eustachian tubes, throat, larynx and bronchial tubes. The mucus membranes become inflamed and emit a watery discharge. Symptoms such as runny nose or blocked nose, sore throat, cough and headache are common.

Foods	Health Benefits	How To Use	Composition (based on Cup)
Bananas	Bananas contain vitamin B6, which plays a role in over 200 biochemical reactions in the body. Vitamin B6 is crucial to maintaining a healthy immune system.[1]	Baked Banana Oatmeal: Combine 1 cup rolled oats, 1 mashed banana, 1 cup non-dairy milk, 1 teaspoon chia seeds, ½ teaspoon vanilla extract, ¼ cup raisins, and a pinch of salt. Bake in greased dish at 350°F for 25 minutes.	Fresh Bananas Carbohydrate: 34 g Fat: 0 g Protein: 2 g Sodium: 2 mg Vitamin A: 96 IU Vitamin C: 13.1 mg Vitamin B6: 0.6 mg
Oranges	Vitamin C in oranges may not be able to cure a cold, but it may well help to shorten the duration of the cold.[2] Vitamin C is an antioxidant that helps to strengthen the immune system.	Orange, Greens and Cranberry Salad: Place salad greens on each plate, add orange segments, dried cranberries and pecans. Drizzle with Orange Dressing* and enjoy for lunch or a light dinner.	Fresh Oranges Carbohydrate: 21 g Fat: 0 g Protein: 2 g Sodium: 0 mg Vitamin A: 405 IU Vitamin C: 95.8 mg Vitamin B6: 0.1 mg
Cantaloupes	Cantaloupes are high in colorful compounds called carotenoids. The body transforms carotenoids into the antioxidant vitamin A, which strengthens the immune system.[1]	Blender Cantaloupe Juice: Blend the flesh of 1 cold, seeded, peeled cantaloupe with ½ inch peeled chopped ginger, five or six washed mint leaves and a cup of ice, until smooth. Serve immediately.	Fresh Cantaloupe Carbohydrate: 14 g Fat: 0 g Protein: 1 g Sodium: 26 mg Vitamin A: 5,412 IU Vitamin C: 58.7 mg Vitamin B6: 0.1 mg
Almonds	Vitamin E, found in almonds, is a powerful antioxidant that assists the body in fighting infection.[1] Almonds also contain a small amount of vitamin B6 and selenium.[1, 3]	Chopped, sliced or slivered almonds can be added to savory rice dishes or vegetable stir-fry dishes. Blended into soups and smoothies, almonds add creaminess and nutrition.	Almonds Carbohydrate: 31 g Fat: 71 g Protein: 30 g Sodium: 1 mg Vitamin A: 1.4 IU Vitamin E: 37.5 mg Vitamin B6: 0.2 mg
Sesame Seeds	Sesame seeds contain the trace element selenium, which acts like an antioxidant and stimulates the immune system.[3] They also contain vitamin B6, which helps maintain a healthy immune system.[1]	Sesame Banana Smoothie: Toast 2 tablespoons sesame seeds. Blend sesame seeds until finely ground. Add 1 banana, 2 oranges, a pinch of salt, and 1 cup ice cubes. Blend until smooth.	Sesame Seeds Carbohydrate: 34 g Fat: 72 g Protein: 26 g Sodium: 16 mg Vitamin E: 0.4 mg Vitamin B6: 1.1 mg Selenium: 8.2 mcg
Garlic	Garlic acts as an antibiotic and has antiviral properties, and assists in preventing bronchitis and infections of the respiratory system.[4]	Garlic Broth: In a saucepan simmer 8 cups vegetable stock, 1 tablespoon olive oil, 1 head of garlic peeled and minced, 1 bay leaf, a pinch dried sage and thyme for 35 minutes.	Fresh Garlic Carbohydrate: 45 g Fat: 1 g Protein: 9 g Sodium: 23 mg Vitamin A: 12.2 IU Vitamin C: 42.4 mg Selenium: 19.3 mcg

HEALTH TIP: Frequently gargling with warm salt water can soothe and reduce swelling in the throat.

CONSTIPATION

A condition that manifests in slow and difficult transit of contents through the intestines, frequently resulting in less than three bowel movements a week. Improper diet with insufficient fiber, inadequate water intake, and lack of physical exercise contribute to causing constipation.

Foods	Health Benefits	How To Use	Composition (based on Cup)
Apples	Sorbitol, one of the carbohydrates found in apples, can help to increase the frequency of bowel movements. Apple juice also helps to increase the water content of stools.[1]	Chopped apples can be added to fruit salad and fruit smoothies, or added as a topping to hot and cold cereal. Enjoy a fresh crunchy apple for breakfast, lunch or supper. Dried apple can be stewed or added to trail mix.	Fresh Apples Carbohydrate: 17 g Fat: 0 g Protein: 0 g Sodium: 1 mg Vitamin A: 67.5 IU Vitamin C: 5.7 mg Dietary Fiber: 3 g
Kiwifruit	Kiwifruit contains actinidin, which is thought to stimulate receptors in the colon, improving colon function. The high fiber content of kiwifruit also helps to improve bowel function.[2]	Kiwifruit Dessert Kebabs: Slide quartered kiwifruit, pineapple chunks, and medium size strawberries onto skewer stick until full. Arrange on serving plate. Enjoy for breakfast or as part of a light supper.	Fresh Kiwifruit Carbohydrate: 28g Fat: 0 g Protein: 2 g Sodium: 10 mg Vitamin A: 318 IU Vitamin C: 136.4 mg Dietary Fiber: 6 g
Prunes	Prunes contain insoluble fiber, which improves the consistency of stools as well as the frequency of bowel movements.[3]	Prune Energy Bites: Process 1 ½ cup walnuts, 1 cup pitted prunes, 2 tablespoons orange juice, and 1 teaspoon vanilla until sticky. Roll into balls. Store in refrigerator.	Dried Prunes Carbohydrate: 111g Fat: 1 g Protein: 4 g Sodium: 3 mg Vitamin A: 1,359 IU Magnesium: 71.3 mg Dietary Fiber: 12 g
Carrots	Carrots are a good source of beta-carotene, which helps to maintain the health of the intestinal lining.[4] They also contain fiber, which improves frequency of bowel movments.[5]	Blender Carrot Juice: Blend 1 ½ cups diced or shredded carrots, 2 teaspoons fresh lemon juice, ¾ to 1 cup of water and ½ to 1 cup ice cubes, until smooth. Drink immediately.	Fresh Carrots Carbohydrate: 12 g Fat: 0 g Protein: 1 g Sodium: 88 mg Vitamin A: 21,383 IU Vitamin C: 7.6 mg Dietary Fiber: 4 g
Peas	Peas are high in dietary fiber, which helps to increase the bulk of stools as well as to speed up transit time through the intestines.[6]	Green Pea Salad: Combine 2 cups lightly cooked frozen peas, 1 cup sliced thinly sliced carrots, 1 thinly sliced spring onion, 1 tablespoon chopped parsley, ½ tablespoon lemon juice, ½ tablespoon olive oil and salt to taste.	Frozen Green Peas Carbohydrate: 18 g Fat: 1 g Protein: 7 g Sodium: 145 mg Vitamin A: 2757 IU Vitamin C: 24.1 mg Dietary Fiber: 6 g
Flaxseed	Flaxseed helps to relieve constipation because it contains insoluble fiber that helps to increase stool bulk and reduce bowel transit time.[7]	Banana Flaxseed Smoothie: Blend 1 large banana, 1 cup unsweetened almond milk, 1 tablespoon ground flaxseed, 2 tablespoons almond butter, 1 teaspoon honey, and 4 ice cubes until creamy.	Ground Flaxseed Carbohydrate: 32 g Fat: 48 g Protein: 16 g Sodium: 32 mg Calcium: 286.4 mg Magnesium: 438.4 mg Dietary Fiber: 32 g

HEALTH TIP: Sipping a quart of warm water before breakfast will help to develop regular morning bowel movement.[4]

COPD

Chronic Obstructive Pulmonary Lung disease is a term used for progressive inflammatory lung diseases, which result in obstruction of airflow from the lungs and increasing breathlessness. COPD includes diseases such as chronic bronchitis, emphysema and non-reversible asthma.

Foods	Health Benefits	How To Use	Composition (based on Cup)
Pineapples	The antioxidants in pineapples, in particular vitamin C, act to decrease inflammation in the lungs, and are important for the hydration of airway surfaces.[1]	Serve freshly sliced pineapple as a side dish at breakfast, or diced with other fruit as a topping for hot or cold cereal, or as a topping for pancakes, or as a filling for crepes.	Fresh Pineapples Carbohydrate: 22g Fat: 0 g Protein: 1 g Sodium: 2 mg Vitamin C: 78.9 mg Calcium: 28.5 mg Magnesium: 19.8 mg
Celery	Celery contains phosphorous, which is important for building healthy cells and for repairing body tissue.[2] Celery also contains a small amount of calcium and magnesium.	Celery Soup: Sauté 1 chopped onion and 2 cloves minced garlic in a little olive oil. Add 4 cups vegetable stock, 1 chopped potato, 1 head of celery chopped. Simmer 25 minutes. Blend. Add salt to taste.	Cooked Celery Carbohydrate: 6 g Fat: 0 g Protein: 1 g Sodium: 136 mg Calcium: 63 mg Magnesium: 18 mg Phosphorous: 37.5 mg
Tomatoes	The antioxidant lycopene found in tomatoes may be helpful in improving the forced expiratory volume, and in suppressing inflammation in the airways.[3]	Tomato Gravy: Blend 1 cup canned tomatoes, ½ cup cashews, ½ cup cooked rice until very smooth. Add 3 cups canned tomatoes, ¼ teaspoon each onion powder, garlic powder, oregano and salt, 2 teaspoons honey. Simmer 10 minutes, stirring often.	Fresh Tomatoes Carbohydrate: 7 g Fat: 0 g Protein: 2 g Sodium: 9 mg Vitamin C: 22.9 mg Magnesium: 19.8 mg Phosphorous: 43.2 mg
Corn	Corn contains magnesium, which helps to maintain the health of the breathing muscles. Along with calcium, it helps to regulate the activity of the bronchial tubes.[2]	Simple Boiled Corn: Place corn on the cob in boiling water to cover, and put the lid on the saucepan. Return to boil and turn heat off. Allow to cook for about 10 minutes until tender. Remove corn from the water as soon as it is cooked.	Cooked Corn Carbohydrate: 41 g Fat: 2 g Protein: 5 g Sodium: 0 mg Calcium: 4.9 mg Magnesium: 42.6 mg Phosphorous: 123 mg
Kidney Beans	The protein in kidney beans helps to maintain the health of individuals with COPD by assisting in the production of antibodies that help to resist infections.[2]	Kidney Bean Salad: Combine 1 ½ cup cooked kidney beans, 1 clove garlic minced, 2 cups diced tomato, ⅓ cup chopped walnuts, ½ cup chopped parsley. Add a little olive oil and lemon juice. Salt to taste.	Cooked Kidney Beans Carbohydrate: 40 g Fat: 1 g Protein: 15 g Sodium: 2 mg Calcium: 62 mg Magnesium: 74.3 mg Phosphorous: 244 mg
Almonds	Almonds contain calcium, which his essential for lung function and muscle contraction. It also helps to prevent calcium deficiency often caused by COPD medications.[2]	Almond Banana Smoothie: Blend 1 cup almond milk, ⅓ cup blanched, slivered almonds, 1 medium banana and ½ cup chopped pineapple until smooth.	Almonds Carbohydrate: 31 g Fat: 71 g Protein: 30 g Sodium: 1 mg Calcium: 378 mg Magnesium: 255 mg Phosphorous: 460 mg

ENCOURAGEMENT: As we live in communion with God we will grow strong in God's strength and become a blessing to others.

CROHN'S DISEASE

A chronic disease causing inflammation and ulceration of the intestinal tract. This inflammation can occur anywhere from the mouth through to the anus, but is commonly found in the lower part of the small intestine. Common symptoms are abdominal pain, vomiting, diarrhea, fever and weight loss.

Foods	Health Benefits	How To Use	Composition (based on Cup)
Blueberries	Blueberries are a rich source of quercetin, which acts as an intestinal barrier-protective agent, and helps to main mucosal integrity.[1] The omega-3 fatty acids in blueberries may help to reduce inflammation.[2]	Berry Green Smoothie: Blend ½ cup almond milk, ½ cup frozen blueberries, ½ cup strawberries, 1 banana, ½ cup spinach, and 1 tablespoon honey until creamy.	Fresh Blueberries Carbohydrate: 21 g Fat: 0 g Protein: 1 g Sodium: 1 mg Vitamin A: 79.9 IU Calcium: 8.9 mg Omega-3: 85.8 mg
Spinach	The omega-3 fatty acids found in spinach may be helpful in fighting inflammation and may assist in reducing the recurrence of flare-ups.[2] Spinach also contains vitamin A and calcium.	Spinach Soup: Sauté 1 onion and 3 cloves garlic in a little olive oil. Add 1 diced sweet potato, 1 diced apple, 2 cups vegetable broth. Simmer until soft. Add 12 ounces spinach, 2 cups unsweetened almond milk, and salt to taste. Blend when spinach is cooked.	Cooked Spinach Carbohydrate: 7 g Fat: 0 g Protein: 5 g Sodium:126 mg Vitamin A: 18,867 IU Folate: 58.2 mcg Omega-3: 41.4 mg
Cabbage	The glutamine in cabbage plays a role in protecting the mucosa, which is the lining of the gastrointestinal tract. Individuals suffering with Crohn's disease may be glutamine deficient.[3]	Cabbage and Sweet Potato Hash: Sauté 1 onion cut in wedges, and 3 leaves shredded cabbage in one tablespoon olive oil. Add chopped cooked sweet potato and a dash of soy sauce or salt to taste. Serve warm.	Cooked Cabbage Carbohydrate: 70 g Fat: 1 g Protein: 16 g Sodium: 101 mg Vitamin A: 1,010 IU Folate: 379 mcg Calcium: 606 mg
Sweet Potatoes	Sweet potatoes are a good source of vitamin A. The mucosal integrity as well as the protective barrier function of the intestinal wall are compromised when there is a vitamin A deficiency.[1]	Sweet Potato Hummus: Process 2 cans garbanzos, 1 medium baked sweet potato, 1 tablespoon lemon juice, ½ cup water, 1 teaspoon paprika and 1 teaspoon garlic powder until smooth.	Sweet Potatoes Carbohydrate: 41 g Fat: 0 g Protein: 4 g Sodium: 72 mg Vitamin A: 38,433 IU Folate: 12 mcg Calcium: 76 mg
Oats	Oats contain folate and zinc, which are minerals the body needs in order to repair the cells in the intestine.[2] They also contain omega-3 fatty acids which fight inflammation.[2]	Blueberry Overnight Oats: Combine ½ cup oats, ½ cup almond milk, 1 teaspoon vanilla, and 1 teaspoon honey. Seal container, place in the refrigerator overnight. Layer with banana, blueberries and slivered almonds in the morning.	Raw Oats Carbohydrate: 103 g Fat: 11 g Protein: 26 g Sodium: 3 mg Calcium: 84.3 mg Folate: 87.4 mcg Zinc: 6.2 mg
Almonds	Individuals with Crohn's disease are often calcium deficient,[2] which may lead to osteoporosis. Almonds contain a good amount of calcium, which may help overcome this deficiency.	Almond Milk: Soak 1 cup almonds in filtered water overnight. Rinse and drain. Blend with 3 cups filtered water, 4 pitted dates and 1 teaspoon vanilla. Strain. Add a pinch of salt. Stir well before using. Serve cold. Keeps 3 to 4 days in a refrigerator.	Almonds Carbohydrate: 27 g Fat: 73 g Protein: 30 g Sodium: 1 mg Calcium: 251 mg Folate: 45. Mcg Zinc: 2.9 mg

HEALTH TIP: After the regular meal is eaten, the stomach should be allowed to rest for five hours.[4]

DEPRESSION

A mood disorder where there is a continual feeling of sadness, hopelessness, and a general loss of interest in life, often manifesting in an inability to carry out normal day-to-day activities. Symptoms can include loss of weight or weight gain, fatigue, insomnia, restlessness, memory problems, headaches, digestive disorders, social withdrawal, and even thoughts of suicide or death.

Foods	Health Benefits	How To Use	Composition (based on Cup)
Peanuts	Peanuts contain folate, which is essential for the normal function of the nervous system. It also plays an important role in the healthy production of serotonin and other neurotransmitters.[1]	Peanut Banana Smoothie: Blend 1 cup non-dairy milk, 2 bananas, 1 tablespoon honey, ½ cup of ice cubes and ¼ cup of sugar-free peanut butter until smooth.	Dry Roasted Peanuts Carbohydrate: 31 g Fat: 73 g Protein: 35g Sodium: 9 mg Folate: 212 mcg Magnesium: 257 mg Potassium: 961 mg
Walnuts	The omega-3 fatty acids found in walnuts improve cognitive function, help to maintain the normal functioning of the mitochondria, and improve the neurotransmitter signaling in the brain.[2]	Walnut Trail Mix: Combine 2 cups toasted walnut halves, 1 cup unsalted pumpkin seeds, 1 cup dried cranberries, 1 cup chopped dried apricots and 1 cup banana chips.	English Walnuts Carbohydrate: 16 g Fat: 76 g Protein: 18 g Sodium: 2 mg Magnesium: 185 mg Potassium: 516 mg Omega-3: 10,623 mg
Pumpkin Seeds	Pumpkin seeds are high in zinc, one of the antioxidant minerals. Adequate intake of zinc is important for maintaining normal mitochondrial function.[3]	Avocado Pumpkin Seed Salad: On individual plates place spinach leaves, sliced avocado, mandarin slices, sprinkle with green pumpkin seeds, and drizzle with Tahini Dressing.[4]	Dried Green Pepitas Carbohydrate: 25 g Fat: 63 g Protein: 34 g Sodium: 25 mg Magnesium: 738 mg Potassium: 1,114 mg Zinc: 10.3 mg
Raisins	The potassium in raisins may help to maintain electrolyte balance, preventing changes in the neurophysiological system, and dysfunction of the autonomous nervous system.[1]	Oatmeal Raisin Energy Bites: Process ¾ cup rolled oats, 1 tablespoon flaxseed, ½ cup raisins, 1 teaspoon vanilla, 2 teaspoons honey and ¼ cup almond butter to make sticky dough. Roll into balls, Store in refrigerator.	Seedless Raisins Carbohydrate: 131 g Fat: 1 g Protein: 5 g Sodium: 18 mg Folate: 8.3 mcg Magnesium: 52.8 mg Potassium: 1,236 mg
Bananas	Bananas provide a good source of magnesium which is essential for creating and maintaining healthy neurons. A deficiency in magnesium results in neuron damage.[1]	Banana Ice Cream: Slice one or two ripe bananas and freeze in an airtight bag or bowl overnight. Process in food processor until bananas become creamy. Eat right away or freeze until solid.	Fresh Bananas Carbohydrate: 34 g Fat: 0 g Protein: 2 g Sodium: 2 mg Magnesium: 40.5 mg Potassium: 537 mg Omega-3: 40.5 mg
Grapefruit	The antioxidants in grapefruit may improve the function and resilience of the central nervous system, help to improve cognitive function, and protect against oxidative damage to the mitochondria.[2]	Broiled Grapefruit: Slice grapefruit in half. Place sliced side up on a lined baking tray. Brush lightly with coconut oil. Drizzle with honey. Broil for 5 to 8 minutes. Allow to cool and serve.	Fresh Grapefruit Carbohydrate: 25 g Fat: 0 g Protein: 2 g Sodium: 0 mg Vitamin A: 2,645 IU Vitamin C: 71.8 mg Folate: 29.9 mcg

DID YOU KNOW? Practicing deep breathing outdoors, twice a day, reduces a sense of gloom.[3]

DIABETES

A complex condition that affects how the body uses glucose, resulting in too much glucose in the blood. If diabetes is not well controlled, or left untreated, it leads to health complications such as blindness, kidney failure, loss of circulation in the extremities resulting in amputation, and increased risk of heart attack and stroke.

Foods	Health Benefits	How To Use	Composition (based on Cup)
Apples	Apples contain pectin, as well as fiber, which helps to reduce the intensity of insulin and blood glucose responses, resulting in better glucose control and less risk of heart disease.[1]	Breakfast is the best time for diabetics to eat apples. Fresh apples are definitely preferable to canned apples that may be sweetened, or dried apples where the sugar is more concentrated.	Fresh Apples Carbohydrate: 17 g Fat: 0 g Protein: 0 g Sodium: 1 mg Vitamin C: 5.7 mg Vitamin E: 0.2 mg Dietary Fiber: 3 g
Blueberries	Blueberries contain vitamins C and E which improve glucose tolerance[2] as well as reduce inflammation.[3] Both these vitamins protect against damage to eyes, kidneys and blood vessels.[2]	Blueberry Waffles: Blend ½ cup cashews, 1 tablespoon honey and 1 cup water until smooth. Add 1 ¼ cups water, 2 cups rolled oats, 1 teaspoon vanilla, ½ teaspoon salt and blend well. Stir in 1 cup blueberries. Bake in waffle iron until steaming stops.	Fresh Blueberries Carbohydrate: 21 g Fat: 0 g Protein: 1 g Sodium: 1 mg Vitamin C: 14.4 mg Vitamin E: 0.8 mg Dietary Fiber: 4 g
Avocados	Avocados may help to normalize the fat composition of the blood, reduce cholesterol levels and may help to maintain a reasonable blood glucose level.[4] They also contain a reasonable amount of dietary fiber.	Avocado Guacamole: Combine mashed avocado, a little fresh chopped onion and tomato, minced garlic, lemon juice and salt to taste. Chill for 30 minutes to allow flavors to blend. Eat with carrot and celery sticks or on baked potatoes.	Fresh Avocados Carbohydrate: 13 g Fat: 22 g Protein: 3 g Sodium: 11 mg Vitamin C: 15 mg Vitamin E: 3.1 mg Dietary Fiber: 10 g
Olives	The nutrients found in olives have been found to be effective in improving endothelial function, normalizing lipids, reducing blood pressure, preventing clotting and reducing inflammation.[5]	Consume one serving of olives (usually 10 olives or 2 tablespoons of tapenade) daily. Choose olives simply cured with water and salt. It is best to avoid olives preserved with vinegar and other substances.	Small Canned Olives Carbohydrate: 8.06 g Fat: 14.8 g Protein: 1.34 g Sodium: 1,172 mg Vitamin C: 1.2 mg Vitamin E: 2.28 mg Dietary Fiber: 4.03 g
Potatoes	During digestion, the fiber and complex carbohydrates found in potatoes cause glucose to be released slowly. Used in moderation they prevent a sharp drop in blood glucose levels.[4]	Perfect Baked Potatoes: Pierce the skin of a scrubbed potato a number of times with a fork. Rub olive oil over the skin of the potato. Place in a baking dish and bake in the oven for 90 minutes at 300°F, or until soft.	Baked Potatoes Carbohydrate: 63 g Fat: 0 g Protein: 7 g Sodium: 30 mg Vitamin C: 28.7 mg Vitamin E: 0.1 mg Dietary Fiber: 7 g
Black Beans	Beans are rich in fiber and have a low glycemic index. Consumption of beans helps to lower postprandial glucose and insulin concentrations, contributing to better glycemic control, and reduced hemoglobin A1C levels.[6]	Black Bean Butternut Bowl: Place shredded lettuce in a bowl. Separately combine ⅓ cup warm Roasted Butternut Cubes,* ⅓ cup warm cooked black beans and ⅓ cup warm cooked quinoa. Spoon into the bowl with lettuce. Drizzle with Avocado Ranch Dressing.*	Cooked Black Beans Carbohydrate: 41 g Fat: 1 g Protein: 15 g Sodium: 2 mg Folate: 256 mcg Omega-3: 181 mg Dietary Fiber: 15 g

HEALTH TIP: A ten-minute walk after each meal helps move sugar out of the blood stream and into the cells.[2]

DIARRHEA

An acute or chronic condition which results in frequent bowel movements and a decrease in the consistency of bowel movements. The most common causes of this condition are viral and bacterial infections; however, it can also be a sign of other conditions such as inflammatory bowel disease or irritable bowel syndrome.

Foods	Health Benefits	How To Use	Composition (based on Cup)
Bananas	Bananas contain magnesium, which helps to combat magnesium deficiency that can cause diarrhea and also results from diarrhea.[1] Bananas are also easy on the intestinal mucosa and aid in halting diarrhea.[2]	Bananas are best eaten as simply as possible when trying to halt diarrhea. Sliced or mashed banana can be eaten as needed at any meal and makes a good accompaniment for oatmeal.	Sliced Bananas Carbohydrate: 34 g Fat: 0 g Protein: 2 g Sodium: 2 mg Magnesium: 40.5 mg Potassium: 537 mg Omega-3: 40.5 mg
Papayas	Papayas provide significant antiseptic action against some pathogens, and are helpful in treating infectious diarrhea. They have emollient properties that protect the intestinal mucosa.[2]	Make sure papaya is properly ripe. It is gentle on the stomach and best eaten alone when treating diarrhea. It may also be eaten with simple foods such as banana, oatmeal or applesauce.	Fresh Papayas Carbohydrate: 14 g Fat: 0 g Protein: 1 g Sodium: 4 mg Vitamin A: 1,531 IU Vitamin C: 86.5 mg Magnesium: 14 mg
Apples	Apples contain antiseptic organic acids, pectin for detoxification, emollients and astringent tannins, which all play a role in the healing of intestinal disorders.[2]	Applesauce, baked apples and stewed apples are the best way to eat apples when suffering with diarrhea. Plain applesauce without added sugar or additives is recommended.	Cooked Apples Carbohydrate: 23 g Fat: 1 g Protein: 0 g Sodium: 2 mg Vitamin A: 75.2 IU Magnesium: 5.1 mg Potassium: 150 mg
Carrots	Carrots are a good source of pectin, which aids in absorbing intestinal toxins and works to protect the intestinal mucosa. The nutrients in carrots help to restore normal intestinal function.[2]	Baked Carrots: Toss whole, peeled, diagonally sliced carrots lightly with olive oil and salt. Place them in a baking dish and roast them in a 400°F oven for 20 minutes or until tender.	Cooked Carrots Carbohydrate: 12 g Fat: 0 g Protein: 2 g Sodium: 90 mg Vitamin A: 26,576 IU Magnesium: 7.8 mg Potassium: 183 mg
Rice	Rice is very easy to digest as it does not contain any gluten. Rice water helps to restore fluid balance in the body and assists in replacing lost electrolytes.[3]	Rice Water: Bring ½ cup brown rice and 3 cups of water to boil. Reduce heat and simmer 45 minutes. Remove from the heat. Strain out rice. Rice water should be refrigerated and drank throughout the day.	Cooked Brown Rice Carbohydrate: 45 g Fat: 2 g Protein: 5 g Sodium: 10 mg Magnesium: 83.9 mg Potassium: 83.9 mg Zinc: 1.2 mg
Oats	Oats are nutritious and provide the soluble fiber needed to protect the intestine. They help promote normal intestinal function by regulating intestinal movement.[2]	Warm oatmeal cereal is the best way to consume oats when dealing with diarrhea. It can be topped with sliced banana, diced papaya and a little nondairy milk.	Cooked Oats Carbohydrate: 29 g Fat: 3 g Protein: 6 g Sodium: 115 mg Magnesium: 60.8 mg Potassium: 143 mg Zinc: 1.5 mg

ENCOURAGEMENT: God often uses the simplest means to accomplish the greatest results.[4]

DIVERTICULAR DISEASE

Diverticulosis is the formation of many little pockets called diverticula in the lining of the colon. When inflammation and infection occur in the diverticula it is called diverticulitis. Diverticular bleeding is a result of injury to the tiny blood vessels next to the diverticula. Symptoms may include constipation and diarrhea, abdominal bloating and pain, and fever.

Foods	Health Benefits	How To Use	Composition (based on Cup)
Peaches	All fruits, including peaches, provide the body with soluble fiber that aids in softening the stool and improving intestinal movement. This helps prevent the formation of new diverticula.[1]	Summer Fruit Salad: Combine 2 cups sliced strawberries, 4 diced peaches, 1 cup blueberries, 1 tablespoon fresh chopped mint. Mix 2 tablespoons lemon juice with 1 tablespoon honey and gently stir through fruit salad.	Fresh Peaches Carbohydrate: 22 g Fat: 1 g Protein: 2 g Sodium: 0 mg Vitamin A: 730 IU Vitamin C: 14.8 mg Dietary Fiber: 3.4 g
Pears	Pears provide dietary fiber that helps to relieve the symptoms of most severe cases of colon disease. Adequate intake of dietary fiber reduces the risk of developing new diverticula.[2]	Baked Pears: Cut pears in half from top to bottom. Scoop out seeds. Place on a baking sheet. Drizzle with ½ teaspoon honey. Top with chopped walnuts. Bake for 30 minutes at 350°F.	Fresh Pears Carbohydrate: 25 g Fat: 0 g Protein: 1 g Sodium: 2 mg Vitamin A: 37 IU Vitamin C: 6.8 mg Dietary Fiber: 5 g
Flaxseed	Consumption of flaxseed provides dietary fiber which works as a bulk forming laxative, softening the stool and shortening transit time through the intestines.[3]	Chia Flax Crackers: Combine ½ cup ground flaxseed, ¼ cup chia seeds, ¼ cup flaxseed, 1 cup water, ¼ teaspoon garlic salt, 2 tablespoons soy sauce. Set aside for 10 minutes. Spread on a lined baking sheet. Bake at 350°F for 15 minutes. Cut into squares. Turn crackers over and bake 10 to 15 more minutes.	Ground Flaxseeds Carbohydrate: 32 g Fat: 48 g Protein: 16g Sodium: 32 mg Omega-3: 1,597 mg Magnesium: 438.4 mg Dietary Fiber: 32 g
Cauliflower	All vegetables, including cauliflower, are a particularly good source of soluble fiber. Fiber improves how the intestines function and reduces the excess pressure which causes diverticula.[1]	Cauliflower Casserole: Place 4 cups lightly boiled cauliflower florets in a baking dish. Stir in 2 chopped leeks. Blend 1 cup cashews, 2 cloves garlic, ⅔ cup sesame seeds, ¾ teaspoon salt. Pour over vegetables. Bake at 380°F for approximately 45 minutes.	Cooked Cauliflower Carbohydrate: 6 g Fat: 0 g Protein: 2 g Sodium: 18 mg Vitamin A: 14.8 IU Vitamin C: 55 mg Dietary Fiber: 2.8 g
Brown Rice	The dietary fiber in whole grain brown rice helps to soften stools, helping to prevent constipation and inflammation. This decreases pressure in the colon and reduces the risk of flareups of diverticulitis.[4]	Mexican Brown Rice: Sauté 1 diced onion, 1 diced tomato and 2 cloves minced garlic until tender. Stir in 2 tablespoons tomato paste, ½ teaspoon cumin, ¾ teaspoon paprika, and 4 cups hot cooked rice. Add salt to taste.	Cooked Brown Rice Carbohydrate: 45 g Fat: 2 g Protein: 5 g Sodium: 10 mg Magnesium: 83.9 mg Potassium: 83.9 mg Dietary Fiber: 4 g
Pinto Beans	Legumes such as pinto beans provide dietary fiber which helps to improve colon function and lessen the pain and symptoms caused by diverticular disease.[5]	Pinto Bean Soup: In a soup pot simmer 1 diced onion, 2 sliced carrots, 3 diced potatoes in 6 cups vegetable stock until tender. Add 3 cups cooked pinto beans. Add herbs and salt to taste. Blend to desired consistency.	Cooked Pinto Beans Carbohydrate: 45 g Fat: 1 g Protein: 15 g Sodium: 2 mg Magnesium: 85.5 mg Folate: 294 mcg Dietary Fiber: 15 g

DID YOU KNOW? If we would exercise faith in the word of the living God we should have the richest blessings.[6]

ECZEMA

A common, chronic skin condition in which patches of skin become rough, red and inflamed, with blistering and scaling. Flareups occur periodically and then subside. The cause of eczema is unknown, but heredity and environment seem to play a role. It is also known as atopic dermatitis.

Foods	Health Benefits	How To Use	Composition (based on Cup)
Blueberries	The antioxidants found in blueberries may help to reduce allergic reactions, decrease inflammation and strengthen connective tissue.[1]	Blueberry Avocado Smoothie: Blend 1 banana, flesh of ½ avocado, 1 cup fresh or frozen blueberries, nondairy milk as needed, and a little honey to taste.	Fresh Blueberries Carbohydrate: 21 g Fat: 0 g Protein: 1 g Sodium: 1 mg Vitamin A: 79.9 IU Vitamin C: 14.4 mg Vitamin E: 0.8 mg
Sweet Potatoes	The body converts the beta-carotene in sweet potatoes to vitamin A, which is important for normal cell reproduction. A deficiency in vitamin A is known to cause skin problems.[2]	Mashed Sweet Potatoes: Peel, cut in 1˝cubes, cover with cold water, simmer until soft — don't boil. Drain water off and mash. Season with a little olive oil and rosemary.	Sweet Potatoes Carbohydrate: 58 g Fat: 0 g Protein: 4 g Sodium: 89 mg Vitamin A: 51,631 IU Vitamin C: 42 mg Dietary Fiber: 8 g
Broccoli	The vitamin C in broccoli functions as an antihistamine and may help to lessen eczema symptoms.[1] Broccoli also contains vitamin A, vitamin E and fiber which are essential for healthy skin.	Steamed Broccoli: Place fresh broccoli florets in a steamer basket over a saucepan of boiling water, making sure there is no contact with the water. Cover. Steam for 4 to 5 minutes until tender.	Cooked Broccoli Carbohydrate: 12 g Fat: 0 g Protein: 4 g Sodium: 64 mg Vitamin A: 2,414 IU Vitamin C: 101.2 mg Dietary Fiber: 6 g
Lentils	Lentils supply a good amount of fiber, which has been found to be helpful in reducing inflammation, as well as providing protection against eczema.[3]	Sweet Potato Lentil Soup: Sauté 1 diced onion and 2 small tomatoes until soft. Add 7 cups vegetable stock, 1 cup brown lentils and 3 peeled, cubed sweet potatoes. Simmer about 30 minutes until soft. Cook 10 minutes. Add salt to taste.	Cooked Lentils Carbohydrate: 40 g Fat: 1 g Protein: 18 g Sodium: 4 mg Vitamin A: 15.8 IU Selenium: 5.5 mcg Dietary Fiber: 16 g
Sunflower Seeds	The antioxidant vitamin E, found in sunflower seeds, may help to limit itching and reduce the extent of lesions. It also helps to maintain the health of the immune system.[4]	Sunflower Seed Energy Balls: Process ½ cup pitted dates, 1 cup unsweetened dried apricots, ½ cup unsweetened coconut flakes, ½ cup raw sunflower seeds and ¼ cup tahini.* Roll into bite-size balls. Freeze or refrigerate.	Freeze or refrigerate. Sunflower Seeds Carbohydrate: 28 g Fat: 72 g Protein: 29 g Sodium: 13 mg Vitamin E: 46.5 mg Selenium: 74.2 mcg Dietary Fiber: 12 g
Molasses	The minerals and trace elements found in molasses are important to skin health.[5] Molasses contains selenium and zinc, which are important for normal healthy skin.[6]	Drizzle molasses on hot oatmeal that has been topped with sliced banana and chopped nuts. It can also be stirred into yogurt, or blended into smoothies.	Molasses Carbohydrate: 252 g Fat: 0 g Protein: 0 g Sodium: 125 mg Iron: 15.9 mg Selenium: 60 mcg Zinc: 1 mg

HEALTH TIP: Soaking in a tub of lukewarm water with two cups of oatmeal for 20 minutes may relieve itching.[7]

EPILEPSY

A disorder of the central nervous system that disrupts the nerve cell activity of the brain, resulting in temporary disturbance of mental, sensory or motor function, also known as a seizure. Symptoms may include staring blankly and twitching arms and legs. Symptomatic epilepsy may be caused by a tumor, chemical imbalance, head injury, stroke, alcohol withdrawal, and drug abuse. In many cases the cause of seizures is unknown.

Foods	Health Benefits	How To Use	Composition (based on Cup)
Avocados	The use of anticonvulsant drugs may cause deficiencies in biotin, folic acid and vitamin B6. Avocados are a good source of all of these essential nutrients.[1]	Avocado Ranch Dressing: Blend 1 avocado, ½ cup unsweetened almond milk, 2 tablespoons lemon juice, 1 tablespoon olive oil, 1 teaspoon each of garlic powder, onion powder, dried parsley, dried dill and ½ teaspoon salt.	Fresh Avocados Carbohydrate: 13 g Fat: 22 g Protein: 3 g Sodium: 11 mg Vitamin B6: 0.4 mg Folate: 122 mcg Magnesium: 43.5 mg
Swiss Chard	Inadequate magnesium levels may contribute to increased frequency of seizures. Swiss chard provides dietary magnesium that will help to increase and maintain magnesium levels in the body.[1]	Swiss Chard Salad: Wash and finely slice Swiss chard. Combine with sliced celery, sliced cucumber and toasted walnuts. To serve drizzle with Avocado Ranch Dressing.	Raw Swiss Chard Carbohydrate: 1 g Fat: 0 g Protein: 1 g Sodium: 77 mg Folate: 5 mcg Magnesium: 29.2 mg Omega-3: 2.5 mg
Brussels Sprouts	Brussels sprouts provide a good source of thiamine. Severe thiamine deficiency can lead to seizures. Adequate thiamine levels have been associated with improved cognitive function in epilepsy patients.[1]	Roasted Brussels Sprouts: Cut off ends and remove damaged outer leaves. Toss with a little olive oil and a little salt. Place in a baking pan and roast at 400°F for approximately 40 minutes until tender inside.	Cooked Brussels Sprouts Carbohydrate: 12 g Fat: 0 g Protein: 4 g Sodium: 32 mg Vitamin B6: 0.2 mg Thiamin: 0.2 mg Folate: 93.6 mcg
Broccoli	Broccoli contains dietary folate and omega-3 fatty acids which help to improve levels of these nutrients. Both of these nutrients may help to reduce the frequency of seizures.[1,2]	Broccoli Dip: Process 2 cups cooked white beans, 2 cups steamed tender broccoli florets, 1 clove garlic, 1 ½ tablespoons lemon juice, 1 teaspoon olive oil and ½ teaspoon salt. Enjoy with carrot and celery sticks.	Cooked Broccoli Carbohydrate: 12 g Fat: 0 g Protein: 4 g Sodium: 64 mg Vitamin A: 2,414 IU Vitamin C: 101.2 mg Dietary Fiber: 6 g
Sunflower Seeds	In some cases vitamin B6 deficiency can cause epileptic seizures.[2] Sunflower seeds provide dietary vitamin B6, which may help to reduce deficiency and frequency of seizures.[1]	Roasted Sunflower Seeds: Rinse off raw sunflower seeds. Blot dry. Place a single layer on parchment paper on a baking sheet. Roast at 300°F for about 40 minutes. Sprinkle on vegetable dishes.	Sunflower Seeds Carbohydrate: 31 g Fat: 64 g Protein: 25 g Sodium: 4 mg Vitamin B6: 1 mg Magnesium: 165 mcg Omega-3: 88.3 mg
Walnuts	Walnuts contain omega-3 fatty acids which may help to reduce seizure frequency. They also contain vitamin B6 and biotin to help prevent deficiency, and thiamine which may improve cognitive function.[1]	Walnut Crackers: Process 2 cups walnuts until crumbly. Place in bowl. Process 2 cups zucchini into tiny pieces. Add to bowl. Stir in ½ cup ground flaxseed and 1 teaspoon salt. Mix. Add water to make spreadable dough. Spread on lined baking sheets. Dehydrate in oven at 105°F until dry.	English Walnuts Carbohydrate: 16 g Fat: 76 g Protein: 18 g Sodium: 2 mg Magnesium: 185 mg Thiamin: 0.4 mg Omega-3: 10,623 mg

ENCOURAGEMENT: The very feeblest prayer that we can offer, Jesus will hear.[3]

EYE CONDITIONS

Common eye conditions include conjunctivitis, which may be caused by infection, irritants or deficiency; and glaucoma, where the pressure in the eyeball increases, causing a gradual loss of sight. Cataracts, the progressive clouding of the lens of the eye causing blurred vision, are common, as well as age related macular degeneration of the retina. There are many reasons for the loss of visual acuity, including diabetes and arteriosclerosis.

Foods	Health Benefits	How To Use	Composition (based on Cup)
Oranges	Oranges contain flavonoids, carotenoids, vitamin C and other antioxidants which help to protect against macular degeneration of the retina and help to reduce intraocular pressure in glaucoma.[1]	Orange Kale Smoothie: Blend 2 peeled, chopped oranges, 1 cup of chopped kale, 1 banana, ½ cup nondairy milk and 4 ice cubes, until perfectly smooth.	Fresh Oranges Carbohydrate: 21 g Fas: 0 g Protein: 2 g Sodium: 0 mg Vitamin A: 405 IU Vitamin C: 95.8 mg Vitamin B6: 0.1 mg
Apricots	Provitamin A and the B vitamins found in apricots assist in keeping the delicate conjunctive membrane of the eye healthy, fighting conjunctivitis. The nutrients in apricots improve the function of the retina, thus improving visual acuity.[1]	Dried Apricot Jam: Boil 1 pound chopped unsweetened dried apricots with just under 2 cups water for approximately 7 minutes. Blend a little if you want a smoother jam. Add 3 tablespoons lemon juice. Stir. Store in sterilized glass bottles. Refrigerate.	Dried Apricots Carbohydrate: 81 g Fat: 1 g Protein: 4 g Sodium: 13 mg Vitamin A: 4,686 IU Vitamin B6 0.2 mg Zinc: 0.5 mg
Cashews	Zinc found in cashews may help in slowing down and perhaps even halting the process of macular degeneration of the retina.[1,2] They also contain the antioxidants zeaxanthin and lutin, which fight macular degeneration[3] and the loss of visual acuity.[1]	Cashew, Carrot and Apricot Spread: Simmer 3 chopped carrots in a little water until tender. Add ¾ cup cashews and 10 chopped dried apricots and simmer until apricots are soft. Drain. Process. Chill. Serve on crackers.	Raw Cashews Carbohydrate: 47 g Fat: 63 g Protein: 26 g Sodium: 17 g Vitamin B6 0.6 mg Zinc: 8.3 mg Omega-3: 417.3 mg
Kale	Kale contains a large number of antioxidants including zeaxanthin and lutin, which may help reduce the risk of cataracts[3] as well as help prevent macular degeneration of the retina and loss of visual acuity.[1]	Kale, Apricot and Walnut Salad: Combine finely shredded kale, unsweetened cranberries, chopped unsweetened dried apricots, and chopped walnuts. Serve with Tahini Dressing.*	Fresh Kale Carbohydrate: 7 g Fat: 0 g Protein: 2 g Sodium: 29 mg Vitamin A: 10,302 IU Vitamin C: 80.4 mg Omega-3: 121 mcg
Carrots	Provitamin A in carrots helps the retina to perform well in dim lighting, thus helping with night blindness. Provitamin A also helps to fight conjunctivitis and loss of visual acuity.[1]	Keep a bag of fresh, crunchy baby carrots in the refrigerator which can be added whole or sliced to green salads, or eaten dipped in hummus or guacamole for a light supper.	Fresh Carrots Carbohydrate: 12 g Fat: 0 g Protein: 1 g Sodium: 88 mg Vitamin A: 21,383 IU Vitamin C: 7.6 mg Vitamin B6 0.1 mg
Flaxseed	Flaxseed contains omega-3 and omega-6 essential fatty acids which may assist in lowering inflammation on the ocular surface, aid in tear production, and help in treating dry eye symptoms.[4]	Almond Granola: Combine 8 cups oats, 1 cup shredded coconut, ¾ cup flaxseed, 1 cup almonds, 1 teaspoon salt. Blend ¾ cup sunflower seeds, ¾ cup water, ¾ cup honey, 2 teaspoons vanilla. Stir into oat mixture. Bake in shallow pans at 225˚F, stirring occasionally until golden brown.	Ground Flaxseed Carbohydrate: 32 g Fat: 48 g Protein: 16 g Sodium: 32 mg Omega-3: 25,552 mg Omega-6: 6,624 mg Zinc: 4.8 mg

DID YOU KNOW? The eye muscles are the most active muscles in the body.[5]

FATIGUE

A state of extreme tiredness which does not abate. Some typical symptoms include feelings of weakness, lack of energy, lethargy, shortness of breath and poor concentration. Inadequate diet, exercise and rest as well as overwork, stress, medication, and mental or physical disease may all trigger fatigue.

Foods	Health Benefits	How To Use	Composition (based on Cup)
Raspberries	The antioxidants found in raspberries neutralize free radicals, reducing oxidative stress on the mitochondria, which play an important role in healthy energy production.[1]	Raspberry Orange Smoothie: Blend 1 banana, 1 cup frozen raspberries, 1 cup orange juice, ⅓ cup nondairy milk and 2 teaspoons sesame seeds until creamy. Add honey to taste if needed.	Fresh Raspberries Carbohydrate: 15 g Fat: 1 g Protein: 1 g Sodium: 1 mg Vitamin A: 40.6 IU Vitamin C: 32.2 mg Vitamin E: 1.1 mg
Oranges	Oranges contain essential nutrients such as vitamins, minerals and fiber, all of which are essential to the healthy functioning of the body.[2]	Orange Avocado Salad: Place salad greens on each plate. Layer with a little chopped cilantro, slivered red onion, diced avocado, and orange segments. Drizzle with a little orange juice and olive oil or Sunflower Seed Dressing.*	Fresh Oranges Carbohydrate: 21 g Fat: 0 g Protein: 2 g Sodium: 0 mg Vitamin A: 405 IU Vitamin C: 95.8 mg Dietary Fiber: 4 g
Sesame Seeds	The calcium, potassium and sodium found in sesame seeds help to maintain adequate levels of electrolytes in the body, preventing deficiency and fighting fatigue.[3]	Banana Tahini Toast: Spread whole grain toast with a layer of tahini,* followed by a thin layer of honey, and top with slices of fresh banana.	Sesame Seeds Carbohydrate: 34 g Fat: 72 g Protein: 26 g Sodium: 16 mg Calcium: 1,404 mg Potassium: 674 mg Iron: 20.9 mg
Brown Rice	Brown rice contains magnesium, a mineral essential for energy production in the body. Inadequate magnesium blocks the healthy functioning of the mitochondria, which play a role in energy production for the body.[1]	Stir-Fry Brown Rice: Stir-fry sliced carrots, zucchini, onions, bell peppers and cashews with a little olive oil, soy sauce and garlic salt until just tender. Add cooked brown rice and stir fry for 2 to 3 minutes longer. Remove from heat and serve.	Cooked Brown Rice Carbohydrate: 45 g Fat: 2 g Protein: 5 g Sodium: 10 mg Magnesium: 83.9 mg Potassium: 83.9 mg Iron: 0.8 mg
White Beans	The iron in white beans helps to overcome iron deficiency, that causes a feeling of faintness and tiredness. The complex carbohydrates in white beans digest slowly, releasing energy gradually.[3]	White Bean Pasta Sauce: Sauté 1 diced shallot and a little minced garlic for 2 minutes, add two cups white beans, 1 ½ to 2 cups vegetable stock and salt to taste. Simmer 5 to 6 minutes. Blend until creamy. Adjust seasoning as needed.	Cooked White Beans Carbohydrate: 45 g Fat: 1 g Protein: 17 g Sodium: 11 mg Magnesium: 113 mg Iron: 6.6 mg Dietary Fiber: 11 g
Potatoes	The B vitamins in potatoes are essential for maintaining the biochemical reactions which enable our bodies to convert the food we eat into energy for our cells.[1]	Baked Potato Wedges: Slice washed potatoes into wedges, thoroughly coat with lemon juice. Toss until evenly coated with dried herbs and minced garlic. Bake a single layer on a lined baking sheet at 400°F, stirring occasionally until crisp and lightly browned.	Baked Potatoes Carbohydrate: 63 g Fat: 0 g Protein: 7 g Sodium: 30 mg Vitamin C: 28.7 mg Magnesium: 83.7 mg Dietary Fiber: 7 g

ENCOURAGEMENT: Come to me, all ye that labour and are heavy laden, and I will give you rest (Matthew 11:28).

FIBROMYALGIA

A chronic condition with complex, chronic, widespread musculoskeletal pain. Common symptoms include muscular pain and tenderness, joint stiffness, fatigue, insomnia, headaches, cognitive difficulties, anxiety and depression. The exact cause of this disease is not known, and it is often misdiagnosed.

Foods	Health Benefits	How To Use	Composition (based on Cup)
Apples	Apples are high in malic acid, which helps to reduce the number of tender points in the body. It also assists in binding aluminum and removing it from the body.[1,2]	Raw Applesauce: Process or blend 3 cored, chopped apples, 2 teaspoons lemon juice, 1 soft date (optional) and water as needed. Enjoy as is, on pancakes or in smoothies.	Fresh Apples Carbohydrate: 17 g Fat: 0 g Protein: 0 g Sodium: 1 mg Omega-3: 11.2 mg Magnesium: 6.3 mg Folate: 3.8 mcg
Bananas	Bananas contain magnesium, which is key to many of the enzymatic reactions in the body. Adequate magnesium, along with malic acid has been found to decrease muscular pain and tenderness.[1]	Banana Pudding: Process 1 cup soaked cashews, 1 frozen ripe banana and 1 regular ripe banana, 4 dates, and approximately ⅓ cup almond milk, until perfectly smooth. Serve topped with fresh berries.	Fresh Bananas Carbohydrate: 34 g Fat: 0 g Protein: 2 g Sodium: 2 mg Magnesium: 60.8 mg Thiamin: 0.1 mg Folate: 45 mcg
Walnuts	Walnuts are a good source of omega-3 fatty acids, which are known to help reduce inflammation and which also help to build the immune system.[3]	Chopped walnuts, along with sliced banana can be used to top oatmeal or be stirred into non-dairy yogurt. They can also be sprinkled on pasta dishes, and added to grain dishes and fresh vegetable salads.	English Walnuts Carbohydrate: 16 g Fat: 76 g Protein: 18 g Sodium: 2 mg Magnesium: 185 mg Folate: 115 mcg Omega-3: 10,623 mg
Avocados	Avocado contains magnesium to help reduce tenderness[1] and omega-3 to help reduce inflammation.[3] It also contains vitamin E, which has been found to be helpful in improving quality of life.[4]	Avocado Toast: Peel and mash one ripe avocado and spread it on three or four slices of wholegrain bread toast. Sprinkle with garlic or celery salt to taste.	Carbohydrate: 13 g Fat: 22 g Protein: 3 g Sodium: 11 mg Vitamin E: 3.1 mg Magnesium: 43.5 mg Omega-3: 165 mg
Spinach	Dark leafy greens like spinach are high in folate, which helps to regulate the central nervous system, thus preventing deficiency which leads to peripheral neuropathy pain.[4]	Green Smoothie: Blend 1 cup apple juice, 2 cups chopped baby spinach, 1 peeled, cored, and chopped apple, 1 cup chopped pineapple and ½ to 1 diced avocado, together until smooth.	Fresh Spinach Carbohydrate: 1 g Fat: 0 g Protein: 1 g Sodium: 24 mg Folate: 58.2 mcg Magnesium: 23.7 mg Omega-3: 41.4 mg
Black Beans	Black beans contain thiamine, which is essential for normal functioning of the central nervous system, and has been observed to reduce fatigue and related symptoms.[5]	Mexican Black Bean Salad: Combine diced cucumber, cooked black beans, cooked corn kernels, diced red pepper, cherry tomatoes, diced avocado, a little chopped cilantro and a little lime juice. Add salt to taste.	Cooked Black Beans Carbohydrate: 41 g Fat: 1 g Protein: 15 g Sodium: 2 mg Folate: 256 mcg Thiamin: 0.4 mg Omega-3: 181 mg

HEALTH TIP: Regular exercise helps to decrease pain and stiffness.

GALLBLADDER DISEASE

Cholecystitis is the most common gallbladder disease, in which the gallbladder becomes inflamed, often due to irritation of the gallbladder walls by gallstones, or by gallstones blocking the ducts that lead from the gallbladder. While in many cases symptoms may not be obvious right away, common symptoms include intermittent pain, nausea, vomiting, and jaundice.

Foods	Health Benefits	How To Use	Composition (based on Cup)
Papayas	Papaya is high in vitamin C, which may help to reduce the risk of forming gallstones.[1] Due to the fact that fruit has almost no fat, if eaten alone this gives the gallbladder time to rest.[2]	Papaya Blackberry Smoothie: Blend 1 cup papaya, ½ cup of fresh or frozen blackberries, ½ cup fresh or frozen strawberries, ½ cup nondairy milk and 1 tablespoon of honey.	Fresh Papaya Carbohydrate: 14 g Fat: 0 g Protein: 1 g Sodium: 4 mg Vitamin C: 86.5 mg Calcium: 33.6 mg Folate: 53.2 mcg
Blackberries	The antioxidants, B vitamins and fiber found in blackberries may help to reduce the symptoms of gallbladder disease, including inflammation.[3] They also contain calcium which may help to reduce the risk of developing gallstones.[4]	Blackberry Banana Ice Cream: In a food processor process 1 frozen sliced banana, ½ cup frozen blackberries, ¼ cup almond milk (optional), and 1 tablespoon honey until creamy.	Frozen Blackberries Carbohydrate: 24 g Fat: 1 g Protein: 2 g Sodium: 2 mg Niacin: 1.8 mg B6: 0.1 mg Dietary Fiber: 8 g
Peas	Adequate intake of dietary fiber helps to lower cholesterol and decreases the risk of gallstones.[4] Peas are a good source of fiber, as well as antioxidants and B vitamins which may help to reduce gallbladder disease symptoms.[3]	Asparagus Pea Salad: Combine 1 cup lightly steamed asparagus, 1 cup cooked quinoa, 1 cup fresh or frozen peas, 1 cup baby spinach, ¼ cup grated butternut, ¼ cup sliced almonds, ¼ cup spinach pesto, and 1 tablespoon lemon juice.	Frozen Green Peas Carbohydrate: 18 g Fat: 1 g Protein: 7 g Sodium: 145 mg Niacin: 2.3 mg Folate: 71 mcg Dietary Fiber: 6 g
Broccoli	Broccoli contains fiber and antioxidants and is a good source of vitamin C. All these nutrients may help to lower the risk of gallbladder disease and gallstones. [1,3,4]	Broccoli Soup: In a large pot combine 6 cups vegetable stock, 7 medium potatoes, peeled and cubed, 1 chopped onion, 1 chopped broccoli head, 1 teaspoon ground coriander, 1 teaspoon garlic powder, cook until tender. Blend. Salt to taste as needed.	Fresh Broccoli Carbohydrate: 6 g Fat: 0 g Protein: 3 g Sodium: 30 mg Vitamin C: 81.2 mg Folate: 57.3 mcg Dietary Fiber: 2 g
Almonds	Almonds are a good source of fiber and calcium. It has been shown that people who consume these nutrients, and in particular eat nuts regularly, are less likely to develop gallstones.[4,5]	Almond Apricot Balls: Combine 5 ounces ground almonds, 7 ounces finely chopped dried apricots, 1 tablespoon unsweetened shredded coconut, 1 tablespoon honey. Roll into little balls. Store in refrigerator.	Almonds Carbohydrate: 31 g Fat: 71 g Protein: 30 g Sodium: 1 mg Folate: 71.5 mcg Calcium: 378 mg Dietary Fiber: 17.4 g
Red Kidney Beans	The B vitamins, calcium and fiber that red kidney beans supply, may help to reduce inflammation as well as reduce the risk of gallstone formation.[3,4]	Three Bean Salad: Combine ½ cup chopped lightly cooked green beans, ¾ cup cooked garbanzos, ¾ cup cooked red kidney beans, ½ chopped orange bell pepper, 1 tablespoon chopped parsley, 1 green onion chopped, and a little olive oil, lemon juice and salt to taste.	Red Kidney Beans Carbohydrate: 40 g Fat: 1 g Protein: 15 g Sodium: 4 mg Niacin: 1 mg Calcium: 49.6 mg Dietary Fiber: 13 g

DID YOU KNOW? Gallstones can range in size from as small as a grain of sand to the size of a golf ball.[6]

GASTRITIS

A condition in which the stomach lining becomes irritated and inflamed, and which may occur gradually or suddenly. Gastritis commonly results from infection or medication use; however, it may also be caused by injury, critical illness and alcohol use. Symptoms may include indigestion, bloating, burning pain in the upper abdomen, nausea, vomiting and loss of appetite.

Foods	Health Benefits	How To Use	Composition (based on Cup)
Papayas	The vitamin C found in papayas plays an important role in protecting and healing the gastric mucosa. Vitamin C also helps to prevent and reduce gastric inflammation.[1]	Papaya Oatmeal Smoothie: Blend 1 cup fresh or frozen cubed papaya, 1 banana, 1 tablespoon oats, 1 teaspoon honey and 1 cup unsweetened nondairy milk until smooth.	Fresh Papayas Carbohydrate: 14 g Fat: 0 g Protein: 1 g Sodium: 4 mg Vitamin A: 1,531 IU Vitamin C: 86.5 mg Vitamin E: 1.0 mg
Oats	Oats contain mucilage, which helps to protect and soothe the gastric mucosa, the mucous membrane layer of the stomach, and is usually a recommended food for individuals suffering with gastritis.[2]	Raspberry Papaya Overnight Oats: Combine ½ cup oats, ½ cup almond milk, 1 teaspoon vanilla and 1 teaspoon honey. Seal container, refrigerate overnight. Layer with chopped papaya and fresh raspberries in the morning.	Raw Oats Carbohydrate: 103 g Fat: 11 g Protein: 26 g Sodium: 3 mg Dietary Fiber: 17 g Folate: 87.4 mcg Magnesium: 276 mg
Beets	Beets contain powerful antioxidants which aid in protecting cells from free radical damage. The nutrients found in beets also play a vital role in reducing inflammation and pain.[3]	Roasted Beet Soup: Sauté 1 sliced leek in a little olive oil until tender. Add 3 chopped Roasted Beets,* 7 cloves Roasted Garlic,* 1 teaspoon dried thyme, 1 bay leaf, 3 cups water. Bring to boil, simmer 8 minutes. Cool. Blend. Add 2 tablespoons lemon juice and salt to taste.	Cooked Beets Carbohydrate: 16 g Fat: 0 g Protein: 4 g Sodium: 130 mg Vitamin A: 60 IU Vitamin C: 6.2 mg Magnesium: 39.2 mg
Potatoes	Baked, boiled or puréed potatoes have a soft texture and an antacid effect on the stomach. They contain nutrients that are sedating and soothing and aid in curing gastritis.[2]	Boiled Potatoes: Place small potatoes in a pot, and cover with 1 inch of water. Bring to the boil. Reduce heat to medium, and simmer until tender. Drain. Cool. Peel and cut in half. Place in a bowl and coat with a drizzle of olive oil. Sprinkle with chopped chives and a little salt.	Boiled Potatoes Carbohydrate: 32 g Fat: 0 g Protein: 2 g Sodium: 374 mg Vitamin A: 4.6 IU Vitamin C: 20.2 mg Dietary Fiber: 4 g
Broccoli	Broccoli contains sulforaphane which has been found to kill *H. pylori* bacteria in the lining of the stomach. Broccoli sprouts are over 20 times higher in sulphoraphane than mature broccoli.[4]	Broccoli Sprouts: Rinse and then soak two tablespoons broccoli seeds in water to cover for 8 hours. Drain. Rinse. Place in jar and cover top with cheesecloth and hold cloth on with an elastic. Keep in cool dark place. Rinse and drain every 12 hours for 2-5 days until sprouted.	Fresh Broccoli Carbohydrate: 6 g Fat: 0 g Protein: 3 g Sodium: 30 mg Vitamin A: 567 IU Vitamin C: 81.2 mg Vitamin E: 0.7 mg
Rice	Rice has astringent properties that help to dry the gastric mucosa. Rice is also known to be an excellent anti-inflammatory for the stomach and intestines.[2]	Pesto Brown Rice: Combine 4 cups cooked brown rice, ½ cup Spinach Pesto,* ½ cup toasted pine nuts and salt to taste. Serve warm.	Cooked Brown Rice Carbohydrate: 45 g Fat: 2 g Protein: 5 g Sodium: 10 mg Iron: 1.0 mg Magnesium: 83.9 mg Dietary Fiber: 4 g

HEALTH TIP: Avoiding caffeine helps to reduce inflammation in the body.[5]

GERD

A chronic digestive disease also known as gastroesophageal reflux disease. This disease is often caused by a weak esophageal sphincter which allows stomach acid to flow back into the esophagus, irritating the lining. This acid reflux causes heartburn pain, inflammation, chest pain, and a sore throat.

Foods	Health Benefits	How To Use	Composition (based on Cup)
Blackberries	Blackberries provide a good source of antioxidants and dietary fiber, both of which may be helpful in reducing the risk of GERD symptoms.[1,2]	Blackberry Beet Smoothie: Blend ¾ cup fresh or frozen blackberries, 1 banana, ¼ cup grated beet, ¾ cup nondairy milk, 1 tablespoon chia seed, and 2 teaspoons honey until smooth.	Frozen Blackberries Carbohydrate: 24 g Fat: 1 g Protein: 2 g Sodium: 2 mg Vitamin A: 172 IU Vitamin C: 4.7 mg Dietary Fiber: 8 g
Beets	Beets contain antioxidant vitamins A, C, E and B vitamins along with trace minerals magnesium, calcium, zinc and selenium which may help to improve digestive health.[1]	Beet and Arugula Salad: Combine 3 cups arugula, 3 cooked, peeled, cubed beets, ⅓ cup walnuts, 2 tablespoons olive oil and 2 tablespoons lemon juice. Season to taste.	Cooked Beets Carbohydrate: 8 g Fat: 0 g Protein: 4 g Sodium: 347 mg Vitamin C: 35.9 mg Folate 20.2 mcg Zinc: 0.7 mg
Spinach	Leafy greens such as spinach that are high in B vitamins and calcium may help to reduce GERD symptoms. They also contain other antioxidants and trace minerals which may improve digestive health.[1]	Spinach Cashew Spread: Process 1 cup soaked, drained, raw, unsalted cashews, 1 clove garlic, 1 tablespoon nutritional yeast, 1 tablespoon water and ¼ teaspoon salt until creamy. Add 3 cups spinach and process until smooth. Enjoy with crackers, toast or corn chips.	Fresh Spinach Carbohydrate: 1 g Fat: 0 g Protein: 1 g Sodium: 24 mg Calcium: 29.7 mg Folate: 58.2 mcg Omega-3: 41.4 mg
Chia Seeds	Omega-3 fatty acids in chia seeds may help to reduce the inflammation caused by acid reflux.[1] Chia seeds are a good source of dietary fiber, which helps to reduce the risk of GERD symptoms.[2]	Blackberry Chia Jam: Bring 1 pound frozen blackberries to boil; simmer until soft. Mash lightly. Stir in 2 tablespoons honey and 3 tablespoons chia seeds. Cook about 5 minutes on low until thick, stirring often. Remove from heat and stir in ½ teaspoon vanilla extract.	Chia Seeds Carbohydrate: 72 g Fat: 51 g Protein: 26 g Sodium: 31 g Calcium: 1,029 mg Zinc: 5.71 g Omega-3: 28,610 mg
Oats	Oats are a good source of B vitamins, calcium and dietary fiber, which may help to reduce GERD symptoms. Oatmeal helps to absorb acid in the stomach.[2,3]	Almond Oatmeal: Bring 1 cup coconut milk to boil. Add ½ cup oats, reduce heat. Add 1 mashed banana. Once most liquid is absorbed add ¼ teaspoon almond extract, pinch of salt and 1 tablespoon carob powder. Cook to desired consistency. Top with blackberries and chia seeds.	Raw Oats Carbohydrate: 103 g Fat: 11 g Protein: 26 g Sodium: 3 mg Thiamin: 1.2 mg Niacin: 1.5 mg Dietary Fiber: 17 g
Ginger	Ginger acts as an antacid and has natural anti-inflammatory properties that may help to reduce the inflammation caused by GERD.[3,4]	Fresh Ginger Tea: Peel and grate ginger. Add 1 tablespoon freshly grated ginger to 2 cups boiled filtered water. Steep for 10 minutes. Remove ginger and add 1 tablespoon honey.	Fresh Ginger Carbohydrate: 18 g Fat: 1 g Protein: 2 g Sodium: 13 g Vitamin B6: 0.2 mg Folate: 11 mcg Magnesium: 43 mg

DID YOU KNOW? Caffeine relaxes the sphincter, allowing stomach contents to move back up into the esophagus.[4]

GOUT

A form of arthritis that occurs when excess uric acid builds up in the body, bringing on sudden attacks of severe pain, inflammation and swelling in the joints. This occurs particularly in the smaller joints of the feet, and most often in the joint at the base of the big toe.

Foods	Health Benefits	How To Use	Composition (based on Cup)
Cherries	The consumption of cherries or cherry juice has been found to reduce the risk of gout attacks recurring. Cherries contain high levels of flavonoids called anthocyanins that may help to protect against inflammation.[1]	Research suggests that half a pound of fresh or frozen cherries be consumed daily for two weeks.[2] Fresh or frozen cherries can be added to fruit smoothies, used as a topping for cereal, or added to fruit salad.	Fresh Cherries Carbohydrate: 22 g Fat: 0 g Protein: 1 g Sodium: 0 g Vitamin A: 88.3 IU Vitamin C: 9.7 mg Magnesium: 15.2 mg
Pineapples	Pineapples contain a nutrient called bromelain, which may be helpful in dealing with the pain and inflammation caused by gout. Pineapples also contain vitamin C, which may lower the risk of gout attacks.[2]	Pineapple Salad: Combine small cubes of pineapple, chopped cucumber, diced tomato, a few sliced green onions, a little chopped mint and some fresh lime juice.	Fresh Pineapples Carbohydrate: 22g Fat: 0 g Protein: 1 g Sodium: 2 mg Vitamin C: 78.9 mg Thiamin: 0.1 mg Folate: 29.7 mcg
Avocados	The B vitamins, including folate, found in avocado assist in changing the uric acid in the body into harmless compounds, thus lowering the risk of gout attacks.[2]	Avocado Topping for Baked Potato: Mash one avocado well, add a little chopped onion and tomato, fresh lime juice, fresh parsley and dill. Add salt to taste. Serve on hot baked potato.	Fresh Avocados Carbohydrate: 13 g Fat: 22 g Protein: 3 g Sodium: 11 mg Vitamin C: 15 mg Folate: 122 mcg Fiber: 10 g
Potatoes	Potatoes are a good source of magnesium, are low in calcium, and are a source of dietary fiber. These nutrients are recommended as part of a healthy diet for treating gout.[2]	Potato Salad: Combine cooked, peeled, cubed potatoes, chopped red onion, red bell pepper, a little fresh chopped mint and oregano, salt to taste, fresh lemon juice and a little olive oil. Refrigerate until an hour before serving.	Boiled Potatoes Carbohydrate: 32 g Fat: 0 g Protein: 2 g Sodium: 374 mg Vitamin C: 20.2 mg Magnesium: 34.4 mg Dietary Fiber: 4 g
Oats	Oats contain B vitamins, which help to lower uric acid levels[3] as well as provide a good source of magnesium and are low in calcium. They also add fiber to the diet. Fiber is an important nutrient for individuals prone to gout.[2]	Simple Granola: Combine 8 cups quick oats, 1 cup coconut, 1 teaspoon salt. Blend ¾ cup sunflower seeds, ¾ cup water, ¾ cup honey, 2 teaspoons vanilla. Add blended mixture to oats, mix well. Bake in large shallow pans at 225°F, stirring occasionally until golden brown.	Raw Oats Carbohydrate: 103 g Fat: 11 g Protein: 26 g Sodium: 3 mg Thiamin: 1.2 mg Folate: 87.4 mcg Dietary Fiber: 17 g
Turmeric	Curcumin is a naturally occurring chemical compound found in turmeric. It works to decrease the levels of two enzymes that are known to cause inflammation.[4]	Turmeric Vegetable Soup: Sauté 1 cup chopped onion, 1 sliced carrot, 2 cloves minced garlic in a little olive oil. Stir in 1 tablespoon ground turmeric, 6 cups vegetable broth, 3 cups cauliflower, 2 cups cooked white beans, 3 cups baby spinach and simmer until vegetables are soft.	Turmeric Powder Carbohydrate: 65 g Fat: 16 g Protein: 16 g Sodium: 48 mg Vitamin C: 27.2 g Folate: 41.6 mcg Magnesium: 208 mg

ENCOURAGEMENT: Let patience, gratitude, and love keep sunshine in the heart though the day may be ever so cloudy.[5]

GUM DISEASE

A condition in which the soft tissue of the gums become inflamed, starting with gingivitis and progressing to periodontitis. Advanced periodontitis includes abnormal loss of bone that surrounds and holds the teeth in place, and can result in loss of teeth. Symptoms may include bleeding gums, infection, swelling and pain.

Foods	Health Benefits	How To Use	Composition (based on Cup)
Kiwifruit	Kiwifruit contains vitamin C, which plays an important role in forming collagen and connective tissue essential for healthy gums. Vitamin C deficiency increases the risk of developing periodontal disease.[1]	Kiwifruit Pancake Sauce: Combine 8 peeled, finely diced kiwifruit with 5 tablespoons passion fruit pulp and two tablespoons of honey. Place sliced banana and strawberries on pancakes and top with kiwifruit sauce.	Fresh Kiwifruit Carbohydrate: 28g Fat: 0 g Protein: 2 g Sodium: 10 mg Vitamin C: 136.4 mg Calcium: 47.4 mg Magnesium: 54.7 mg
Chia Seeds	Chia seeds are a good source of omega-3 fatty acids, which have anti-bacterial properties. An adequate supply of omega-3 fatty acids may reduce the risk of periodontal disease.[1]	Pudding: Blend 2 cups coconut milk, 3 tablespoons of honey and ½ teaspoon of vanilla. Whisk in ½ cup chia seeds. Refrigerate overnight. In the morning top with chopped fruit and nuts.	Chia Seeds Carbohydrate: 72 g Fat: 51 g Protein: 26 g Sodium: 31 g Calcium: 1,029 mg Zinc: 5.71 g Omega-3: 28,610 mg
Cashews	Cashews contain zinc, a mineral that plays an essential role in new tissue formation and wound healing. Adequate zinc levels support immune system health and help to control periodontal disease.[1]	Vanilla Cashew Shake: Blend ½ cup raw cashews, ⅓ cup water, 1 banana, 1 tablespoon honey, ½ teaspoon vanilla extract, pinch of salt, and 6 large ice cubes until smooth.	Raw Cashews Carbohydrate: 47 g Fat: 63 g Protein: 26 g Sodium: 17 g Magnesium: 417.3 mg Zinc: 8.3 mg Omega-3: 417.3 mg
Corn	The mineral magnesium, found in corn, fights magnesium deficiency, which is linked to swelling and inflammation of the gums, as well as deterioration of the health of the gums.[1]	Corn Salad: Combine 3 cups cooked corn, 1 diced tomato, ½ green bell pepper diced, ½ red onion diced. Blend ½ cup cilantro, ¼ cup olive oil, 2 cloves garlic, 1 ½ tablespoons lime juice and salt to taste. Pour over salad and mix well.	Cooked Corn Carbohydrate: 41 g Fat: 2 g Protein: 5 g Sodium: 0 mg Calcium: 4.9 mg Magnesium: 42.6 mg Zinc: 1 mg
Soybeans	Green soybeans, also called edamame, are a good source of calcium. Inadequate calcium in the body has been linked to greater risk of gingival detachment and more severe periodontal disease.[1]	Plain Green Soybeans: Bring 3 ½ cups water to a boil. Add ½ pound shelled edamame and ½ teaspoon salt. Boil five minutes. Drain. Rinse with cold water. Serve plain or cold in a green salad.	Green Soybeans Carbohydrate: 20 g Fat: 12 g Protein: 22g Sodium: 25 mg Calcium: 261 mg Magnesium: 108 mg Zinc: 1.6 mg
Buckwheat	Buckwheat is high in amino acids, which help to repair tissue and maintain healthy gums. Inadequate amino acid levels result in vulnerability to infection, slower wound healing and degeneration of periodontal tissue.[1]	Savory Buckwheat: Sauté 1 chopped onion in a little olive oil. Add 1 cup buckwheat groats, 2 cloves garlic, ½ teaspoon cumin. Sauté 3 minutes. Add 2 cups vegetable stock, bring to a boil then simmer until liquid is absorbed. Stir in 1 chopped tomato, ½ teaspoon salt. Serve while hot.	Buckwheat Carbohydrate: 122 g Fat: 6 g Protein: 23 g Sodium: 2 mg Calcium: 30.6 mg Magnesium: 393 mg Zinc: 4.1 mg

HEALTH TIP: Brushing teeth with a soft toothbrush after every meal helps to fight gum disease.[2]

HAIR LOSS

A condition that can affect the entire body or just the scalp and may be temporary or permanent. There are many reasons for hair loss, but some of the most common causes are hereditary hair loss with age, hormonal changes, scalp infections, medications and radiation. The risk of hair loss is also increased by stress and poor nutrition.

Foods	Health Benefits	How To Use	Composition (based on Cup)
Avocados	Avocados contain the essential amino acid l-lysine which has been found helpful in reducing hair loss.[1] They also contain minerals and trace elements that help to build healthy hair.[2]	Avocado Garbanzo Salad Tacos: Combine 1 ½ cups cooked garbanzos slightly mashed with 1 mashed avocado, ¼ cup grated carrot, ½ teaspoon minced garlic, ½ tablespoon lime juice and salt to taste. Place into tacos and add salsa.	Fresh Avocados Carbohydrate: 13 g Fat: 22 g Protein: 3 g Sodium: 11 mg Lysine: 198 mg Beta-carotene: 93 mcg Niacin: 2.6 mg
Tomatoes	Tomatoes supply the body with iron, a nutrient that helps fight hair loss.[3] Tomatoes also contain Vitamin A, which is essential for building healthy hair.[2]	Creamy Tomato Pasta Sauce: Blend 2 tomatoes, ½ cup raw cashews, ¼ cup water, and 1 teaspoon tomato paste. Sauté 2 teaspoons chopped garlic in a little olive oil. Add blender mixture and simmer for five minutes, add water if needed. Stir into pasta and enjoy right away.	Fresh Tomatoes Carbohydrate: 7 g Fat: 0 g Protein: 2 g Sodium: 9 mg Beta-carotene: 808 mcg Iron: 0.5 mg Calcium: 18 mg
Carrots	Orange vegetables such as carrots are a good source of beta-carotene, which is converted to Vitamin A in the body. This vitamin is key to having healthy skin, hair and nails.[2]	Roasted Carrot Pâté: Wrap 4 cloves garlic and 12 ounces carrots in foil and bake at 350°F until soft. Remove from oven and process with 2 tablespoons tahini,* ½ teaspoon ground cumin, 1 teaspoon olive oil and ½ teaspoon salt. Use as a dip or spread.	Cooked Carrots Carbohydrate: 12 g Fat: 0 g Protein: 2 g Sodium: 90 mg Vitamin A: 26,576 IU Iron: 0.6 mg Calcium: 46.8 mg
Peanuts	Peanuts are a good supply of vitamin B3, also known niacin. A deficiency in this vitamin has been correlated with premature hair loss.[2]	Chopped peanuts can be sprinkled on oatmeal, pancakes, waffles and even ice cream. Peanuts can also add flavor and texture to vegetable and vegetable stir-fry dishes.	Dry Roasted Peanuts Carbohydrate: 31 g Fat: 73 g Protein: 35g Sodium: 9 mg Niacin: 19.7 mg Iron: 3.3 mg Zinc: 4.8 mg
Almonds	The antioxidant vitamin E, found in almonds, has been shown to help improve hair growth on the scalp as well as reduce hair thinning caused by alopecia.[4]	Almond Clusters: Thoroughly combine 1 ½ cups ground roasted almonds, 1 ½ cups whole roasted almonds and ½ cup honey. Use damp hands to divide into clusters, place on lined, oiled baking sheet and bake 32 minutes. Cool before storing in an airtight container.	Almonds Carbohydrate: 31 g Fat: 71 g Protein: 30 g Sodium: 1 mg Vitamin E: 37.5 mg Niacin: 4.8 mg Calcium: 378 mg
Molasses	Molasses is particularly high in minerals and trace elements, including calcium, iron, silicone and zinc, all of which are essential building blocks for healthy hair.[2]	Hot Molasses: Heat 8 ounces of soy milk until almost boiling. Pour into a mug and add 1 to 1 ½ teaspoons of blackstrap molasses. Stir well before drinking.	Molasses Carbohydrate: 252 g Fat: 0 g Protein: 0 g Sodium: 125 mg Calcium: 691 mg Iron: 15.9 mg Zinc: 1 mg

DID YOU KNOW? Physical endurance and ability to work is increased by as much as 80% with adequate water consumption.[5]

HEADACHES

A condition in which pain occurs in any region of the head. Headaches may cause pain on both sides of the head or only one side, occur in one particular place on the head, or radiate across the head. Headache pain may be dull, sharp or throbbing. Headaches can occur gradually or suddenly with a duration of less than sixty minutes up to several days. There are multiple types of headaches with multiple causes.

Foods	Health Benefits	How To Use	Composition (based on Cup)
Blackberries	High fiber foods, as well as calcium and magnesium, have been used in treating and curing migraines. Fresh and frozen blackberries are a good source of these nutrients.[1]	Blackberry Smoothie: Blend 1 cup coconut milk, ½ cup almond milk, 1 sliced banana, ¾ cup of blackberries and 1 tablespoon of honey until fairly smooth.	Frozen Blackberries Carbohydrate: 24 g Fat: 1 g Protein: 2 g Sodium: 2 mg Calcium: 43.8 mg Magnesium: 33.2 mg Dietary Fiber: 8 g
Spinach	Spinach is a source of riboflavin, otherwise known as vitamin B2. This nutrient supports normal function of the mitochondria, and may help to prevent migraine[2] and reduce the frequency of headaches.[3]	Spinach Pesto: Process 2 cups baby spinach, ¾ cup Italian parsley, ¾ cup walnuts, ½ teaspoon crushed garlic, ½ teaspoon salt. Add 2 tablespoons lemon juice, ¼ cup olive oil and water as needed and process until smooth and creamy.	Fresh Spinach Carbohydrate: 1 g Fat: 0 g Protein: 1 g Sodium: 24 mg Riboflavin: 0.1 mg Magnesium: 23.7 mg Calcium: 29.7 mg
Quinoa	Quinoa is a good source of magnesium. Magnesium deficiency seems to increase the frequency, severity and duration of headaches.[3]	Breakfast Quinoa: Bring 2 cups nondairy milk to a boil. Add ¾ cup uncooked quinoa. Simmer until milk is absorbed. Remove from heat. Add a little nondairy milk, 1 teaspoon nut butter (optional), chopped fruit, unsweetened dried cranberries and a drizzle of honey.	Cooked Quinoa Carbohydrate: 39 g Fat: 4 g Protein: 8 g Sodium: 13 mg Magnesium: 118 mg Riboflavin: 0.2 mg Dietary Fiber: 5.2 g
Potatoes	Alpha lipoic acid is a fatty acid found in many foods, including potatoes. This nutrient supports efficient mitochondrial function and may help to reduce frequency, severity and duration of headaches.[3]	Scalloped Potatoes: Blend 1 cup cashews, 2 cups cold water, 1 teaspoon onion powder, and 1 teaspoon salt. Layer with five peeled, thinly sliced potatoes. Cover with foil. Bake 45 minutes. Remove foil and bake another 15 minutes.	Boiled Potatoes Carbohydrate: 32 g Fat: 0 g Protein: 2 g Sodium: 8 mg Calcium: 12.4 mg Magnesium: 31.2 mg Dietary Fiber: 2.8 g
Black Beans	Black beans are high in folic acid and fiber, which contribute to overall health. These nutrients have been found to play an important role in treating and curing migraines.[1]	Simple Black Bean Salad: Sauté a little chopped onion and garlic in 2 tablespoons olive oil. Add 2 cups cooked quinoa, 1 ½ cups cooked black beans, 1 cup corn kernels, 2 teaspoons chopped cilantro and two tablespoons lime juice and salt to taste.	Cooked Black Beans Carbohydrate: 41 g Fat: 1 g Protein: 15 g Sodium: 2 mg Folate: 256 mcg Magnesium: 120 mg Dietary Fiber: 15 g
Broccoli	The antioxidant coenzyme Q10 helps boost mitochondrial function, which helps to reduce nausea as well as the frequency, severity and duration of headaches.[4]	Mashed Potato and Broccoli: Steam 3 cups broccoli florets and 1 pound peeled, chopped potatoes until soft. Place in bowl and mash, adding a little olive oil and salt to taste.	Cooked Broccoli Carbohydrate: 12 g Fat: 0 g Protein: 4 g Sodium: 64 mg Folate: 168.4 mcg Magnesium: 32.8 mg Dietary Fiber: 6 g

ENCOURAGEMENT: Our heavenly Father has a thousand ways to provide for us, of which we know nothing.[5]

HEARING LOSS

A condition in which the ability to hear sound has been impaired. There are varying degrees of hearing loss. It can be caused by auditory dysfunction, chronic exposure to excessively loud noise, aging, or a large amount of ear wax.

Foods	Health Benefits	How To Use	Composition (based on Cup)
Strawberries	Strawberries contain antioxidants such as vitamins A, C, and E as well as magnesium, all of which work against the formation of free radicals caused by noise exposure, and which contribute to hearing loss.[1,2]	Strawberry Banana Smoothie: Blend 1 sliced banana, 1 ½ cups fresh or frozen strawberries, 1 cup nondairy milk, and 1 tablespoon unsalted cashews until smooth. Optional extra: four ice cubes if not using frozen fruit.	Fresh Strawberries Carbohydrate: 12 g Fat: 0 g Protein: 1 g Sodium: 2 mg Vitamin A: 18.2 IU Vitamin C: 89.4 mg Magnesium: 19.8 mg
Kale	Kale provides a good source of beta carotene as well as a smaller amount of folate. An adequate supply of these nutrients may lower the risk of hearing loss.[3]	Sautéed Kale: Sauté 2-3 cloves minced garlic in a little olive oil until soft. Add destemmed, chopped kale, and ½ cup vegetable stock. Cover and cook about 6 minutes until soft. Remove lid and cook until liquid is evaporated. Season to taste.	Cooked Kale Carbohydrate: 7 g Fat: 1 g Protein: 2 g Sodium: 30 mg Beta-Carotene: 10,626 mcg Folate: 16.9 mcg Selenium: 1.2 mcg
Pumpkin	Pumpkin is high in the carotenoids beta-carotene and beta-crypotxanthin. Sufficient intake of these nutrients has been associated with a decreased risk of hearing loss.[3]	Baked Pumpkin: Scoop out the seeds and insides of the pumpkin. Cut slices about 1 inch thick. Place on a baking sheet, brush lightly with olive oil on both sides. Season with salt. Bake at 400°F for about 25 minutes until soft.	Cooked Pumpkin Carbohydrate: 12 g Fat: 0 g Protein: 2 g Sodium: 2 mg B-Carotene: 5,135 mcg B-Cryptoxanthin: 3,552 mcg Zinc: 0.6 mg
Garbanzos	Garbanzos contain a nutrient called folate, and folate deficiency may contribute to poor blood flow to the cochlea, and be linked to age-related hearing loss.[3,4]	Garbanzo Salad: Combine 3 cups cooked garbanzos, 1 small chopped red onion, 1 chopped red bell pepper, 1 minced clove of garlic, 3 ribs thinly sliced celery, 3 tablespoons of olive oil and 2 tablespoons lemon juice. Season with salt and a little rosemary.	Cooked Garbanzos Carbohydrate: 45 g Fat: 4 g Protein: 15 g Sodium: 11 mg Folate: 282 mcg Magnesium: 78.7 mg Selenium: 6.1 mcg
Brazil Nuts	Brazil nuts contain both magnesium and selenium, both of which, along with other dietary nutrients such as vitamin A, vitamin C and vitamin E, found in other food sources, may be helpful in the recovery of sudden sensorineuralural hearing impairment.[5]	Brazil Nut Balls: Process 1 cup brazil nuts, ½ cup cashews, with 6-8 pitted, softened medjool dates. Roll into little balls. Roll in unsweetened desiccated coconut. Refrigerate.	Raw Brazil Nuts Carbohydrate: 16 g Fat: 88 g Protein: 19 g Sodium: 4 mg Magnesium: 500 mg Selenium: 2,550 mcg Zinc: 5.4 mg
Cashew Nuts	The mineral zinc, found in cashew nuts, has been found to assist in recovery from sudden sensorineural hearing loss. Cashews also contain magnesium and selenium, which assist, in recovery from hearing loss.[5]	Cashew Gravy: Blend ½ cup cashews, 2 cups water, 2 tablespoons cornstarch, 2 teaspoons onion powder, ½ teaspoon garlic powder, and ½ teaspoon salt until smooth. Place in a saucepan and cook over medium heat until thick.	Raw Cashews Carbohydrate: 47 g Fat: 63 g Protein: 26 g Sodium: 17 mg Folate: 35.7 mcg Magnesium: 116.9 mg Zinc: 8.3 mg

HEALTH TIP: Choosing to use nondairy milk reduces the fat in your diet and helps keep your arteries clear.

HEMORRHOIDS

A common unpleasant and painful condition also known as piles, where veins in the walls of the anus, and occasionally around the rectum, become swollen and inflamed. Hemorrhoids are often the result of untreated constipation, but have also been infrequently associated with chronic diarrhea.

Foods	Health Benefits	How To Use	Composition (based on Cup)
Oranges	Oranges are a good source of vitamin C and contain the bioflavonoids hesperidin and rutin. It is suggested that these nutrients aid in the healing of and recovery from hemorrhoids.[1]	Creamy Orange Smoothie: Blend 1 banana, 1 peeled and quartered orange, ¼ cup unsweetened desiccated coconut, ¼ cup sunflower seeds, 1 cup nondairy milk, and 3 blocks of ice until smooth and creamy. Serve in a tall glass.	Fresh Oranges Carbohydrate: 21 g Fat: 0 g Protein: 2 g Sodium: 0 mg Vitamin A: 405 IU Vitamin C: 95.8 mg Dietary Fiber: 4 g
Grapes	The consumption of grapes has been found to increase the circulation in the veins of the portal system. They also contain anthocyanin, which helps to reduce inflammation and shrink hemorrhoids.[2]	It is recommended that two to six pounds of fresh washed grapes be consumed over a period of three days when suffering from an acute hemorrhoidal attack.[2]	Fresh Grapes Carbohydrate: 16 g Fat: 0 g Protein: 1 g Sodium: 2 mg Vitamin A: 82 IU Vitamin C: 3.7 mg Dietary Fiber: 0.8 mg
Strawberries	The soluble fiber found in strawberries helps to improve intestinal function. Strawberries are also known to improve circulation in the veins of the portal system, and to help reduce swelling.[2]	Consumption of three to four and a half pounds of preferably organic strawberries, for two to three days, may provide some relief during an acute hemmorrhodial attack.[2]	Fresh Strawberries Carbohydrate: 12 g Fat: 0 g Protein: 1 g Sodium: 2 mg Vitamin A: 18.2 IU Vitamin C: 89.4 mg Dietary Fiber: 3 g
Brown Rice	Adequate intake of insoluble fiber, as found in brown rice, helps to regulate bowel movements, helping to prevent constipation and reducing the risk of developing hemorrhoids.[3]	Brown Rice Cereal: Combine 1 ½ cups cooked rice, 1 cup non-dairy milk, and 1 tablespoon honey in saucepan, bring to a boil and cook about 4 minutes. Spoon into bowls and top with sliced banana, slivered almonds and raisins.	Cooked Brown Rice Carbohydrate: 45 g Fat: 2 g Protein: 5 g Sodium: 10 mg Calcium: 19.5 mg Magnesium: 83.9 mg Dietary Fiber: 4 g
Lentils	Lentils contain both soluble and insoluble fiber that help to soften stools, so that straining, which can cause or aggravate hemorrhoids, becomes unnecessary.[4]	Lentil Salad: Combine 3 cups drained hot cooked lentils, 2 cups diced tomatoes, ¾ cup spring onions, ¼ cup chopped fresh dill, ¼ cup fresh chopped basil, ¼ teaspoon garlic powder, 2 tablespoons olive oil and ½ teaspoon salt. Can be served warm.	Cooked Lentils Carbohydrate: 40 g Fat: 1 g Protein: 18 g Sodium: 4 mg Vitamin C: 3 mg Magnesium: 71.3 mg Dietary Fiber: 16 g
Tomatoes	The flavonoids found in tomatoes and other red and orange fruit and vegetables may help to reduce bleeding, pain, itching and recurrence of hemorrhoids.[5]	Stuffed Tomatoes: Scoop flesh out of 6 medium tomatoes. Sauté 1 chopped onion with chopped flesh from inside tomatoes. Add 1 ½ cups cooked lentils, 1 cup cooked brown rice, and salt to taste. Place mixture in tomato shells, brush with a little olive oil and bake 12 minutes at 450°F.	Cooked Tomatoes Carbohydrate: 10 g Fat: 0 g Protein: 2 g Sodium: 26 mg Vitamin C: 54.7 mg Magnesium: 21.6 mg Dietary Fiber: 2 g

DID YOU KNOW? Exercising helps you lose weight, breathe better, sleep more soundly, and feel less fatigued.

HEPATITIS

A condition in which the liver becomes inflamed, most frequently caused by a virus. Hepatitis can also be caused by autoimmune conditions and drug toxicity, including alcohol. There are five main types of hepatitis, with some resulting in swelling of the liver and/or progressing to cirrhosis or liver cancer. Typical symptoms may include joint and muscle pain, stomach pain, poor appetite, nausea, vomiting, mild fever, fatigue and yellow skin or eyes.

Foods	Health Benefits	How To Use	Composition (based on Cup)
Mangos	Mangos contain antioxidants such as vitamin C and beta-carotene, which help to limit free radical damage to liver cells. They also contain folic acid, potassium and fiber, which are important nutrients for individuals with hepatitis.[1]	Mango Smoothie: Blend 1 cup peeled, sliced, ripe mango or frozen mango, 1 ripe banana, 2/3 cup nondairy milk, 1 tablespoon of sunflower seeds and 1 teaspoon of honey until smooth.	Fresh Mangos Carbohydrate: 28 g Fat: 0 g Protein: 1 g Sodium: 3 mg Vitamin C: 45.7 mg Beta-carotene: 734 mcg Folate: 23.1 mcg
Cantaloupes	Cantaloupe is a good source of vitamin A. The liver plays an important role in metabolism and storage of vitamin A and these processes may be compromised by hepatitis, resulting in vitamin A deficiency.[2]	Cantaloupe Fruit Salad: Combine ½ cantaloupe, peeled, seeded and diced, with two mangos peeled and cubed, one cup sliced strawberries and ½ cup orange juice.	Fresh Cantaloupes Carbohydrate: 14 g Fat: 0 g Protein: 1 g Sodium: 26 mg Vitamin A: 5,412 IU Vitamin C: 58.7 mg Potassium: 473 mcg
Corn	The carnitine found in corn acts as an antioxidant in the body, helping to fight damage done by free radicals. It also works as an antiviral in the body.[3] Carnitine deficiency can result from liver disease.[4]	Creamed Corn: Simmer 1 ½ cups coconut milk and 2 cups frozen corn until mixture has thickened a little and coconut milk has reduced. Add a little salt to taste and 2 teaspoons finely chopped parsley and serve.	Cooked Corn Carbohydrate: 41 g Fat: 2 g Protein: 5 g Sodium: 0 mg Vitamin A: 431 IU Vitamin C: 10.2 mg Dietary fiber: 4.6 g
Cauliflower	The consumption of coenzyme Q10 found in cauliflower works as an antioxidant in the body, and provides support for the immune system as well as the muscular system.[3]	Cauliflower Rice: Wash and dry cauliflower. Process in food processor until it resembles rice. Sauté with 1 tablespoon olive oil in large pan over medium heat for 6 to 8 minutes. Use as you would cooked rice.	Cooked Cauliflower Carbohydrate: 6 g Fat: 0 g Protein: 2 g Sodium: 18 mg Folate: 54.6 mg Potassium: 176 mg Dietary fiber: 2.8 g
Quinoa	An adequate supply of protein, as found in quinoa, is needed for the body to be able to fight infection effectively. Protein is also needed to help the body repair damaged liver cells, and to rebuild and maintain muscles.[1]	Cashew Quinoa Salad: Combine 1 cup cold, cooked quinoa, 1 cup shredded purple cabbage, ½ cup shredded carrots, ½ finely diced red bell pepper, 1 sliced green onion, ¼ cup chopped cilantro, ¼ cup cashews. Serve with Sunflower Seed Dressing.*	Cooked Quinoa Carbohydrate: 39 g Fat: 4 g Protein: 8 g Sodium: 13 mg Folate: 77.7 mcg Potassium: 318 mg Dietary Fiber: 5.2 g
Red Kidney Beans	Red kidney beans contain antioxidants that help to protect the body against liver cell damage. They also improve levels of liver enzymes and work to impair the replication of viruses.[5]	Mexican Beans: Sauté 2 cloves garlic, 1 diced red bell pepper, 1 diced onion and ½ teaspoon cumin. Add 1 ½ cups cooked red kidney beans. Cook 5 minutes. Process, adding water if needed and salt to taste. Use on fajitas, tacos or burritos.	Red Kidney Beans Carbohydrate: 40 g Fat: 1 g Protein: 15 g Sodium: 4 mg Folate: 230 mcg Potassium: 713 mcg Dietary fiber: 13.1 g

ENCOURAGEMENT: Let your heart trust in God … if you abide in Christ, you will grow stronger and stronger.[6]

HIV/AIDS

The human immunodeficiency virus (HIV) remains in the body once an individual has been infected with it. This disease infects and kills white blood cells over time, leaving the immune system impaired and open to opportunistic infections. Acquired immunodeficiency syndrome (AIDS) is caused by HIV and can be deadly. It makes the individual much more susceptible to infection, cancer, tuberculosis, wasting syndromes, and memory problems.

Foods	Health Benefits	How To Use	Composition (based on Cup)
Oranges	Oranges provide vitamin C, which helps to protect the body from infection, and aid in recovery from infection.[1] An adequate supply of vitamin C supports a healthy immune system.[2]	Citrus Berry Salad: Gently combine 1 pint blackberries, 1 pound cut strawberries, segments from 2 oranges. Pour over dressing: 1 tablespoon honey, 4 tablespoons orange juice and 1 tablespoon fresh chopped mint.	Fresh Oranges Carbohydrate: 21 g Fat: 0 g Protein: 2 g Sodium: 0 mg Vitamin A: 405 IU Vitamin C: 95.8 mg Vitamin B6: 0.1 mg
Brazil Nuts	Brazil nuts are a rich source of selenium, which plays a critical role in activating the immune system.[3] Selenium also helps protect the body from infection and oxidative damage.[4]	Brazil Nut Gravy: Blend 2 ½ cups water, ½ cup brazil nuts, 4 tablespoons cornstarch, 1 tablespoon onion powder, 1 tablespoon nutritional yeast flakes, 1 teaspoon vegetarian beef seasoning and 1 teaspoon salt. Cook on medium heat, stirring constantly until thickened.	Raw Brazil Nuts Carbohydrate: 16 g Fat: 88 g Protein: 19 g Sodium: 4 mg Selenium: 2,550 mcg Thiamin: 0.8 mg Vitamin B6: 0.1 mg
Collard Greens	Greens such as collards provide a good source of Vitamin A, a nutrient essential for keeping skin, lung and gastrointestinal tissue healthy. Infections are known to cause vitamin A deficiency.[3]	Collard Carrot Sauté: Sauté 2 cloves minced garlic with 1 chopped onion in a little olive oil. Add 4 peeled, chopped carrots, cook 3 minutes. Set on low heat, add 1 cup vegetable stock, 8 cups chopped collard greens. Cover. Cook about 30 minutes until tender. Add salt to taste.	Cooked Collards Carbohydrate: 9 g Fat: 1 g Protein: 4 g Sodium: 30 mg Vitamin A: 15,416 IU Vitamin C: 34.6 mg Folate: 177 mcg
Rice	The B vitamins found in rice help to build and maintain a healthy immune system. They also support a healthy nervous system[1] which is susceptible to damage by HIV/AIDS.	Perfect Brown Rice: In a large pot boil 8 cups of water, add 1 cup brown rice and 1 ½ teaspoons salt. Cover partially. Cook at medium temperature for 30 minutes. Turn off heat. Drain. Return to pot, cover and let steam for 15 minutes.	Cooked Brown Rice Carbohydrate: 45 g Fat: 2 g Protein: 5 g Sodium: 10 mg Niacin: 3.0 mg Vitamin B6: 0.3 mg Folate: 7.8 mcg
Garbanzos	Garbanzos contain zinc, a nutrient essential for a healthy immune system. It decreases the rate of gastrointestinal inflammation and diarrhea, aids in the repair of tissues, decreases frequency of infections, and may help to reduce inflammation.[5]	Baked Falafels: Process 3 cups cooked garbanzos, 1 cup chopped onion, 3 cloves garlic, ½ cup parsley, 2 tablespoons lemon juice, 3 teaspoons cumin, 1 ½ teaspoons salt until sufficiently mixed. Add flour to bind as needed. Shape into patties. Bake at 360°F for 30 minutes, turning halfway.	Cooked Garbanzos Carbohydrate: 45 g Fat: 4 g Protein: 15 g Sodium: 11 mg Folate: 282 mcg Selenium: 6.1 mcg Zinc: 2.5 mg
Asparagus	Asparagus is a source of carnitine, which may help to reduce nerve pain,[6] as well as neuropathy. It may also slow down the progression of HIV by slowing down the death of lymphocytes.[7]	Asparagus Soup: Sauté 1 chopped onion in a little olive oil. Add 2 pounds washed, chopped asparagus. Cook 6 minutes. Add 6 cups vegetable broth. Simmer 20 minutes. Add ¾ cup soaked cashews. Remove from heat. Purée. Add salt to taste.	Cooked Asparagus Carbohydrate: 8 g Fat: 0 g Protein: 4 g Sodium: 26 mg Vitamin C: 13.8 mg Folate: 268 mcg Zinc: 1 mg

HEALTH TIP: A good breakfast helps you to be less irritable, more efficient and energetic.[8]

HYPERCHOLESTEROLEMIA

This condition occurs when the waxy substance called cholesterol, found in blood lipids, rises above normal levels. Fatty deposits may build up in the blood vessels and leading to inadequate blood flow and complications such as heart attack or stroke. Unhealthy lifestyle choices are a major cause of hypercholesterolemia.

Foods	Health Benefits	How To Use	Composition (based on Cup)
Apples	Apples provide a good source of pectin, a water-soluble fiber that binds cholesterol in the gut, prevents it from being absorbed into the bloodstream, and assists in lowering LDL cholesterol.[1]	Apple and Avocado Salad: Combine finely shredded kale, diced apple, diced avocado, chopped walnuts, lemon juice and salt to taste.	Fresh Apples Carbohydrate: 17 g Fat: 0 g Protein: 0 g Sodium: 1 mg Vitamin A: 67.5 IU Vitamin C: 5.7 mg Omega-3: 11.2 mg
Walnuts	Unsalted walnuts have been shown to decrease LDL cholesterol. They improve endothelial function as well as decrease inflammation markers and oxidative stress.[2]	Walnut Spread: Process 1 ½ cups walnuts, soaked 30 minutes, rinsed and drained; ¼ of an onion, 1 medium carrot, 1 celery stalk, 2 tablespoons soy sauce, and salt to taste.	English Walnuts Carbohydrate: 16 g Fat: 76 g Protein: 18 g Sodium: 2 mg Magnesium: 185 mg Potassium: 516 mg Omega-3: 10,623 mg
Avocados	Avocados are an excellent source of vitamins, minerals, fiber and monounsaturated fatty acids, which help to reduce LDL cholesterol levels.[3]	Avocado Salad Wraps: Layer in a flour tortilla – ½ sliced avocado, ½ cup shredded lettuce, ½ small tomato sliced, a few slices of onion and drizzle with Sunflower Seed Dressing* before folding up.	Fresh Avocados Carbohydrate: 13 g Fat: 22 g Protein: 3 g Sodium: 11 mg Vitamin C: 15 mg Calcium: 18 mg Omega-3: 165 mg
Flaxseed	Flaxseed contain a large proportion of water-soluble fibers that help to prevent absorption of cholesterol and may help in lowering the LDL cholesterol in the body.[4]	Blueberry Flaxseed Smoothie: Blend 1 cup frozen blueberries, 1 banana, 1 to 2 tablespoons ground flaxseeds, 1 ¼ cup non-dairy milk and 1 teaspoon honey. 1/3 cup ice cubes optional.	Ground Flaxseeds Carbohydrate: 32 g Fat: 48 g Protein: 16g Sodium: 32 mg Calcium: 286.4 mg Magnesium: 438.4 mg Omega-3: 38,325 mg
Kale	The phytochemicals, and particularly the sulfur compound phytochemicals, in green leafy vegetables such as kale help to keep cholesterol production down, as well as reduce LDL cholesterol.[5]	Tofu Kale Scramble: Brown 12 ounces chopped tofu in a non-stick skillet with a little olive oil, add ¼ cup vegetable broth, 4 chopped kale leaves. When kale has wilted add 1 cup cooked chopped pumpkin, and season to taste.	Fresh Kale Carbohydrate: 7 g Fat: 0 g Protein: 2 g Sodium: 29 mg Vitamin A: 10,302 IU Vitamin C: 80.4 mg Omega-3: 121 mcg
Kidney Beans	Legumes such as kidney beans contain soluble fiber and phytosterols which have been found to be helpful in lowering total and LDL cholesterol.[6]	Cooked kidney beans can be used as a topping on pizza, and add nutrition and color to a vegetable salad. They can also be used in soups, stews and home-made burger patties.	Cooked Kidney Beans Carbohydrate: 40 g Fat: 1 g Protein: 15 g Sodium: 2 mg Calcium: 62 mg Folate: 230 mg Omega-3: 301 mg

DID YOU KNOW? About 2,500 different kinds of apples are grown in the United States.[7]

HYPERTENSION

This condition is commonly known as high blood pressure. The force with which the blood pushes against the walls of the arteries as it flows through them is known as blood pressure. Abnormal blood pressure would be any reading above 120/80 mmHg. Over time, abnormal blood pressure causes damage to the blood vessels leading to complications such as heart attack, heart failure, stroke, kidney disease, eye damage, peripheral artery disease and aneurysms.

Foods	Health Benefits	How To Use	Composition (based on Cup)
Grapefruit	Grapefruit juice has been found to decrease both systolic and diastolic blood pressure, and is more effective in decreasing mean arterial pressure than other citrus fruit.[1]	Grapefruit Juice: Wash two or three ripe grapefruit. Cut them in half and juice them manually. If you are using a juicer, peel grapefruit roughly and slice into segments that will go through your juicer. Juice and serve.	Grapefruit Juice Carbohydrate: 23 g Fat: 0 g Protein: 1 g Sodium: 2 mg Calcium: 22.2 mg Magnesium: 29.6 mg Potassium: 400 mg
Blackberries	Blackberries are high in anthocyanins, and when they are consumed on a regular basis, along with other measures such as weight loss and exercise, they help to decrease the risk of incident hypertension.[2]	Blackberry Sauce: Place 2 cups fresh or frozen blackberries in a saucepan, heat until boiling. Stir in 1 tablespoon honey and 1 teaspoon fresh lemon juice. Mix 1 tablespoon cornstarch with a little water. Stir into berry mixture to thicken. Remove from heat.	Fresh Blackberries Carbohydrate: 15 g Fat: 1 g Protein: 2 g Sodium: 1 mg Calcium: 41.8 mg Magnesium: 28.8 mg Dietary Fiber: 8 g
Spinach	Greens, and in this case spinach, contain magnesium which plays a major role in regulating blood pressure. It also helps to promote the normal functioning of arteries and veins.[1]	Blackberry Green Smoothie: Blend 1 cup washed, shredded spinach, ½ cup blackberries, ½ cup raspberries, 1 ripe banana, ½ cup nondairy milk, 2 tablespoons oats and 2 teaspoons honey.	Fresh Spinach Carbohydrate: 1 g Fat: 0 g Protein: 1 g Sodium: 24 mg Calcium: 29.7 mg Magnesium: 23.7 mg Dietary Fiber: 1 mg
Beets	The nutrients in beets may help preserve or restore the interior surface of blood vessels. Consumption of beets and beet juice has been found to significantly reduce both systolic and diastolic blood pressure.[5]	Blender Beet Juice: Wash and peel fresh beets. Chop as finely as possible. Blend beets with ¼ cup water, add more water if needed. Strain juice to remove pulp and any remaining pieces of beet. Drink 16 ounces daily.[5]	Fresh Beets Carbohydrate: 13 g Fat: 0 g Protein: 2 g Sodium: 106 mg Vitamin A: 44.9 IU Magnesium: 31.3 mg Dietary Fiber: 3.8 g
Peas	Vegetables such as peas are high in dietary fiber. Adequate dietary fiber intake may help to significantly decrease blood pressure.[3,4] They also contain calcium and magnesium which help to normalize blood pressure.[1]	Split Pea Soup: Bring 3 quarts of water to a boil, add 16 ounces split peas, 1 chopped onion, 4 chopped carrots, 2 chopped celery stalks, ½ teaspoon thyme, and ½ teaspoon sage. Simmer uncovered about 1 hour until vegetables are cooked. Add salt to taste.	Cooked Split Peas Carbohydrate: 41 g Fat: 0 g Protein: 16 g Sodium: 4 mg Calcium: 27.4 mg Magnesium: 70.6 mg Dietary Fiber: 16 g
Garlic	Allicin is a sulfur compound found in garlic that inhibits angiotensin (which narrows blood vessels) and promotes the dilation of the blood vessels. It has been found to decrease both systolic and diastolic blood pressure.[1]	Garlic Alfredo Sauce: Simmer 1 chopped onion and 4 cloves minced garlic in a little water until tender. Blend onions, garlic, 1 cup water, and ½ cup cashews. Add 1 cup water, 2 tablespoons cornstarch and ½ teaspoon salt and blend until smooth. Heat in saucepan, stirring until thickened.	Fresh Garlic Carbohydrate: 45 g Fat: 1 g Protein: 9 g Sodium: 23 mg Calcium: 246 mg Magnesium: 34 mg Dietary Fiber: 3 g

ENCOURAGEMENT: Those who take Christ at His word ... will find peace and quietude.[5]

HYPERTHYROIDISM

A condition which in the thyroid gland is overactive and produces an overabundance of thyroid hormone. One of the most common causes of hyperthyroidism is an autoimmune disorder called Graves' disease. Common symptoms include weight loss, increased appetite, shortness of breath, fatigue, muscle weakness, tremors, heart palpitations, skin dryness, increased frequency of bowel movements, insomnia and anxiety.

Foods	Health Benefits	How To Use	Composition (based on Cup)
Avocados 	Avocados provide the body with carnitine. This nutrient has the effect of decreasing thyroid activity.[1] It also may help to reverse and prevent the symptoms of hyperthyroidism.[2]	Avocado Kale Smoothie: Blend ½ ripe avocado, 1 banana, ½ cup berries, 1 cup shredded kale, ¾ cup nondairy milk, and 1 tablespoon flaxseed until perfectly smooth.	Fresh Avocados Carbohydrate: 13 g Fat: 22 g Protein: 3 g Sodium: 11 mg Calcium: 18 mg Selenium: 0.6 mcg Omega-3: 165 mg
Kale 	Kale is a good source of calcium, which helps to prevent thinning of the bones that may occur as the result of hyperthyroidism. Adequate intake of calcium is necessary to prevent osteoporosis.[3]	Kale Pesto: Process ¾ cup walnuts, 2 cloves garlic, juice of one lemon, ¾ teaspoon salt, 1 cup fresh basil leaves, 2 cups fresh kale, and ¼ cup extra virgin olive oil. Serve with pasta.	Fresh Kale Carbohydrate: 7 g Fat: 0 g Protein: 2 g Sodium: 29 mg Calcium: 90.5 mg Selenium: 0.6 mcg Omega-3: 121 mg
Flaxseed 	The regular consumption of omega-3 fatty acids found in flaxseed may help to normalize TSH levels.[4] Omega-3 fatty acids also help to reduce inflammation and strengthen the immune system.[1]	Flaxseed Energy Balls: Process ½ cup ground flaxseed, ¼ cup sunflower seeds, 2 tablespoons sesame seeds, 2 tablespoons carob powder, 1 tablespoon unsweetened desiccated coconut, 3 tablespoons honey and a small pinch of salt. Roll into balls. Refrigerate.	Ground Flaxseed Carbohydrate: 32 g Fat: 48 g Protein: 16g Sodium: 32 mg Calcium: 286.4 mg Selenium: 28.8 mcg Omega-3: 41,522 mg
Brazil Nuts 	Brazil nuts are an excellent source of selenium, which plays an important role in the production and regulation of thyroid hormones. Selenium also helps to normalize thyroid hormone levels.[5]	Brazil Nut Milk: Blend 1 ½ cups brazil nuts, 6 cups filtered water, 6 pitted dates, pinch of salt and ½ teaspoon vanilla extract until completely smooth. Strain a little at a time through a nut milk bag or cheesecloth. Store in sealed container in the refrigerator 2 to 3 days.	Raw Brazil Nuts Carbohydrate: 16 g Fat: 88 g Protein: 19 g Sodium: 4 mg Calcium: 213 mg Selenium: 2,550 mcg Omega-3: 23.9 mg
Black Beans 	Adequate intake of protein helps to compensate for rapid protein loss due to metabolic acceleration caused by an overactive thyroid. Black beans provide a good source of protein.[6]	Black Bean Burgers: Lightly process 1 ½ cups cooked black beans, 1 ½ cups cooked quinoa, ⅓ cup salsa, ½ teaspoon cumin, ½ teaspoon garlic powder, ½ teaspoon salt, and ⅓ cup breadcrumbs until slightly chunky. Form into burgers. Bake at 360°F for 40 minutes, turning after 20 minutes.	Cooked Black Beans Carbohydrate: 41 g Fat: 1 g Protein: 15 g Sodium: 2 mg Calcium: 46.4 mg Selenium: 2.1 mcg Omega-3: 181 mg
Cauliflower 	Mashed cauliflower releases a substance that has an anti-thyroid effect. It limits iodine's being absorbed by the thyroid, thus slowing down its activity.[6]	Mashed Cauliflower: Steam washed cauliflower florets in a steamer basket over boiling water in a large pot for 8 minutes. Drain. Add roasted garlic cloves, thyme or chives. Process in food processor. Add salt to taste.	Cooked Cauliflower Carbohydrate: 6 g Fat: 0 g Protein: 2 g Sodium: 18 mg Calcium: 9.9 mg Selenium: 0.4 mcg Omega-3: 104 mg

DID YOU KNOW? Drinking more water relieves bloating caused by dehydration.[7]

HYPOTHYROIDISM

A condition in which the thyroid gland does not produce an adequate amount of thyroid hormone. The most common cause of hypothyroidism is chronic thyroiditis also known as Hashimoto's disease. Symptoms include weight gain, fatigue, muscle weakness, decreased heart rate, memory problems, constipation, dry skin, depression, numbness in hands, and extreme sensitivity to cold.

Foods	Health Benefits	How To Use	Composition (based on Cup)
Apricots	Apricots are a good source of vitamin A. An adequate supply of vitamin A is needed in order for iodine to be properly absorbed from the body, by the thyroid gland.[1]	Apricot Cranberry Trail Mix: Combine ¾ cup roasted peanuts, ½ cup chopped dried apricots, ½ cup cranberries, ¼ cup banana chips, ¼ cup almonds and ¼ cup pumpkin seed. Store in airtight container.	Dried Apricots Carbohydrate: 81 g Fat: 1 g Protein: 4 g Sodium: 13 mg Vitamin A: 4,686 IU Vitamin B6 0.2 mg Iron: 3.5 mg
Prunes	Vitamin B6 is an essential nutrient found in good quantity in prunes. Vitamin B6 promotes the health of the thyroid, and helps the thyroid to use iodine efficiently in hormone production.[1]	Stewed Prunes: Place dried prunes into a saucepan and cover with water. Bring to a boil, cover and simmer for 10 minutes. Cool. Keep in a sealed container in the refrigerator and enjoy with breakfast.	Dried Prunes Carbohydrate: 111g Fat: 1 g Protein: 4 g Sodium: 3 mg Vitamin A: 1,359 IU Vitamin B6: 0.4 mg Iron: 1.6 mg
Watercress	Watercress contains many important trace elements and minerals, including iron and iodine. These nutrients promote the healthy functioning of the thyroid.[2]	Watercress has a slightly peppery taste and adds taste, color and nutrition to vegetables, salads, vegetable soups, risottos and whole-grain sandwiches.	Watercress Carbohydrate: 0 g Fat: 0 g Protein: 1 g Sodium: 14 mg Vitamin A: 1.085 IU Vitamin C: 14.6 mg Omega-3: 7.8 mg
Radishes	One of the chemicals found in radishes is raphanin, which has been said to be helpful in keeping thyroxine levels in balance.[1]	Radish Cucumber Salad: Combine 1 ½ cups diced radish, ½ cup finely chopped cucumber, ½ cup finely chopped parsley, 1 tablespoon lemon juice, 1 tablespoon olive oil and a pinch of salt.	Fresh Radishes Carbohydrate: 4 g Fat: 0 g Protein: 1 g Sodium: 45 mg Vitamin A: 8.1 IU Vitamin B6: 0.1 mg Omega-3: 36 mg
Oats	Oats supply the body with the amino acid tyrosine. Sufficient tyrosine is vital as the thyroid gland makes thyroid hormone from a combination of iodine and tyrosine.[3]	Easy Oat Waffles: blend 5 cups oats, 3 cups water, 3 cups non-dairy milk, 3 tablespoons olive oil and 1 teaspoon salt. Bake in a preheated waffle iron, and serve while warm.	Raw Oats Carbohydrate: 103 g Fat: 11 g Protein: 26 g Sodium: 3 mg Vitamin B6: 0.2 mg Iron: 7.4 mg Omega-3: 173 mg
Chia Seeds	The omega-3 fatty acids found in chia seeds are helpful in treating immune disorders as they help to reduce inflammation as well as normalize the immune system.[3]	Apricot Chia Energy Bars: Process 1 cup pitted dates, 1 cup dried apricots, 1 cup raw pumpkin seeds, and 2 tablespoons chia seeds. Press into lined pan. Refrigerate for 45 minutes before slicing.	Chia Seeds Carbohydrate: 72 g Fat: 51 g Protein: 26 g Sodium: 31 g Calcium: 1,029 mg Potassium: 261 mg Omega-3: 28,610 mg

HEALTH TIP: Soaking the feet in hot water can relieve a headache or nasal congestion.[4]

INFLUENZA

An acute respiratory condition of the respiratory system, also known as flu, which is caused by the influenza virus. Onset is often sudden, and the nose, throat and lungs are commonly affected. Symptoms include aching muscles, fever, chills and sweats, headache, sore throat, nasal congestion, coughing, fatigue and weakness.

Foods	Health Benefits	How To Use	Composition (based on Cup)
Oranges	The antioxidants in oranges help to boost the immune system.[1] Fluids such as orange juice, which are easily ingested, provide good nutrition and help to replace fluids lost as a result of fever.[2]	Blender Orange Juice: Blend 3 peeled, quartered navel oranges, ⅓ cup water, 1 cup ice cubes, and 1 tablespoon honey (optional), until smooth enough to drink.	Fresh Orange Juice Carbohydrate: 26 g Fat: 0 g Protein: 2 g Sodium: 2 mg Folate: 74.4 mcg Iron: 0.5 mg Vitamin C: 124 mg
Mangos	Mangos are a good source of antioxidants vitamin A and vitamin Cm which may stimulate as well as help to maintain a healthy immune system.[1,3]	Ripe chopped mango can be used to top oatmeal, be added to fruit salads or fruit smoothies, or chopped and stirred into nondairy yogurt. It is best eaten properly ripe and chilled.	Fresh Mangos Carbohydrate: 28 g Fat: 0 g Protein: 1 g Sodium: 3 mg Vitamin A: 1,262 IU Vitamin C: 45.7 mg Vitamin E: 1.8 mg
Tomatoes	Vegetables, and in this case tomatoes, made into a warm broth or soup have a soothing effect on a sore throat and help to loosen mucus, thus easing congestion. They are also a good source of antioxidants, which help to strengthen immunity.[1]	Tomato Soup: Sauté 1 cup chopped onion in a little olive oil. Blend ½ cup cashews with ½ cup water until creamy. Add onions and 4 cups stewed tomatoes. Blend. Put in saucepan and add 1 tablespoon honey, ¼ cup coconut milk, 1 teaspoon basil and salt to taste. Serve hot.	Cooked Tomatoes Carbohydrate: 10g Fat: 0 g Protein: 2 g Sodium: 26 mg Vitamin A: 1,174 IU Vitamin C: 54.7 mg Zinc: 0.3 mg
Garbanzos	The zinc found in garbanzo beans helps the immune system to function properly. Zinc may help to reduce the risk of contracting influenza, as well as possibly ease its symptoms.[1]	Garbanzo Stew: Sauté 1 minced onion, ½ diced red bell pepper, 1 chopped tomato, 1 sliced carrot. Add 1 cup cooked garbanzos, 1 ½ cups water, ½ cup tomato sauce, ½ teaspoon dried basil and simmer 20 minutes. Mash some of the garbanzos to thicken. Enjoy over brown rice.	Cooked Garbanzos Carbohydrate: 45 g Fat: 4 g Protein: 15 g Sodium: 11 mg Vitamin A: 44.3 IU Vitamin C: 2.1 mg Zinc: 2.5 mg
Pumpkin	Pumpkin contains a good quantity of the antioxidant vitamin A which helps to strengthen the immune system, and which also helps to protect the lining of the throat.[4]	Mashed Pumpkin: Peel and cube pumpkin and simmer in vegetable stock until pumpkin is soft. Drain. Mash. Stir in a little olive oil, garlic powder, cumin and salt to taste.	Cooked Pumpkin Carbohydrate: 12 g Fat: 0 g Protein: 2 g Sodium: 2 mg Vitamin A: 12,231 IU Vitamin C: 11.5 mg Zinc: 0.6 mg
Garlic	Regular consumption of garlic may help lower the risk of, or prevent, upper respiratory infections.[1] Allicin in garlic is known to function as an antiviral and anti-inflammatory agent.[5]	Roasted Garlic: Cut ¼ inch off garlic heads to expose cloves. Place in small pan with cut side up. Brush with olive oil. Cover pan tightly with foil. Bake at 350°F for 45 minutes until soft. Cool. Squeeze garlic from skins. Add to your favorite dish, or spread on whole-grain toast.	Fresh Garlic Carbohydrate: 45 g Fat: 1 g Protein: 9 g Sodium: 23 mg Vitamin A: 12.2 IU Vitamin C: 42.4 mg Zinc: 1.2 mg

ENCOURAGEMENT: They that wait upon the Lord shall renew their strength (Isaiah 40:31).

INSOMNIA

An acute or chronic condition in which the individual has difficulty falling asleep, staying asleep, and wakes too early even though there is adequate opportunity for sleep. Symptoms include waking unrefreshed, low energy, fatigue, concentration problems, mood disturbances, and irritability. Insomnia can be caused by life stress, emotional or physical discomfort, environmental factors, medications and interference with the sleep cycle.

Foods	Health Benefits	How To Use	Composition (based on Cup)
Red Grapefruit	Adequate intake of lycopene, which is found in red fruits such as grapefruit, has been found to be associated with being able to sleep for longer periods. Deficiency in lycopene leads to short sleep periods.[1]	Grapefruit Avocado Salad: Combine 1 cup diced cucumber, 1 cup chopped grapefruit, 2 diced avocados, ¼ cup chopped almonds, 2 sliced spring onions, 1 tablespoon lemon juice, ½ tablespoon olive oil and salt to taste.	Fresh Grapefruit Carbohydrate: 25 g Fat: 0 g Protein: 2 g Sodium: 0 mg Tryptophan: 18.4 mg Magnesium: 20. Mg Omega-3: 18.4 mg
Cherries	The consumption of the nutrients found in cherries, particularly cherry juice, has been shown to increase melatonin levels and this results in an increased amount, and better quality, of sleep.[2]	Eight ounces of tart cherry juice consumed twice a day is recommended.[7] When choosing cherry juice, select options that are unsweetened and pure as possible.	Tart Cherry Juice Carbohydrate: 34 g Fat: 0 g Protein: 1 g Sodium: 20 mg Calcium: 20 mg Iron: 1.44 mg Potassium: 410 mg
Peanuts	Peanuts contain healthy unsaturated fats, which help to improve serotonin levels.[3] The neurotransmitter serotonin plays a key role in regulating a normal sleep/wake cycle.[4]	Peanut Snack Balls: Process 2 cups pitted dates, 1 cup of oats, 1 cup of roasted peanuts, 2 tablespoons peanut butter and 2 tablespoons coconut oil. Roll into balls. Refrigerate.	Dry Roasted Peanuts Carbohydrate: 31 g Fat: 73 g Protein: 35g Sodium: 9 mg Tryptophan: 336 mg Magnesium: 257 mg Omega-3: 4.4 mg
Sunflower Seeds	Sunflower seeds are a good source of magnesium, which has been found to help increase sleep time, sleep efficiency and melatonin, and decrease the time taken to fall asleep and the severity of insomnia.[5]	Sunflower Seed Butter: Process 2 cups unsalted, roasted sunflower seeds with 1 teaspoon olive oil, and ¼ teaspoon salt until smooth butter forms.	Sunflower Seeds Carbohydrate: 28 g Fat: 72 g Protein: 29 g Sodium: 13 mg Tryptophan: 487 mg Magnesium: 455 mg Omega-3: 104 mg
Corn	Corn is low in fat and protein and high in carbohydrates. These kind of foods may help to promote the production of serotonin and melatonin, brain chemicals that play a role in good sleep.[2]	Corn Grits: Boil 3 cups of water, add a pinch of salt and 1 cup fine yellow corn grits. Turn heat to low, stir continuously for five or six minutes until thick and cooked. Dish into bowls and top with chopped fruit, sunflower seed, honey and a little nondairy milk.	Corn Grits: Carbohydrate: 124 g Fat: 2 g Protein: 14 g Sodium: 2 mg Tryptophan: 96.7 mg Magnesium: 42.1 mg Omega-3: 23.4 mg
Kidney Beans	Tryptophan, found in kidney beans, is an essential amino acid that plays a key role in the production of serotonin in the body. Increased consumption of tryptophan is associated with improved sleep.[6]	Kidney Bean Soup: Sauté 1 chopped onion, and 2 chopped carrots until tender. Add 2 cups vegetable stock, 2 cups kidney beans, 1 cup frozen corn. Bring to a boil. Purée 2 cups kidney beans and 2 cups stewed tomatoes. Add to saucepan. Simmer 15 minutes. Season to taste.	Cooked Kidney Beans Carbohydrate: 40 g Fat: 1 g Protein: 15 g Sodium: 2 mg Tryptophan: 184 mg Magnesium: 74.3 mg Omega-3: 301 mg

DID YOU KNOW? Overeating close to bedtime can cause insomnia.[8]

IRRITABLE BOWEL SYNDROME

A common, chronic gastrointestinal disorder that affects the large intestine. Typical symptoms of irritable bowel syndrome are nausea, intestinal gas, abdominal cramping and pain, diarrhea, and constipation. Common triggers for irritable bowel syndrome include food allergy or intolerance, stress, and hormonal imbalance.

Foods	Health Benefits	How To Use	Composition (based on Cup)
Apples	The dietary fiber found in apples helps the intestines to function better, and may also help to lessen bloating and pain and make the stools softer, thus reducing constipation.[1]	Stewed Apples: Simmer 6 peeled, cored, diced apples, ½ cup sultanas and ½ cup of water in a covered pan for 15 to 20 minutes until soft. Serve hot or cold for breakfast or for dessert.	Cooked Apples Carbohydrate: 23 g Fat: 1 g Protein: 0 g Sodium: 2 mg Magnesium: 5.1 mg Potassium: 150 mg Dietary Fiber: 4 g
Papayas	The pulp from the papaya has a healing effect on the intestinal mucosa, helping to soothe and protect it. It can also help to relieve the spasms associated with irritable bowel syndrome.[2]	Papaya Coconut Smoothie: Blend 2 cups cubed papaya, 1 sliced banana, 1 cup coconut milk, 1 tablespoon flaxseed, 1 tablespoon lemon juice, and 1 tablespoon honey until smooth.	Fresh Papayas Carbohydrate: 14 g Fat: 0 g Protein: 1 g Sodium: 4 mg Magnesium: 14 mg Potassium: 360 mg Dietary Fiber: 3 g
Corn	Corn is fairly easily tolerated by sensitive digestive systems. The nutrients found in corn help to soothe and protect the innermost layer of the gastrointestinal tract.[3]	Roasted Corn Soup: Roast 1 pound thawed, frozen corn on a baking sheet for 15 minutes at 440°F. Blend corn with 2 to 3 cups vegetable stock, 1 tablespoon thyme, and 2 teaspoons onion powder until smooth. Salt to taste. Serve warm.	Cooked Corn Carbohydrate: 41 g Fat: 2 g Protein: 5 g Sodium: 0 mg Magnesium: 42.6 mg Potassium: 348 mg Dietary Fiber: 4.6 g
Navy Beans	Navy beans contain soluble fiber, which may help diarrhea because they slow down the transit of food from the stomach to the intestines and help to give form to stools.[1]	Navy Bean Sandwich Spread: Process 1 ½ cup navy beans, ¼ cup fresh basil, 2 tablespoons olive oil, 1 tablespoon lemon juice, ½ teaspoon garlic powder and salt to taste.	Cooked Navy Beans Carbohydrate: 48 g Fat: 1 g Protein: 15 g Sodium: 0 mg Magnesium: 96.4 mg Potassium: 708 mg Dietary Fiber: 19 g
Potatoes	Diarrhea robs the body of electrolytes such as potassium. Potatoes are a good source of potassium,[3] thus fighting deficiency and helping the healing process.	Mashed Potatoes: Boil 2 pounds of peeled, cubed potatoes and 4 cloves peeled garlic about 15 minutes until soft. Drain. Keep 1 cup of liquid. Mash. Mix in 3 tablespoons olive oil and then add reserved liquid as needed. Salt to taste.	Boiled Potatoes Carbohydrate: 32 g Fat: 0 g Protein: 2 g Sodium: 374 mg Magnesium: 34.4 mg Potassium: 256 mg Dietary Fiber: 4 g
Sesame Seeds	A lactose-free diet helps to prevent bloating and gas. Sesame seeds contain the calcium that the body needs to maintain health.[1]	Toasted sesame seeds can be sprinkled on salads, vegetables, rice, and pasta dishes. They can also be sprinkled on hot or cold cereal, added to smoothies or used in baking.	Sesame Seeds Carbohydrate: 34 g Fat: 72 g Protein: 26 g Sodium: 16 mg Potassium: 674 mg Dietary Fiber: 17 g Omega-3: 541 mg

HEALTH TIP: Regular outdoor exercise contributes to good bowel health.[4]

KIDNEY DISEASE

Kidney disease, also known as chronic kidney failure, is the slow progressive loss of kidney function over a number of years. Eventually permanent kidney failure necessitates dialysis on a regular basis. Uncontrolled diabetes and hypertension are the most common causes of kidney failure. Symptoms may include anemia, edema, fatigue, blood in urine, decreased urine output, nausea, muscle cramps, headaches, and insomnia.

Foods	Health Benefits	How To Use	Composition (based on Cup)
Pears	Pears help to improve the function of the kidneys and increase the production of urine. They are a mild diuretic and help with the elimination of salts and fluids that are retained in the tissues.[1]	Pear Sauce: Place 3 pounds cored, chopped pears in saucepan with ½ cup orange juice, boil, reduce heat and simmer for 30 minutes, stirring often. When fruit has softened process gently until desired texture is achieved. Freeze in small quantities until needed.	Fresh Pears Carbohydrate: 25 g Fat: 0 g Protein: 1 g Sodium: 2 mg Vitamin C: 6.8 mg Calcium: 14.5 mg Iron: 0.3 mg
Apples	Apples are diuretic, helping to eliminate fluid from the tissues and increase urine output. They also help to purify the blood by increasing the elimination of toxins.[1]	Apples are best eaten fresh, rather than cooked or in recipes with multiple ingredients that might not promote kidney health. Try to eat at least one apple daily.	Fresh Apples Carbohydrate: 17 g Fat: 0 g Protein: 0 g Sodium: 1 mg Vitamin C: 5.7 mg Calcium: 7.5 mg Iron: 0
Blueberries	Blueberries contain vitamin C, which helps to maintain the health of the tissues in the body. Vitamin C plays a role in wound and bruise healing and might aid in preventing infections.[2]	Simple Blueberry Sauce: Heat two to three cups frozen berries in a saucepan with ½ cup unsweetened apple juice until bubbling. Mix 2 tablespoons cornstarch with a little apple juice and add to saucepan and stir until thickened. Enjoy on hot cereal, pancakes and waffles.	Frozen Blueberries Carbohydrate: 19 g Fat: 1 g Protein: 1 g Sodium: 2 mg Vitamin C: 3.9 mg Calcium: 12.4 mg Iron: 0.3 mg
Spinach	Leafy green vegetables, such as spinach, are a source of iron, which helps to overcome the anemia that is usually caused by kidney failure.[3]	Apple Berry Green Smoothie: Blend 1 large apple, peeled and cored, 1 cup blueberries, 1 cup strawberries, 2 cups spinach and 1 cup unsweetened nondairy milk.	Fresh Spinach Carbohydrate: 1 g Fat: 0 g Protein: 1 g Sodium: 24 mg Vitamin C: 8.4 mg Calcium: 29.7 mg Iron: 0.8 mg
Cauliflower	Cauliflower helps to stimulate the production of urine and also helps to cleanse the blood. It helps to fight edema by promoting the elimination of fluids from the tissues.[1]	Steamed Cauliflower: Fill a large pot with two inches of water, set steamer basket in the pot and steam cauliflower florets on medium to high heat for about seven minutes until soft.	Cooked Cauliflower Carbohydrate: 6 g Fat: 0 g Protein: 2 g Sodium: 18 mg Vitamin C: 55 mg Calcium: 19.8 mg Iron: 0.4 mg
Squash	Squash benefits kidney function in that it is a mild diuretic. It contains limited sodium, phosphorous and protein, so is a safe food for patients with kidney failure.[1]	Oven Baked Spaghetti Squash: Slice squash in half lengthwise and remove seeds. Place face down on roasting pan. Cover base of the pan with a little water. Cover with foil. Cook at 400°F for at least 30 minutes until tender. Scrape out flesh and serve with a little olive oil.	Cooked Squash Carbohydrate: 10 g Fat: 0 g Protein: 1 g Sodium: 28 mg Vitamin C: 10.8 mg Calcium: 65.2 mg Iron: 1 mg

ENCOURAGEMENT: Eat slowly and with cheerfulness, your heart filled with gratitude to God for all His blessings.[4]

LUPUS

A chronic inflammatory condition in which the immune system starts to attack the individual's own organs and body tissues. Any part of the body can be affected. Symptoms may include inflammation, swelling, and joint deterioration. Lupus may also affect the skin, brain, blood cells, blood vessels, heart and lungs.

Foods	Health Benefits	How To Use	Composition (based on Cup)
Kiwifruit	Kiwifruit are high in vitamin C, which helps to reduce the risk of inflammation by modulating immune functions and releasing inflammatory mediators. It also helps to prevent the cardiovascular complications associated with lupus.[1]	Kiwifruit Banana Ice Cream: Process 1 banana, sliced and frozen overnight, with 1 peeled sliced kiwifruit until completely smooth. Serve right away.	Fresh Kiwifruit Carbohydrate: 28g Fat: 0 g Protein: 2 g Sodium: 10 mg Vitamin A: 318 IU Vitamin C: 136.4 mg Calcium: 47.4 mg
Prunes	Prunes contain vitamin B6, which helps to lower homocysteine levels, and may help to reduce the risk of atherosclerosis associated with lupus. Vitamin B6 also helps to decrease the serum levels of some of the inflammatory markers.[1]	Quinoa Dried Plum Salad: Combine 2 cups cooked quinoa, ½ cup quartered prunes, ½ cup orange segments, 2 tablespoons each of chopped mint, parsley, cilantro, ½ cup chopped pecans, 2 tablespoons olive oil, 2 tablespoons lemon juice, ½ teaspoon ground cumin and salt to taste.	Dried Prunes Carbohydrate: 111g Fat: 1 g Protein: 4 g Sodium: 3 mg Vitamin A: 1,359 IU Vitamin B6: 4 mg Dietary Fiber: 12 g
Sweet Potatoes	Sweet potato provides a good source of vitamin A, which has been shown to decrease the severity of lupus symptoms. Inadequate vitamin A leads to an excessive number of antibodies and autoantibodies in the blood.[1]	Sweet Potato Soup: Blend ½ cup cooked red lentils, 2 cooked sweet potatoes, 2 cooked carrots, 2 cups warm vegetable broth, 1 teaspoon onion powder, ¼ teaspoon garlic powder, 1 teaspoon turmeric, 1 teaspoon cumin, ½ teaspoon ginger powder. Heat. Add salt to taste.	Sweet Potatoes Carbohydrate: 41 g Fat: 0 g Protein: 4 g Sodium: 72 mg Vitamin A: 38,433 IU Vitamin B6 0.6 mg Vitamin C: 39.2 mg
Kale	Some lupus medications deplete calcium in the body, which increases the risk of osteoporosis. The consumption of kale supplies calcium to the body, helping to keep the bones strong.[2]	Pineapple Kale Smoothie: ½ cup coconut milk, ½ cup nondairy milk, 1 large ripe banana, 1 ½ cups chopped pineapple, 1 ¾ cups chopped kale (stems removed). Blend until smooth.	Cooked Kale Carbohydrate: 7 g Fat: 1 g Protein: 2 g Sodium: 30 mg Vitamin A: 17,709 IU Vitamin B6: 0.2 mg Calcium: 93.6 mg
Barley	High in fiber, barley helps to reduce inflammation and the severity of lupus, and decreases homocysteine and some of the inflammatory markers. Fiber also helps control elevated cholesterol and triglycerides associated with lupus.[1]	Barley Tomato Risotto: In a large pot simmer 1 cup barley, 1 tablespoon olive oil, ½ teaspoon dried basil, ½ teaspoon dried oregano, 1 ½ cups diced tomatoes, 1 cup unsweetened almond milk, ½ cup water. Cook covered for 45 minutes, stir every five minutes until cooked.	Cooked Pearl Barley Carbohydrate: 44 g Fat: 1 g Protein: 4 g Sodium: 5 mg Vitamin B6: 0.2 mg Calcium: 17.3 mg Dietary Fiber: 6 g
Pecan Nuts	The omega-3 fatty acids are integral to healthy cell function and help to regulate hormones which control inflammation. Adequate intake of this nutrient may help to control lupus.[2]	Sprinkle chopped pecans on hot or cold cereal, or on top of pancakes or waffles. Whole or chopped pecans can be used in green salads, and added to rice and pasta dishes.	Pecan Nuts Carbohydrate: 15 g Fat: 78 g Protein: 10 g Sodium: 0 mg Vitamin B6: 0.2 mg Omega-3: 1,075 mg Dietary Fiber: 10.5 g

DID YOU KNOW? Avoiding nightshade plants such as tomatoes, eggplant, and peppers can be helpful in managing lupus.[3]

MIGRAINE

A common type of vascular headache that occurs on either one or both sides of the head. This results from an abnormal sensitivity of arteries in the brain that respond to various triggers, and consequently some of them constrict and others dilate, causing throbbing and often disabling pain. Migraine attacks may last from hours to days. Symptoms include nausea, vomiting, blurred vision, and increased sensitivity to light and/or sound.

Foods	Health Benefits	How To Use	Composition (based on Cup)
Bananas	Vitamin B6 and folic acid, found in bananas, help to reduce homocysteine levels and thus may help to reduce frequency and intensity of pain and disability from migraines.[1]	Baked Banana Chips: Slice two ripe bananas into ¼ inch slices. Dip in 1 cup freshly squeezed lemon juice. Place on baking tray coated with cooking spray. Bake at 210°F for about 3 ¼ hours until golden. Turn once while baking. They will become crisp as they cool.	Sliced Bananas Carbohydrate: 34 g Fat: 0 g Protein: 2 g Sodium: 2 mg Vitamin B6: 0.6 mg Folate: 30 mcg Magnesium: 40.5 mg
Collard Greens	Greens, and in this case collard greens, are a good source of calcium, which has been found to be helpful in treating migraines as well as in preventing them.[2]	Collard Wraps: Wash and tear the collard leaves away from the stem. On each half spread a little nondairy Sunflower Seed Cheese Spread,* add red pepper slices, sliced avocado, alfalfa sprouts and grated carrot. Roll up and serve immediately.	Fresh Collards Carbohydrate: 2 g Fat: 0 g Protein: 1 g Sodium: 7 mg Vitamin B6: 0.1 mg Folate: 59.8 mcg Calcium: 52.2 mg
Quinoa	Quinoa contains magnesium, which may dilate blood vessels and relax muscles, helping to maintain normal function. Adequate magnesium intake helps to prevent and decrease migraines.[3]	Quinoa Veggie Bowl: Combine 1 cup diced cooked broccoli, 1 cup cooked quinoa, 1 diced small red onion, ½ cup grated carrots, ½ cup sliced green onions, ¼ cup chopped peanuts, 2 teaspoons sesame seeds, 1 tablespoon olive oil, 1 tablespoon lime juice, and salt to taste.	Cooked Quinoa Carbohydrate: 39 g Fat: 4 g Protein: 8 g Sodium: 13 mg Riboflavin: 0.2 mg Calcium: 31.5 mg Magnesium: 118 mg
Sesame Seeds	Sesame seeds are a good source of riboflavin, which helps with normal mitochondrial function and helps to reduces the symptoms of migraine, as well as the frequency and length of migraines.[1]	Honey Banana Tahini Smoothie: Blend 1 ½ cups unsweetened almond milk, 2 ripe bananas sliced and frozen overnight, 1 tablespoon tahini,* and 1 tablespoon honey.	Tahini Carbohydrate: 48 g Fat: 128 g Protein: 48 g Sodium: 80 g Riboflavin: 0.24 mg Calcium: 338 mg Magnesium: 227 mg
Sunflower Seeds	The vitamin E found in sunflower seeds is an anti-prostaglandin agent and may be helpful in reducing pain and functional disability associated with menstrual migraines.[1]	Sunflower Seed Cheese Spread: Soak 1 cup hulled sunflower seeds in water overnight. Rinse. Drain. Process with ¼ onion, 1 tablespoon dill, 1 garlic clove, and salt to taste. Chill two hours. Serve on wholegrain crackers.	Sunflower Seeds Carbohydrate: 28 g Fat: 72 g Protein: 29 g Sodium: 13 mg Vitamin E: 46.5 mg Magnesium: 455 mg Tryptophan: 487 mg
Navy Beans	Adequate intake of tryptophan, found in legumes such as navy beans, helps in normalizing serotonin in the brain and may lead to fewer and milder migraines.[4]	Navy Bean Salad: Combine ½ cup cooked quinoa, 2 cups black beans, 2 cups navy beans, 1 cup diced cucumber, ¼ cup diced onion, ¼ cup fresh cilantro, 1 clove minced garlic, 2 tablespoons olive oil, 2 tablespoons lime juice, ½ teaspoon dried oregano and salt to taste.	Cooked Navy Beans Carbohydrate: 48 g Fat: 1 g Protein: 15 g Sodium: 0 mg Calcium: 126 mg Magnesium: 96.4 mg Tryptophan: 182 mg

HEALTH TIP: Maintaining a regular meal and sleep schedule helps to prevent migraine attacks.[5]

MULTIPLE SCLEROSIS

A chronic autoimmune disease in which the immune system attacks the protective myelin sheath that covers nerve fibers of the central nervous system, causing deterioration and resulting in communication problems between the brain and the body. It commonly affects the brain, spinal cord and optic nerves. Symptoms include numbness, weakness, dizziness, tremors, incoordination of muscles, slurred speech, fatigue, visual changes, and incontinence.

Foods	Health Benefits	How To Use	Composition (based on Cup)
Pineapples	Pineapples contain two enzymes, bromelain and pancreatin, which reduce circulating immune complexes. If not stopped, these cause the immune system to initiate an attack on the body.[1]	Blender Pineapple Juice: Blend four cups of peeled, cubed pineapple with ½ cup coconut milk (optional) and 1 cup of ice cubes.	Fresh Pineapples Carbohydrate: 22g Fat: 0 g Protein: 1 g Sodium: 2 mg Vitamin B6: 0.2 mg Thiamin: 0.1 g Selenium: 0.1 mcg
Blueberries	The oligomeric procyanidins in blueberries help to protect against the destruction of the myelin sheath, as well as helping to inhibit the inflammatory activity of multiple sclerosis.[1]	Blueberry Chia Seed Jam: In a medium pot bring 3 cups of blueberries and 2 tablespoons of honey to a boil. Simmer 5 minutes. Slightly mash blueberries. Stir in 2 tablespoons chia seeds and cook 1 more minute. Cool for a couple of hours. Serve once thickened. Keep refrigerated.	Fresh Blueberries Carbohydrate: 21 g Fat: 0 g Protein: 1 g Sodium: 1 mg Vitamin B6: 0.1 mg Folate: 8.9 mcg Selenium: 0.1 mcg
Pecan Nuts	Pecan nuts are high in polyphenols which have an anti-inflammatory effect in the body, and also help to regulate the immune system.[2]	Pecan Nut Pâté: Process 1 cup soaked pecans, 1 tablespoon lemon juice, 1 tablespoon olive oil, ¼ teaspoon garlic salt. Place in bowl. Stir in 2 chopped green onions and ½ tablespoon fresh chopped parsley. Eat on crackers.	Pecan Nuts Carbohydrate: 15 g Fat: 78 g Protein: 10 g Sodium: 0 mg Vitamin B6: 0.2 mg Folate: 24 mcg Selenium: 4.1 mcg
Chia Seeds	Chia seeds are a good source of selenium, one of the trace elements most effective in slowing down the progression of multiple sclerosis.[3]	Raspberry Chia Pudding: Blend 2 cups unsweetened almond milk, 2 teaspoons honey, 2 cups raspberries. Place in bowl and mix in ½ cup chia seeds. Refrigerate at least four hours before serving.	Chia Seeds Carbohydrate: 72 g Fat: 51 g Protein: 26 g Sodium: 31 g Niacin: 14.4 mg Riboflavin: 0.28 mg Selenium: 90 mcg
Sweet Potatoes	The carotenoids and polyphenols found in sweet potato may help to restore oxidative balance, function as anti-inflammatories and help to regulate the immune system.[4]	Sweet Potato Black Bean Salad: Combine 1 pound baked, peeled, cubed sweet potatoes, 2 cups black beans, ½ chopped onion, ½ cup chopped cilantro, 3 tablespoons olive oil, ½ teaspoon ground cumin, and salt to taste.	Sweet Potatoes Carbohydrate: 41 g Fat: 0 g Protein: 4 g Sodium: 72 mg Vitamin A: 38,433 IU Vitamin B6 0.6 mg Selenium: 0.4 mcg
Millet	Millet is a source of B vitamins, which help to support the nervous system. The fiber found in millet helps to prevent constipation, which is often associated with multiple sclerosis.[3]	Millet Burgers: Sauté 3 medium chopped onions and 3 cloves minced garlic. Place in bowl. Add 2 finely grated carrots and 1 finely grated red bell pepper. Add 2 cups cooked millet, 1 teaspoon lemon juice, 1 teaspoon salt. Shape into burgers. Bake at 350°F for 30 minutes.	Cooked Millet Carbohydrate: 41 g Fat: 2 g Protein: 6 g Sodium: 3 mg Vitamin B6: 0.2 mg Selenium: 1.6 mcg Dietary Fiber: 2 g

ENCOURAGEMENT: Nothing tends more to promote health of body and of soul than does a spirit of gratitude.[5]

MUSCLE CRAMPS

The sudden, involuntary and usually painful contraction of one or more of the muscles. Muscle cramps may last from a few seconds to as long as fifteen minutes and occasionally longer. A number of muscles, one muscle or even part of a muscle may be involved. Cramping may result from an inadequate supply of minerals, dehydration, overuse, injury, and medications. The frequency of muscle cramps increases with age.

Foods	Health Benefits	How To Use	Composition (based on Cup)
Cantaloupes	Cantaloupes contain potassium, a major electrolyte found in muscle and nerve cells. Deficiency can be caused by fasting, diarrhea, use of diuretics and may result in muscle cramps.[1]	Cantaloupe Green Smoothie: Blend ¼ medium cantaloupe flesh cubed, with ½ cup fresh or frozen berries and 1 cup spinach. Add ¼ cup water if needed.	Fresh Cantaloupes Carbohydrate: 14 g Fat: 0 g Protein: 1 g Sodium: 26 mg Vitamin B6: 0.1 mg Magnesium: 19.2 mg Potassium: 427 mg
Avocados	Avocados provide vitamin E. Muscle cramps may result as a deficiency in this vitamin. Adequate intake of Vitamin E may be able to reduce frequency of muscle cramps.[3]	Avocado Navy Bean Sandwiches: Combine 1 cup mashed navy beans with 1 teaspoon olive oil and 1 teaspoon lemon juice. Spread on whole-grain bread. Add sliced onion, cucumber, avocado, baby spinach and salt to taste. Top with another slice of whole-grain bread and enjoy.	Fresh Avocados Carbohydrate: 13 g Fat: 22 g Protein: 3 g Sodium: 11 mg Vitamin E: 3.1 mg Calcium: 18 mg Potassium: 727 mg
Prunes	Deficiency in vitamin B, and in particular vitamins B2 and B6, is associated with muscle cramps.[4] Prunes contain B vitamins that may be helpful in treating leg cramps.[5]	Soft dried prunes can be eaten dried or stewed for breakfast. They can be substituted for dates and raisins in baking. Sliced prunes can be added to green salads, rice dishes and stews.	Dried Prunes Carbohydrate: 111g Fat: 1 g Protein: 4 g Sodium: 3 mg Vitamin B2: 0.3 mg Vitamin B6: 0.4 mg Vitamin E: 0.7 mg
Pecan Nuts	Pecan nuts provide magnesium, which helps to maintain healthy nerve and muscle function. Deficiency can result in muscle cramps.[6] Magnesium is involved in helping muscles relax.[4]	Pecan Nut Pesto: Process ½ cup pecans, 1 or 2 cloves fresh peeled garlic, 2 cups washed, stemmed basil, ¼ cup extra virgin olive oil and salt to taste.	Pecan Nuts Carbohydrate: 15 g Fat: 78 g Protein: 10 g Sodium: 0 mg Vitamin B6: 0.2 mg Calcium: 76.3 mg Magnesium: 132 mg
Collard Greens	Consumption of an abundance of green leafy vegetables such as collard greens helps to improve blood quality and helps to maintain mineral balance, thus preventing muscle cramping.[2]	Collard Coleslaw: Combine 1 bunch destemmed and finely shredded collard greens, 2 shredded carrots, 1 shredded parsnip, 1 shredded apple, ¼ cup olive oil and salt to taste.	Raw Collard Greens Carbohydrate: 2 g Fat: 0 g Protein: 1 g Sodium: 7 mg Calcium: 52.2 mg Magnesium: 3.2 mg Potassium: 60.8 mg
Navy Beans	Navy beans contain calcium, which plays a role in muscle contraction as well as the generation of nerve impulses. Adequate intake of dietary calcium has been associated with relief from muscle cramps.[1]	Navy Bean Soup: Bring to a boil and slowly simmer 2 cups soaked, drained navy beans, 8 cups vegetable stock, 4 sliced carrots, 1 cup sliced celery, 1 cup shredded cabbage, 1 cup chopped tomato, 5 cloves minced garlic, 2 bay leaves, and salt to taste, until beans are soft.	Cooked Navy Beans Carbohydrate: 48 g Fat: 1 g Protein: 15 g Sodium: 0 mg Calcium: 126 mg Magnesium: 96.4 mg Potassium: 708 mg

DID YOU KNOW? Nicotine from smoking, and secondhand smoke, disrupts the normal circulation of blood.[2]

OBESITY

A condition in which the weight of the individual is usually at least 20% more than what would be considered healthy. More calories are consumed than the body can use, and extra calories are stored as fat. Obesity predisposes one to life-threatening conditions such as diabetes, hypertension, heart attack, and cancer and increases risk of disability and death.

Foods	Health Benefits	How To Use	Composition (based on Cup)
Peaches	Peaches are low in calories, but give a greater sense of satiety than other fruit, thus decreasing feelings of hunger. They also help with the elimination of acidic waste from the body.[1]	Stewed Peaches: Place 1 cup dried peaches in a saucepan with 1 ½ cups orange juice. Simmer 15 minutes. Let cool and stand until peaches are plump.	Fresh Peaches Carbohydrate: 22 g Fat: 1 g Protein: 2 g Sodium: 0 mg Tryptophan: 22.4 mg Zinc: 0.4 mg Dietary Fiber: 3.4 g
Grapefruit	Consumption of grapefruit is very beneficial for individuals wanting to lose weight, as it acts as an excellent depurant, helping to purify the blood of waste products.[1]	Half a grapefruit or half of glass of freshly squeezed grapefruit juice can be enjoyed before each meal. Grapefruit can also be enjoyed alone as a light supper.	Fresh Grapefruit Carbohydrate: 25 g Fat: 0 g Protein: 2 g Sodium: 0 mg Tryptophan: 18.4 mg Zinc: 0.2 mg Dietary Fiber: 4 g
Zucchinis	Zucchinis are low in fat and sodium and has a diuretic effect that helps the body to eliminate unnecessary water from the tissues. It also helps to soothe the digestive tract.[1]	Zucchini Salad: Cut 1 medium zucchini into spaghetti-thin strands. Combine with 1 diced avocado, ½ cup shelled, cooked, cooled edamame, ½ tablespoon olive oil, ½ tablespoon lemon juice and salt to taste.	Fresh Zucchini Carbohydrate: 4 g Fat: 0 g Protein: 2 g Sodium: 12 mg Tryptophan: 12.4 mg Zinc: 0.4 mg Dietary Fiber: 1 g
Cashews	The tryptophan found in cashews boosts serotonin levels in the central nervous system, which may help to reduce appetite and decrease craving for food.[2] Nuts are rich in fiber and protein, digest slower and help to lessen hunger.[3]	Cashew Caramel Balls: Process 1½ cup raw, unsalted or salted cashews, 1½ cup fresh or unsweetened dry dates, and 3 teaspoons of vanilla extract. Roll into balls. Refrigerate.	Raw Cashews Carbohydrate: 47 g Fat: 63 g Protein: 26 g Sodium: 17 g Tryptophan: 410 mg Zinc: 8.3 mg Dietary Fiber: 4.7 g
Garbanzos	Garbanzos provide the body with zinc, which raises the level of leptin in the body, a hormone that helps one feel full. It may also help to increase lean body mass and decrease fat.[2]	Garbanzo Avocado Sandwich Filling: Process ½ avocado, 1 spring onion, ¼ cup fresh parsley, 1 tablespoon lemon juice. Transfer to bowl and add 1 cup mashed garbanzo, 1 stalk celery diced, and salt to taste.	Cooked Garbanzos Carbohydrate: 45 g Fat: 4 g Protein: 15 g Sodium: 11 mg Tryptophan: 139 mg Zinc: 2.5 mg Dietary Fiber: 12 g
Brown Rice	Grains like brown rice help to reduce weight gain. They have a gentler effect on blood sugar and insulin due to slower digestion, which helps one not to feel hungry as quickly.[3]	Brown Rice Lettuce Rolls: Combine 1 cup cooked rice, 1 cup cooked black beans, ¼ diced onion, ¼ cup corn kernels, ¼ cup diced tomatoes, ¼ cup golden raisins, 2 tablespoons cilantro, 1 teaspoon olive oil, ½ teaspoon honey. Salt to taste. Roll in washed lettuce leaves and enjoy.	Cooked Brown Rice Carbohydrate: 45 g Fat: 2 g Protein: 5 g Sodium: 10 mg Tryptophan: 64.4 mg Zinc: 1.2 mg Dietary Fiber: 4 g

HEALTH TIP: Walking is one of the best exercises and burns up to 120 calories an hour.[4]

OSTEOPOROSIS

A condition in which bone mass decreases and bones become weak and brittle. This occurs when new bone tissue is not replaced as fast as the old bone tissue is removed, and may be as a result of hormonal changes and mineral deficiency. The risk of fractures is greatly increased with fractures to the hip, wrist and spine occurring most frequently.

Foods	Health Benefits	How To Use	Composition (based on Cup)
Raisins	Raisins are an excellent source of the mineral boron, which is essential for the development and regeneration of bone. Adequate boron in the body helps to reduce the urinary loss of calcium and magnesium.[1]	Raisin Overnight Oats: Combine 1 cup oats, 1 cup nondairy milk, 1 teaspoon honey, ¼ cup raisins, ¼ cup sliced almonds, 1 tablespoon chia seeds and ½ teaspoon cinnamon. Refrigerate overnight. Serve cold.	Raisins Carbohydrate: 115 g Fat: 1 g Protein: 4 g Sodium: 16 mg Vitamin K: 5.1 mcg Calcium: 72.5 mg Omega-3: 10.2 mg
Cantaloupes	The regular consumption of the orange carotenoids found in cantaloupes has been found to have a protective effect on bone mineral density in older men and women.[2]	Cantaloupe Berry Salad: Combine ½ cantaloupe cubed, 1 cup sliced strawberries, 1 cup blueberries, 1 tablespoon fresh lemon juice and 2 teaspoons chopped mint leaves.	Fresh Cantaloupes Carbohydrate: 14 g Fat: 0 g Protein: 1 g Sodium: 26 mg Vitamin A: 5,987 IU Vitamin K: 4.4. mcg Calcium: 15.9 mg
Cabbages	Cabbages contain vitamin K, which helps to bind calcium to the bone[2] and increase bone strength. Adequate vitamin K has been associated with reduced vertebral and non-vertebral fractures.[3]	Crunchy Cabbage Salad: Combine 2 cups shredded green cabbage, 2 cups shredded purple cabbage, 6 chopped green onions, 1 cup sliced almonds, salt to taste. Dressing: Whisk 2 tablespoons honey, 2 tablespoons lemon juice and 2 tablespoons olive oil together and stir into salad mix.	Fresh Cabbage Carbohydrate: 4 g Fat: 0 g Protein: 1 g Sodium: 13 mg Vitamin A: 6.6 IU Vitamin K: 53.2 mcg Calcium: 28 mg
Chia Seeds	The omega-3 fatty acids found in chia seed may help to increase calcium absorption, decrease urinary calcium loss, improve bone strength and promote bone growth.[2]	Blueberry Chia Seed Smoothie: Place 2 tablespoons chia seed in ½ cup almond milk overnight. Place in blender and add 1 cup almond milk, 1 cup blueberries, 1 tablespoon unsweetened shredded coconut, 1 teaspoon vanilla, and 1 teaspoon honey. Blend until smooth.	Chia Seeds Carbohydrate: 72 g Fat: 51 g Protein: 26 g Sodium: 31 mg Calcium: 1,029 mg Zinc: 5.71 g Omega-3: 28,610 mg
Almonds	Almonds are high in calcium, an essential mineral needed for building strong bones. Inadequate calcium intake is associated with low bone mass and high fracture rates.[4]	Almond French Toast: Blend 1 cup unsweetened vanilla almond milk, ½ cup tofu, 3 tablespoons almond butter. Dip wholegrain bread in this mixture, drain off excess. Brown on both sides in lightly oiled skillet at medium heat.	Almonds Carbohydrate: 31 g Fat: 71 g Protein: 30 g Sodium: 1 mg Calcium: 378 mg Magnesium: 383 mg Omega-3: 8.6 mg
Soybeans	Soybean isoflavones may help to protect against bone loss and osteoporosis.[2] Higher intake of soy has been linked to lower incidence of osteoporosis.[5]	Spinach Tofu Dip: Blend 1 ½ cups tofu, ¾ cup soaked raw cashews, ¼ cup nutritional yeast, 2 teaspoons lemon juice, ½ teaspoon salt. Sauté 1 chopped onion, 2 cloves chopped garlic, three cups spinach until soft. Add blender mixture to spinach mixture, stir until heated through.	Regular Tofu Carbohydrate: 4 g Fat: 12 g Protein: 20 g Sodium: 18 mg Calcium: 868 mg Phosphorus: 240 mg Omega-3: 792 mg

ENCOURAGEMENT: Put your trust in the Lord, and be not afraid.[6]

PARKINSON'S DISEASE

A chronic and progressive nervous system disorder that is linked to decreased dopamine production in the body as a result of malfunctioning or dying nerve cells in the brain. Symptoms include tremors affecting hands, arms, legs, jaw and face, stiff muscles, slow movement and walking with a shuffling gait, and impaired coordination and balance.

Foods	Health Benefits	How To Use	Composition (based on Cup)
Red Grapefruit	Red grapefruit contains phytochemicals and carotenoids that help to decrease the functional decline related to aging, and may slow down the progression and reduce the risk of Parkinson's disease.[1]	Citrus Pomegranate Salad: Arrange peeled, carefully skinned segments of two red grapefruit and two navel oranges in suitable bowls. Drizzle with a little orange juice. Sprinkle with fresh pomegranate seeds.	Fresh Grapefruit Carbohydrates: 25 g Fats: 0 g Protein: 2 g Sodium: 0 mg Vitamin C: 71.8 mg Calcium: 50.6 mg Dietary Fiber: 4 g
Papayas	Papaya is a good source of vitamin C, which may help to reduce the risk of Parkinson's disease.[1] The antioxidants in papaya help to prevent free radical damage, which may cause cell death in some neurodegenerative disorders.[2]	Papaya Grapefruit Smoothie: Blend 2 cups cubed papaya, 1 peeled grapefruit, ½ cup raspberries, blueberries or strawberries and ½ cup nondairy milk.	Fresh Papayas Carbohydrate: 14 g Fats: 0 g Protein: 1 g Sodium: 4 mg Vitamin C: 86.5 mg Folate: 53.2 mcg Dietary Fiber: 3 g
Sesame Seeds	Individuals with Parkinson's are often prone to osteoporosis, which is caused by low bone mineral density. The calcium contained in sesame seeds helps to prevent deficiency of this vital mineral.[3]	Tahini Bites: Process ⅓ cup tahini,* 1 cup dried apricots, ½ cup unsweetened shredded coconut, and 2 teaspoons of honey. Shape into balls, roll in shredded coconut. Refrigerate.	Tahini Carbohydrates: 48 g Fats: 128 g Protein: 48 g Sodium: 80 g Calcium: 338 mg Folate: 235 mcg Dietary Fiber: 11.2 g
Broccoli	The fiber in vegetables such as broccoli may assist in protecting the healthy functioning of nerve cells. Fiber is also important in preventing constipation and aids weight management.[4]	Avocado Broccoli Soup: Sauté 1 diced onion in a little olive oil. Add 6 cups vegetable stock, 4 cups broccoli florets and simmer until tender. Add Swiss chard and simmer until wilted. Add 1 avocado, 1 tablespoon lime juice and salt to taste. Blend until creamy.	Cooked Broccoli Carbohydrates: 12 g Fats: 0 g Protein: 4 g Sodium: 64 mg Folate: 168.4 mcg Calcium: 62.4 mg Dietary Fiber: 6 g
Collard Greens	Folate, found in greens such as collards, can help to prevent deficiencies that can accelerate Parkinson's disease.[5] Folate helps to increase mitochondrial health, and this assists in preventing or delaying neurodegenerative diseases.[6]	Collard Greens Salad: Finely shred 1 bunch collard greens. Toss lightly with 1 chopped avocado, 1 cup cooked quinoa, 2 cups fresh sliced strawberries, and ¼ cup chopped almonds, 1 tablespoon olive oil and 1 tablespoon lemon juice.	Raw Collard Greens Carbohydrates: 2 g Fats: 0 g Protein: 1 g Sodium: 7 mg Calcium: 52.2 mg Folate: 59.8 mcg Dietary Fiber: 1.3 g
Fava Beans	Fava beans contain natural C-dopa and L-dopa, and increase C-dopa and L-dopa in the blood, leading to marked improvement in motor performance.[7]	Fava Beans: Boil eight cups salted water, add 2 lbs fresh fava beans and cook 2-3 minutes until tender. Drain. Place in ice water. Slip off skins. Place beans in bowl and combine with 1 tablespoon lemon juice, 1 tablespoon olive oil, 1 clove minced garlic and salt to taste.	Boiled Fava Beans Carbohydrates: 33g Fats: 1 g Protein: 13 g Sodium: 9 mg Calcium: 61.2 mg Folate: 177 mcg Dietary Fiber: 9 g

DID YOU KNOW? A faithful exercise program is more effective in fighting Parkinson's disease than anything else.[8]

PEPTIC ULCERS

A condition in which open sores, called gastric ulcers, form on the inner lining of the stomach and in the upper portion of the small intestine, where they are called duodenal ulcers. Peptic ulcers are most commonly caused by *Helicobacter pylori* bacteria and the extended use of some types of painkillers. The most frequently reported symptom of peptic ulcers is pain.

Foods	Health Benefits	How To Use	Composition (based on Cup)
Grapes	Resveratrol, a polyphenol found in grapes, is a powerful anti-oxidant, anti-inflammatory and anti-bacterial agent. Resveratrol is useful in fighting *H.pylori* infections, which frequently are the cause of peptic ulcers.[1]	Red Grape Smoothie: Blend 1 cup washed seedless red grapes, 1 banana, 5 large fresh or frozen strawberries with ½ cup non-dairy milk, until smooth.	Fresh Grapes Carbohydrate: 16 g Fat: 0 g Protein: 1 g Sodium: 2 mg Vitamin A: 92 IU Vitamin C: 3.7 mg Folate: 3.7 mcg
Strawberries	Strawberries contain a good amount of the anti-oxidant vitamin C, which plays an important role in the eradication of the *H.pylori* bacteria in patients with peptic ulcers.[2]	Strawberry Banana Ice Cream: Process or blend 2 frozen, sliced bananas, ½ cup sliced frozen strawberries, 2 tablespoons coconut cream and ½ teaspoon vanilla until smooth.	Fresh Strawberries Carbohydrates: 12 g Fat: 0 g Protein: 1 g Sodium: 2 mg Vitamin C: 89.4 mg Folate: 36.5 mcg Dietary Fiber: 3 g
Cabbage	All types of cabbage are helpful in treating peptic ulcers. The nutrients in cabbage have an anti-inflammatory and cauterizing effect on the gastric mucosa.[3]	Cabbage Juice: Place ½ cup water in the blender, add each ingredient individually, blending until smooth— ¼ cabbage, 1 stick chopped celery, 1 diced red beet, 1 diced apple, and 1 sliced carrot. Remove from blender and strain through very fine sieve.	Fresh Cabbage Carbohydrate: 4 g Fat: 0 g Protein: 1 g Sodium: 13 mg Vitamin C: 25.6 mg Iron: 0.3 mg Folate: 30.1 mcg
Peas	The fiber in peas acts a buffer, lowering the concentration of bile acids in the stomach. It reduces intestinal transit time and lessens bloating, helping to decrease discomfort and pain.[2]	Pea Soup: Sauté ½ to 1 chopped onion, and 1 clove garlic in 1 tablespoon olive oil. Add 2 cups vegetable broth and 1 bag frozen peas. Simmer until peas are heated through. Blend and add salt to taste.	Frozen Green Peas Carbohydrate: 18 g Fat: 1 g Protein: 7 g Sodium: 145 mg Vitamin C: 24.1 mg Iron: 2.1 mg Dietary Fiber: 6 g
Cashews	Cashews contain iron, which assists in preventing anemia. Anemia is caused by gastrointestinal bleeding of ulcers and *H.pylori* infections. Taking antacids decreases normal absorption of iron.[2]	Sweet Cashew Sauce: Cover 2 cups cashews with water, soak for 2 hours. Drain. Blend until creamy with ½ cup almond milk, 2 tablespoons lemon juice, 1 teaspoon vanilla, a pinch of salt, and ¼ cup honey. Use as a dip for fresh fruit.	Raw Cashews Carbohydrate: 47 g Fat: 63 g Protein: 26 g Sodium: 17 g Folate: 35.7 mcg Iron: 9.6 mg Dietary Fiber: 4.2 g
Lentils	Lentils provide folic acid, which is essential for healthy tissue.[4] The use of antacids can decrease the normal absorption of folic acid, resulting in deficiency.	Lentil Sandwich Spread: Sauté 2 cloves minced garlic in a little olive oil. Remove from heat. Process 1 ½ cups cooked lentils with sautéed garlic, ½ teaspoon ground cumin, ½ teaspoon ground coriander and salt to taste. Add a little water to reach desired consistency.	Cooked Lentils Carbohydrate: 40 g Fat: 1 g Protein: 18 g Sodium: 4 mg Vitamin C: 3 mg Folate: 358 mcg Dietary Fiber: 16 g

ENCOURAGEMENT: A merry heart doeth good like a medicine (Proverbs 17:22).[4]

PREMENSTRUAL SYNDROME

A condition that includes a variety of physical, mental and behavioral symptoms, that are linked to the female menstrual cycle, and usually occur in the two weeks before menstruation begins. The most common symptoms include fatigue, irritability, mood swings, crying, oversensitivity, food cravings, bloating, tender breasts, acne, headaches and insomnia.

Foods	Health Benefits	How To Use	Composition (based on Cup)
Apricots 	Apricots provide a good source of magnesium, which aids in muscle relaxation. A deficiency in magnesium can lead to cramping.[1]	Apricot Bars: Process 4 soft pitted dates, ¾ cup soft dried apricots, 1 cup walnuts, 1 tablespoon lemon juice, 1 tablespoon chia seed, 1 tablespoon flaxseed. Pat into a baking tray. Freeze for 15 minutes. Slice into bars and refrigerate.	Dried Apricots Carbohydrate: 81 g Fat: 1 g Protein: 4 g Sodium: 13 mg Riboflavin: 0.1 mg Magnesium: 41.6 mg Dietary Fiber: 9.5 g
Beet Greens 	Greens such as beet greens contain B vitamins as well as iron, which help to fight the fatigue that is frequently associated with premenstrual syndrome.[2]	Beet Greens Pesto: Process 2 cups beet greens, ¼ cup basil, ½ cup walnuts, ¼ cup olive oil, 2 cloves garlic, 1 tablespoon lemon juice, and ½ teaspoon salt. Serve with pizza, pasta, salads or sandwiches.	Fresh Beet Greens Carbohydrate: 2 g Fat: 0 g Protein: 1 g Sodium: 86 mg Riboflavin: 0.1 mg Calcium: 44.5 mg Iron: 1 mg
Chia Seeds 	The dietary calcium found in chia seeds helps to prevent calcium deficiency and reduces the risk of PMS.[3] It also helps to alleviate PMS symptoms such as insomnia, headaches, nervousness and depression.[4]	Berry Tahini Chia Pudding: Combine ¼ cup chia seeds, 1 cup coconut milk, ¼ cup raspberries, 1 tablespoon tahini,* and 2 teaspoons honey. Refrigerate overnight. Top with fresh berries and serve for breakfast.	Chia Seeds Carbohydrate: 72 g Fat: 51 g Protein: 26 g Sodium: 31 g Calcium: 1029 mg Thiamin: 1.3 mg Dietary Fiber: 61.5 g
Sesame Seeds 	Tahini, made from sesame seeds, contains both thiamin and riboflavin. Dietary thiamine and riboflavin are associated with a reduced risk of developing premenstrual syndrome.[5]	Apricot Tahini Balls: Process 1 cup soft dried apricots, 4 tablespoons Tahini.* Add ⅓ cup shredded coconut and process until forms soft dough. Form into balls and roll in coconut. Refrigerate.	Tahini Carbohydrate: 48 g Fat: 128 g Protein: 48 g Sodium: 80 g Calcium: 338 mg Thiamin: 3.2 mg Riboflavin: 0.24 mg
Garbanzos 	Garbanzos contain dietary fiber that helps to reduce pain associated with PMS.[1] Adequate intake of fiber helps with the elimination of excess estrogen from the body.[4,6]	Garbanzo Burgers: Sauté 1 small chopped onion. Blend 1 ½ cups cooked garbanzos, 1 clove garlic, 1 chopped carrot until smooth. Place in bowl with onions. Mix in ½ cup bread crumbs, ½ teaspoon cumin and ½ teaspoon salt. Shape into burgers. Bake at 360°F until golden brown.	Cooked Garbanzos Carbohydrate: 45 g Fat: 4 g Protein: 15 g Sodium: 11 mg Calcium: 80.4 mg Magnesium: 78.7 mg Dietary Fiber: 12.5 g
Millet 	Millet is a whole grain and a complex carbohydrate, which assists in normalizing insulin levels, which in turn helps to control cravings, stabilize mood and ward off depression.[2]	Millet Veggie Bowl: In a cereal bowl place ¾ cup warm cooked millet, ¼ cup warm stir-fried onions and green peppers, ¼ cup warm cooked black beans, ¼ cup corn kernels, and top with two tablespoons of guacamole and 1 tablespoon chopped cilantro.	Cooked Millet Carbohydrate: 41 g Fat: 2 g Protein: 6 g Sodium: 3 mg Thiamin: 0.2 mg Riboflavin: 0.1 mg Magnesium: 76.6 mg

HEALTH TIP: Exposure to sunshine boosts serotonin levels, which help to alleviate depression.[4]

PSORIASIS

A common, chronic autoimmune condition that affects the normal life cycle of skin cells. Thick scaly patches form on the skin and are often dry and itchy, may crack and bleed, and often become red and painful. This condition may occur on one small patch of skin or may affect the whole body.

Foods	Health Benefits	How To Use	Composition (based on Cup)
Peaches	Peaches contain vitamins A, C and E, as well as carotenoids and flavonoids, which all help to reduce tissue inflammation, provide stability to cell membranes and aid in skin lesion healing.[1]	Peach Ice Cream: Process 16 ounces frozen peaches, ½ cup nondairy milk, and 3 tablespoons honey with an s-blade until smooth and creamy. Sprinkle with chopped walnuts when serving.	Fresh Peaches Carbohydrate: 22 g Fat: 1 g Protein: 2 g Sodium: 0 mg Vitamin A: 730 IU Vitamin C: 14.8 mg Vitamin E: 1.6 mg
Lettuce	Lettuce provides a particularly good source of beta-carotene, and adequate intake of this nutrient is associated with a decreased risk of psoriasis[2] and lower levels of inflammation.[3]	Italian Green Salad: Combine 2 cups shredded romaine lettuce, 1 cup halved baby tomatoes, 1 cup diced cucumber, 1 diced avocado, ½ cup sliced pitted olives, 1 tablespoon olive oil, 1 tablespoon lemon juice, ½ teaspoon dill and salt to taste.	Romaine Lettuce Carbohydrate: 2 g Fat: 0 g Protein: 1 g Sodium: 4 mg Beta-carotene: 2,456 mcg Folate: 63.9 mcg Omega-3: 51.3 mg
Celery	Psoralen, a substance that is found in celery as well as many other vegetables, increases photosensitization. Moderate sunbathing may help to improve psoriasis after the consumption of vegetables that contain psoralen.[4]	Thai Celery Salad: Combine diagonally sliced celery stalks, 1 sliced spring onion, ¼ cup fresh cilantro, ⅓ cup grated carrots, ⅛ cup peanuts, 1 tablespoon olive oil, and 1 tablespoon lime juice. Salt to taste.	Fresh Celery Carbohydrate: 3 g Fat: 0 g Protein: 1 g Sodium: 81 mg Vitamin C: 3.1 mg Beta-carotene: 273 mcg Folate: 36.4 mcg
Walnuts	The omega-3 fatty acids found in walnuts are known to assist in decreasing inflammation and are helpful in promoting a healthy immune system.[5]	Walnut Energy Balls: Process 1 cup walnuts with 1 cup soft pitted dates until crumbly. Add ½ cup unsweetened shredded coconut, 1 tablespoon coconut oil, ½ teaspoon vanilla, and a pinch of salt and process until sticky. Roll into balls. Refrigerate.	English Walnuts Carbohydrate: 16 g Fat: 76 g Protein: 18 g Sodium: 2 mg Vitamin E: 0.8 mg Omega-3: 10,623 mg Dietary Fiber: 7.8 g
Barley	The fiber found in cereals such as barley has an important role to play in reducing oxidative stress in the body, which in turn decreases systemic inflammation.[3]	Barley Soup: In a large saucepan sauté 1 diced onion and 3 cloves chopped garlic in 1 teaspoon olive oil. Add ¾ cup barley, 1 stalk chopped celery, 1 diced tomato, 5 cups vegetable stock, 1 teaspoon dried thyme and simmer until barley is cooked. Add salt to taste.	Cooked Pearl Barley Carbohydrate: 44 g Fat: 1 g Protein: 4 g Sodium: 5 mg Vitamin A: 11 IU Folate: 21.5 mcg Dietary Fiber: 6 g
Lentils	Folate is a B vitamin found in legumes such as lentils. The intake of dietary folate may help prevent folate deficiency, which often occurs with psoriasis.[6]	Lentil Burgers: Process 4 cups cooked lentils, ¼ cup raisins, ½ cup walnuts until chunky. Place in bowl. Stir in ½ teaspoon salt and 1 cup bread crumbs and leave to absorb moisture for 10 minutes. Form into burgers. Bake at 380°F for 30 minutes, turning after 15 minutes.	Cooked Lentils Carbohydrate: 40 g Fat: 1 g Protein: 18 g Sodium: 4 mg Vitamin C: 3 mg Folate: 358 mcg Dietary Fiber: 16 g

ENCOURAGEMENT: Cast thy burden upon the Lord, and he shall sustain thee (Psalm 55:22).

RESTLESS LEGS SYNDROME

A condition of the nervous system in which uncomfortable sensations cause an uncontrollable and overwhelming urge to move the legs. The sensations are usually worse when sitting or lying down, and often cause insomnia. Moving the legs helps to relieve discomfort. Insomnia due to restless legs syndrome may lead to fatigue, reduced ability to concentrate and impaired memory.

Foods	Health Benefits	How To Use	Composition (based on Cup)
Oranges	Oranges provide a good source of folate, and the regular consumption of dietary folate may help to alleviate symptoms, particularly in familial restless legs syndrome.[1]	Orange Chia Breakfast Pudding: Blend 1 ¼ cups almond milk, 3 softened dates and zest of one orange. Add ½ cup orange juice. Transfer to a bowl. Add ⅓ cup chia seeds and leave for 30 minutes. Stir in chopped segments from one orange. Refrigerate until ready to eat.	Fresh Oranges Carbohydrate: 21 g Fat: 0 g Protein: 2 g Sodium: 0 mg Vitamin C: 95.8 mg Folate: 54 mcg Magnesium: 18 mg
Strawberries	Strawberries provide a good source of dietary vitamin C. This vitamin may play a role in reducing the severity of restless legs syndrome.[2]	Strawberry Avocado Smoothie: Blend 6 ounces avocado, 4 ounces fresh strawberries, 1 teaspoon honey, 1 fresh sliced banana, 1 tablespoon nondairy milk until creamy.	Fresh Strawberries Carbohydrate: 12 g Fat: 0 g Protein: 1 g Sodium: 2 mg Vitamin C: 89.4 mg Folate: 36.5 mcg Magnesium: 19.8 mg
Avocados	Avocados provide a rich source of dietary vitamin E, which may help to control the symptoms and provide some relief from restless legs syndrome.[3]	Avocado Hummus Veggie Sandwich: Spread two slices of toasted whole-grain bread with hummus. Layer with 4 slices avocado, 3 thin slices cucumber, 2 thin slices tomato and ¼ cup alfalfa sprouts.	Fresh Avocados Carbohydrate: 13 g Fat: 22 g Protein: 3 g Sodium: 11 mg Vitamin C: 15 mg Vitamin E: 3.1 mg Folate: 122 mcg
Almonds	The magnesium found in nuts such as almonds helps to prevent deficiency. Magnesium may help individuals with insomnia related to restless leg syndrome to sleep better.[4]	Roasted Almonds: Place 1 pound of almonds on a baking sheet. Bake at 350°F for approximately 15 minutes. Remove from the oven. Cool. Toss with 1 teaspoon olive oil and 1 teaspoon sea salt.	Almonds Carbohydrate: 27 g Fat: 73 g Protein: 30 g Sodium: 1 mg Vitamin E: 35.9 g Folate: 45 mcg Magnesium: 395 mg
Collard Greens	Iron deficiency is often connected with restless legs syndrome. Collards provide a good source of dietary iron, which may help to reduce symptoms in individuals with mild to moderate symptoms.[5]	Collard Veggie Soup: In a large saucepan simmer 1 cup chopped onion, 1 cup chopped celery, 1 cup diced carrots, 1 diced potato, 1 chopped tomato, 2 cups shredded collards, 6 cups vegetable stock, and 1 teaspoon sage. Simmer until vegetables are tender. Salt to taste. Blend.	Cooked Collards Carbohydrate: 9 g Fat: 1 g Protein: 4 g Sodium: 30 mg Vitamin C: 34.6 mg Folate: 177 mcg Iron: 2.2. mg
Black-Eyed Peas	The dietary iron contained in black-eyed peas may help to improve iron status in the body and assist in eliminating the symptoms of restless legs syndrome.[6]	Black-Eyed Pea Stew: In a saucepan cook 1 chopped onion, 2 diced carrots, ½ cup chopped celery, 1 diced bell pepper, 1 diced sweet potato in four cups vegetable stock until tender. Add 3 cups cooked black-eyed peas, 1 cup puréed tomato, sage, cumin and salt to taste.	Boiled Black-Eyed Peas Carbohydrate: 36 g Fat: 1 g Protein: 13 g Sodium: 7 mg Folate: 358 mcg Iron: 4.3 mg Magnesium: 91.9 mg

HEALTH TIP: Daily cultivating healthy habits leads to improved physical and mental health.[7]

SHINGLES

A viral infection caused by the *Varicella zoster* virus, which manifests as a painful skin rash, usually with blisters or red patches of skin. Shingles usually occur in patches, anywhere on the body. This virus is present in all individuals who have previously had chickenpox and can reactivate decades later causing shingles.

Foods	Health Benefits	How To Use	Composition (based on Cup)
Kiwifruit	Kiwifruit is a good source of vitamin C, and a powerful antioxidant with antiviral properties, which strengthens the immune system and may prevent the replication of the herpes virus.[1]	Kiwifruit Fruit Salad: Combine 6 peeled, chopped kiwifruit, 1 mango cubed, 1 large sliced banana, 6 sliced strawberries, ½ cup fresh pineapple cubed and ½ cup orange juice.	Fresh Kiwifruit Carbohydrate: 28g Fat: 0 g Protein: 2 g Sodium: 10 mg Vitamin A: 318 IU Vitamin C: 136.4 mg Magnesium: 54.7 mg
Mangos	The vitamin A in mangos promotes the generation of healthy cells and assists in healing the skin and keeping it healthy. It also supports normal immune function[2] and decreases the risk of shingles.[3]	Mango Coconut Pudding: Combine 1 cup coconut milk, 1 cup almond milk, 1/3 cup chia seeds, 1/3 cup coconut flakes and 2 tablespoons honey. Refrigerate until set. Blend 2 cups fresh mango until smooth. Layer chia pudding and mango in a glass and top with shredded coconut.	Fresh Mangos Carbohydrate: 28 g Fat: 0 g Protein: 1 g Sodium: 3 mg Vitamin A: 1,262 IU Vitamin B6: 0.2 mg Vitamin C: 45.7 mg
Bananas	Bananas contain vitamins A, B6, C, and E as well as folic acid, iron and zinc. All these nutrients are essential for normal immune function, and adequate intake helps to reduce the risk of shingles.[3]	Tropical Fruit Smoothie: Blend one sliced banana, 1 sliced kiwifruit, ½ mango cubed, 3 brazil nuts, 1 teaspoon Tahini,* 1 teaspoon honey and ½ cup unsweetened nondairy milk.	Sliced Bananas Carbohydrate: 34 g Fat: 0 g Protein: 2 g Sodium: 2 mg Vitamin B6: 0.6 mg Folate: 30 mcg Iron: 0.4 mg
White Beans	Lysine, an amino acid found in beans such as white beans, is known to inhibit the replication of the herpes simplex virus, and thus may do the same with the herpes virus that causes shingles.[4]	White Bean Spread: Lightly sauté 1 chopped onion with 1 clove minced garlic until tender. Process onions, garlic, 2 cups cooked white beans, ¼ cup cooked pimento, 1 tablespoon lemon juice, 1 teaspoon olive oil, 1 teaspoon Tahini,* ½ teaspoon cumin, and salt to taste.	Cooked White Beans Carbohydrate: 45 g Fat: 1 g Protein: 17 g Sodium: 11 mg Lysine: 1,196 mg Magnesium: 113 mg Iron: 6.6 mg
Brazil Nuts	Brazil nuts are one of the best sources of the mineral zinc, which helps to enhance the immune system and which also inhibits the replication of the herpes zoster virus.[1]	Brazil Nut Cream Cheese: Process 1 cup soaked and drained brazil nuts, 1 tablespoon lemon juice, 1 tablespoon olive oil, 2 teaspoons nutritional yeast and ½ teaspoon of dill until creamy. Enjoy on crackers, with vegetable sticks, on baked potatoes or with cooked vegetables.	Raw Brazil Nuts Carbohydrate: 16 g Fat: 88 g Protein: 19 g Sodium: 4 mg Lysine: 654 mg Magnesium: 500 mg Zinc: 5.4 mg
Sesame Seeds	The magnesium found in sesame seeds is an essential mineral which helps to ensure the healthy transmission of nerve impulses in the body.[5]	Avocado Tahini Dressing: Process the flesh of 1 ripe avocado, ¼ cup Tahini,* 1 tablespoon lemon juice, 1 tablespoon fresh cilantro and ½ cup of water until creamy.	Tahini Carbohydrate: 48 g Fat: 128 g Protein: 48 g Sodium: 80 g Folate: 98 mcg Iron: 10.56 mg Magnesium: 227 mg

DID YOU KNOW? Health is the greatest treasure you can have!

SINUSITIS

A condition in which the sinuses and airspaces within the bones of the face become inflamed. Sinusitis may be caused by allergies, fungi, viruses, bacteria or even autoimmune reactions. Common symptoms include nasal congestion, loss of smell, cough, facial pain or pressure, and on occasion fever and fatigue.

Foods	Health Benefits	How To Use	Composition (based on Cup)
Pineapples	Bromelain, an enzyme found in pineapples, may assist in reducing sinusitis symptoms such as inflammation and swelling.[1]	Pineapple Ice Cream: process 1 sliced frozen banana, 1 ¾ cups frozen pineapple chunks and ⅓ cup nondairy milk in a food processor until creamy. Serve immediately.	Fresh Pineapples Carbohydrate: 22g Fat: 0 g Protein: 1 g Sodium: 2 mg Vitamin A: 95.7 IU Vitamin C: 78.9 mg Omega-3: 28.1 mg
Cantaloupes	Cantaloupes contain the antioxidant vitamin C, which helps to counteract histamine, which plays a role in producing symptoms such as runny nose and sneezing.[2]	Pineapple Canteloupe Smoothie: Blend ¾ cup chopped pineapple, ¾ cup chopped cantaloupe, 1 ripe banana, and ½ cup non-dairy milk until creamy.	Fresh Cantaloupes Carbohydrate: 14 g Fat: 0 g Protein: 1 g Sodium: 26 mg Vitamin A: 5,412 IU Vitamin C: 58..7 mg Omega-3: 73.6 mg
Sweet Potatoes	Sweet potato is a good source of vitamin A, which is known to be a natural anti-inflammatory, and may assist in reducing inflammation of the mucous membranes.[3]	Baked Sweet Potato, Onion and Garlic: Place cubed sweet potato, and peeled, quartered onions in baking dish. Sprinkle with minced garlic and a little salt. Drizzle with a little olive oil. Bake uncovered at 425˚ for 25-30 minutes	Sweet Potatoes Carbohydrate: 41 g Fat: 0 g Protein: 4 g Sodium: 72 mg Vitamin A: 38,433 IU Vitamin C: 39.2 mg Omega-3: 8.0 mg
Onions	Onions are a source of quercetin, which has antihistamine properties and assists in reducing nasal congestion and inflammation. Inhaling the compounds from fresh onions also helps to clear the sinuses.[2]	French Onion Soup: In a large pot cook 3 large sliced onions in 2 tablespoons olive oil, on medium heat until soft. Add 6 cups vegetable stock, 1 bay leaf, ½ teaspoon of dried thyme, and salt to taste. Simmer fifteen minutes.	Cooked Onions Carbohydrate: 21 g Fat: 0 g Protein: 3 g Sodium: 6 mg Vitamin A: 4.2 IU Vitamin C: 10.9 mg Omega-3: 8.4 mg
Garlic	The compounds found in garlic (allicin, S-allyl cysteine, and ajoene) are anti-inflammatory and aid in improving the flow of mucous, and this helps to reduce congestion.[2]	Garlicky Potato Soup: Place 4 cups of vegetable stock in a large pot. Add 1 cup chopped onion, 7 large cloves of garlic minced, 2 pounds of potatoes peeled and diced. Bring to a boil. Simmer on medium about 25 minutes until potatoes are tender. Season to taste. Blend until creamy.	Fresh Garlic Carbohydrate: 45 g Fat: 1 g Protein: 9 g Sodium: 23 mg Vitamin A: 12.2 IU Vitamin C: 42.4 mg Omega-3: 27.2 mg
Walnuts	Omega-3 essential fatty acids found in walnuts help to support a healthy immune system, and may bring relief from conditions related to allergies.[2]	Walnut Cheese Spread: Process 1 cup walnuts, 3 ½ teaspoons tomato paste, ½ cup nutritional yeast, 3 teaspoons lemon juice, salt to taste and ½ to ¾ cup water, until spreadable.	English Walnuts Carbohydrate: 16 g Fat: 76 g Protein: 18 g Sodium: 2 mg Vitamin A: 23.4 IU Vitamin C: 1.5 mg Omega-3: 10,623 mg

HEALTH TIP: Sinus pain can be relieved by placing heat on the sinuses.[4]

STRESS

A feeling of mental, emotional or physical tension which may be acute or chronic. Chronic tension is particularly harmful to the body and can result in health conditions such as hypertension, heart disease, diabetes, obesity, skin conditions and depression. Typical symptoms include fatigue, aching muscles, headaches, gastrointestinal problems, memory issues, insomnia and weight loss or weight gain.

Foods	Health Benefits	How To Use	Composition (based on Cup)
Bananas	Carbohydrate-rich foods such as bananas enable the brain to produce the hormone serotonin, which reduces stress[1] and aids in relaxation.[2] The nutrients in bananas also help to replace the extra energy loss caused by stress.[3]	Breakfast Baked Bananas: Slice bananas lengthways and place them on a foil-lined baking tray. Brush each one with a teaspoon of honey. Bake for 10 to 15 minutes until soft.	Fresh Bananas Carbohydrate: 34 g Fat: 0 g Protein: 2 g Sodium: 2 mg Vitamin C: 13.1 mg Vitamin B6: 0.6 mg Magnesium: 40.5 mg
Pineapples	Pineapple contains the antioxidant vitamin C, which has been found to reduce the physical and mental response to stress.[1,4] Stress increases the need for this vitamin, which stimulates the immune system.[3]	Pineapple Banana Smoothie: Blend 1 fresh or frozen sliced banana, ½ cup fresh or frozen cubed pineapple, 1 orange diced, 1 tablespoon oats and ½ cup nondairy milk until smooth.	Fresh Pineapples Carbohydrate: 22g Fat: 0 g Protein: 1 g Sodium: 2 mg Vitamin C: 78.9 mg Magnesium: 19.8 mg Omega-3: 28.1 mg
Oats	Oats are a high-carbohydrate food that promote serotonin production, stress reduction, and a feeling of calmness. They also help to reduce levels of stress hormones in the body.[1]	Oatmeal Power Bowl: Top warm cooked oatmeal with shelled, soaked pumpkin seeds, dried cranberries, almond slivers, toasted flaked coconut, fresh banana slices and a little non-dairy milk.	Cooked Oats Carbohydrate: 32 g Fat: 4 g Protein: 6 g Sodium: 9 mg Thiamine: 0.2 mg Magnesium: 63.2 mg Omega-3: 42.1 mg
Pumpkin Seeds	Omega-3 fatty acids found in pumpkin seeds have been shown to lower the surges of stress hormones and provide protection against depression and heart disease, which are often associated with stress.[1]	Pumpkin Seed Pesto: Process 1 cup hulled, toasted, unsalted pumpkin seeds with 3 tablespoons olive oil, 1 tablespoon lemon juice, ½ teaspoon crushed garlic, ½ cup cilantro and a pinch of salt.	Dried Green Pepitas Carbohydrate: 30 g Fat: 96 g Protein: 75 g Sodium: 41 mg Riboflavin: 0.7 mg Magnesium: 1,212 mg Omega-3: 377 mg
Quinoa	Quinoa contains most of the B vitamins that are essential for the proper functioning of the nervous system, and that also are vital for energy production and metabolism of carbohydrates.[3]	Mexican Quinoa Salad: Place mixed greens on individual plates, layer cooked quinoa, corn kernels, cooked black beans, diced onion, segmented orange, sliced avocado and chopped cilantro. Dressing: blend 1/2 avocado, 4 teaspoons lime juice, 3 tablespoons orange juice. Salt to taste.	Cooked Quinoa Carbohydrate: 39 g Fat: 4 g Protein: 8 g Sodium: 13 mg Vitamin B6: 0.2 mg Riboflavin: 0.2 mg Folate: 77.7 mcg
Black Beans	Black beans are a source of magnesium, which is needed for maintaining a balanced nervous system.[3] Adequate magnesium helps prevent headaches and fatigue, and also may aid in improving sleep quality.[1]	Sweet Potato Black Bean Burgers: Combine 2 cups mashed sweet potato, 1 cup cooked black beans, 1 cup cooked quinoa, ½ cup finely ground walnuts, ½ cup diced onion, 2 teaspoons cumin, and a ¼ teaspoon salt. Form burgers and bake at 350°F for 40 minutes turning halfway.	Cooked Black Beans Carbohydrate: 41 g Fat: 1 g Protein: 15 g Sodium: 2 mg Folate: 256 mcg Magnesium: 120 mg Omega-3: 181 mg

ENCOURAGEMENT: If you will appreciate the valuable gift of salvation ... you will be guided in the way of peace.[5]

STROKE

A condition affecting the arteries leading to and within the brain. Strokes occur when the blood supply to the brain is blocked or when a blood vessel in the brain ruptures. Symptoms include sudden weakness or numbness of the face, arm or leg on one side of the body, sudden vision loss, sudden speech difficulty, sudden mobility problems or sudden headache. Experiencing a stroke may lead to paralysis, vision problems, memory loss, speech and language problems.

Foods	Health Benefits	How To Use	Composition (based on Cup)
Figs	Figs provide a good source of fiber, which helps to reduce cholesterol and correspondingly overall risk for stroke, and diseases associated with stroke such as cardiovascular disease and obesity.[1]	Fresh or dried figs may be eaten on their own or added to other dishes. Dried figs can be simmered in a little water or fruit juice for a few minutes to make them juicier.	Dried Figs Carbohydrate: 95 g Fat: 1 g Protein: 5g Sodium: 15 mg Folate: 13.4 mcg Magnesium: 101 mg Dietary Fiber: 15 g
Strawberries	Strawberries are high in vitamin C, which assists in preventing the development of atherosclerosis and damage to blood vessels, which often lead to stroke. Vitamin C may also aid in improving brain function after a stroke.[2]	Strawberry Pineapple Smoothie: Blend ⅓ cup strawberries, ½ cup sliced banana, ½ cup chopped pineapple, 1 tablespoon shelled pumpkin seeds, soaked overnight and drained, and ½ cup nondairy milk until smooth and creamy.	Fresh Strawberries Carbohydrate: 12 g Fat: 0 g Protein: 1 g Sodium: 2 mg Vitamin C: 89.4 mg Folate: 36.5 mcg Magnesium: 19.8 mg
Pumpkin Seeds	Magnesium deficiency has been indicated as a factor possibly contributing toward strokes. Pumpkin seeds provide dietary magnesium and may also help to reduce hypertension, which is a common risk factor for stroke.[2]	Sweet Pumpkin Seed Balls: Process 1 cup roasted pepitas until crumbly. Add ¾ cup softened, drained dates, ½ cup dried cranberries and ¼ teaspoon of ginger and process until soft dough forms. Roll into little balls and refrigerate.	Dried Green Pepitas Carbohydrate: 25 g Fat: 63 g Protein: 34 g Sodium: 25 mg Folate: 80 mcg Magnesium: 738 mg Dietary Fiber: 5.4 g
Barley	Barley contains soluble fiber, which plays an important role in helping to remove cholesterol and preventing the formation of plaque in the arteries. The risk of stroke is greatly reduced by clear arteries.[3]	Barley Wild Rice Pilaf: Combine 1 ½ cups hot cooked barley and 1 ½ cups hot cooked wild rice with 1 medium chopped onion lightly sautéed, 2 tablespoons of fresh chopped parsley, ½ cup toasted slivered almonds, 1 cup pomegranate seeds. Add a little salt to taste.	Cooked Pearl Barley Carbohydrate: 44 g Fat: 1 g Protein: 4 g Sodium: 5 mg Folate: 25.1 mcg Magnesium 34.5 mg Dietary Fiber: 6 g
Black-Eyed Peas	Black-eyed peas are rich in folate and other B vitamins which help to lower stroke risk. These nutrients help to break down homocysteine, which may cause damage to the artery walls, leading to stroke.[4]	Black-Eyed Peas Dip: Process 1 ½ cups cooked black-eyed peas with ¼ cup chopped parsley, 1 clove of garlic, with 2 tablespoons lemon juice, 1 teaspoon dried thyme and ⅛ teaspoon salt. Enjoy with freshly sliced raw carrot, zucchini and celery sticks.	Black-Eyed Peas Carbohydrate: 36 g Fat: 1 g Protein: 13 g Sodium: 7 mg Folate: 358 mcg Magnesium: 91.9 mg Dietary Fiber: 11.2 g
Garlic	The consumption of garlic may help to prevent the formation of blood clots. It also assists in destroying plaque in the arteries, reducing risk of stroke and hypertension.[2]	Stir a little extra raw chopped garlic into mashed potatoes, cooked beans, pasta dishes, winter soups, vegetable stews, and low fat salad dressings. Fresh Garlic	Fresh Garlic Carbohydrate: 45 g Fat: 1 g Protein: 9 g Sodium: 23 mg Vitamin C: 42.4 mg Folate: 4.1 mcg Magnesium: 34 mg

DID YOU KNOW? The most effective way to prevent a stroke is to lower blood pressure and reduce dietary fat.[5]

ULCERATIVE COLITIS

An inflammatory condition that causes long-lasting ulcers and inflammation on the innermost lining of the colon and rectum. Symptoms include persistent diarrhea with abdominal pain and blood in the stools, as well as loss of appetite, weight-loss, indigestion, headaches and fatigue. The cause of ulcerative colitis is unknown.

Foods	Health Benefits	How To Use	Composition (based on Cup)
Cantaloupes	The soluble fiber in cantaloupes is helpful in absorbing water and forming a gel in the intestines, which makes one feel full longer, slows down digestion and reduces diarrhea.[1]	Cantaloupe Coconut Smoothie: Blend 1 ripe banana, 1 cup of fresh cantaloupe chunks, ½ cup orange juice, 1 tablespoon unsweetened desiccated coconut until creamy.	Fresh Cantaloupes Carbohydrate: 14 g Fat: 0 g Protein: 1 g Sodium: 26 mg Vitamin A: 5,412 IU Vitamin C: 58.7 mg Dietary Fiber: 1 g
Apples	Apples contain emollient and detoxifying pectin, antiseptic organic acids and astringent tannins which are helpful in healing intestinal disorders. When they are eaten alone and cooked, they can help to stop diarrhea.[2]	Honey Baked Apples: Wash and core three or four sweet apples, leaving the bottom intact. Place in an oiled baking dish. Drizzle two teaspoons of honey into the center of each apple. Cover with foil. Bake at 350°F for about 1 hour, until tender.	Cooked Apples Carbohydrate: 23 g Fat: 1 g Protein: 0 g Sodium: 2 mg Vitamin A: 75.2 IU Vitamin C: 0.3 mg Dietary Fiber: 4 g
Avocados	Avocados provide an excellent source of protein, healthy fats, and dietary fiber which is easily digested.[3] They also provide other needed nutrients such as vitamins A, C, E, K and B.[1]	Cheesy Avocado Spread: Combine 2 ripe mashed avocados, 1 tablespoon lemon juice, 2 tablespoons nutritional yeast flakes, ¼ teaspoon salt, ¼ teaspoon garlic powder, onion powder and fresh chopped herbs to taste.	Fresh Avocados Carbohydrate: 13 g Fat: 22 g Protein: 3 g Sodium: 11 mg Vitamin C: 15 mg Calcium: 18 mg Dietary Fiber: 10 g
Carrots	Carrots help to restore intestinal function. They are rich in pectin, which helps to heal intestinal mucosa and absorbs intestinal toxins. Their beta-carotene promotes healthy cells.[2]	Carrot Soup: Sauté 1 large sliced onion and 2 cloves minced garlic in 2 tablespoons olive oil. Add 2 pounds sliced carrots and 1 teaspoon thyme. Cook five minutes. Add 6 cups vegetable stock, boil, reduce heat. Simmer about 20 minutes until carrots are tender. Blend.	Cooked Carrots Carbohydrate: 12 g Fat: 0 g Protein: 2 g Sodium: 90 mg Vitamin A: 26,576 IU Calcium: 23.4 mg Dietary Fiber: 2.7 g
Oats	The soluble fiber in oats protects the intestine and promotes healthy function and healing. It is helpful in cases of constipation as well as diarrhea.[2]	Coconut Oatmeal: In a saucepan combine 1 cup water, ⅓ cup oats, ¼ cup coconut milk, 1 sliced banana. Heat and stir until all liquid is absorbed. Stir in 1 tablespoon almond butter. Add fruit toppings as desired.	Cooked Oats Carbohydrate: 32 g Fat: 4 g Protein: 6 g Sodium: 9 mg Vitamin K: 0.7 mcg Calcium: 21.1 mg Dietary Fiber: 4 g
Soybeans	Calcium deficiency may result from ulcerative colitis. Soy milk is a good source of calcium, which is easily digested and helps to prevent deficiency.[1]	Rice Pudding: Combine 4 cups vanilla soy milk, ⅛ teaspoon salt, ⅓ cup honey, ⅓ cup raisins in a saucepan; heat slowly, boil one minute. Pour into oiled baking dish. Add 1 cup rice, cover, cook at 325°F, stirring once or twice, for 45 minutes or longer until desired creaminess is reached.	Plain Soy milk Carbohydrate: 8 g Fat: 4 g Protein: 7 g Sodium: 119 mg Calcium: 299 mg Vitamin A: 501 IU Riboflavin: 0.5 mcg

UNDERWEIGHT

A condition in which an individual weighs less than what is considered normal, healthy or required for their height, build and age. A BMI of less than 18.5 is usually considered underweight. Underweight can be caused by not eating sufficient calories, an extremely high metabolism or certain medical conditions thats lead to weight loss.

Foods	Health Benefits	How To Use	Composition (based on Cup)
Bananas	Fresh dense fruits such as banana, mango and avocado are high in calories and provide a good range of nutrients and healthy calories for gaining weight.[1]	Breakfast Cookies: Process 1 cup softened dates into small bits. Add 1 banana and 2 tablespoons almond butter and pulse. Add ½ cup almond meal and 1 cup rolled oats. Mix until a soft dough forms. Add ¼ cup raisins. Chill ten minutes. Form cookies and bake at 350°F until golden brown.	Sliced Bananas Carbohydrate: 34 g Fat: 0 g Protein: 2 g Sodium: 2 mg Vitamin A: 96 IU Magnesium: 40.5 mg Calories: 133
Raisins	Raisins are high-energy fruit. The vitamins, minerals and trace elements in raisins help to build the proteins in the body and aid in tissue formation.[2]	Classic Trail Mix: Combine 1 cup banana chips, 1 cup almonds, ¾ cup peanuts, ¾ cup cranberries, ½ cup raisins, and ½ cup sunflower seeds. Store in airtight container.	Seedless Raisins Carbohydrate: 131 g Fat: 1 g Protein: 5 g Sodium: 18 mg Folate: 8.3 mcg Potassium: 1,236 mg Calories: 493
Almonds	Nuts such as almonds are high in calories, providing a good source of protein and healthy fats as well as nutrients that the body needs for tissue formation and weight gain.[1,2]	Almond Butter Gravy: Blend 1 cup nondairy milk, ½ cup almond butter, 1 teaspoon brown sugar. Place in saucepan and stir until thickened. Add salt to taste. Enjoy on whole-grain toast.	Almonds Carbohydrate: 31 g Fat: 71 g Protein: 30 g Sodium: 1 mg Vitamin E: 35.9 g Calcium: 378 mg Calories: 822
Peanuts	Legumes such as peanuts are a concentrated source of carbohydrates, proteins and minerals. Adequate consumption leads to new protein formation and increased body mass.[2]	Peanut Butter Smoothie: Blend 1 large ripe banana, 1 cup soy milk, 2 tablespoons peanut butter, 3 soft dates pitted, ½ teaspoon vanilla, and 1 tablespoon carob powder until smooth and creamy.	Dry Roasted Peanuts Carbohydrate: 31 g Fats 73 g Protein: 35g Sodium: 9 mg Folate: 212 mcg Magnesium: 257 mg Calories: 854
Sweet Potatoes	Starchy vegetables such as sweet potatoes provide more calories than other vegetables, and contain easily digested carbohydrates and vitamins and minerals that contribute to tissue formation and weight gain.[1,2]	Skillet Sweet Potatoes: Cook 1 cup chopped onion in 1 tablespoon olive oil until soft. Add 1 ½ cups sweet potatoes cut in ½ inch cubes, ½ cup vegetable stock. Cover. Stir two or three times while cooking until soft. Season with salt to taste.	Mashed Sweet Potatoes Carbohydrate: 58 g Fat: 0 g Protein: 4 g Sodium: 89 mg Vitamin C: 39.2 mg Magnesium: 54 mg Calories: 249
Quinoa	Liberal use of whole grains such as quinoa are helpful in gaining weight. Most whole grains are a good source of calories as well as nutrients needed to assist the body in forming new tissue.[2,3]	Quinoa Burgers: Combine a heaping ½ cup cooked quinoa, 12 ounces tofu with water squeezed out and mashed, 2 tablespoons nut butter, 2 tablespoons soy sauce. Mix well. Form into burgers. Bake at 360°F for about 40 minutes until golden brown. Turn halfway through baking.	Cooked Quinoa Carbohydrate: 39 g Fat: 4 g Protein: 8 g Sodium: 13 mg Folate: 77.2 mcg Riboflavin: 0.2 mg Calories: 222

ENCOURAGEMENT: God will help those who love the truth, who give themselves, heart and mind and strength, to Him.[4]

URINARY TRACT INFECTION

A condition in which part of the urinary tract system becomes infected. This could include the kidneys, ureters, bladder and urethra. Urinary tract infections (UTIs) are caused by many different health situations. Symptoms often include a frequent urge to urinate and pain and burning when urinating, feeling tired and shaky, and even fever and chills.

Foods	Health Benefits	How To Use	Composition (based on Cup)
Blueberries	Blueberries have a decided antiseptic and antibiotic action in the urinary tract.[3] The proanthocyanadins in blueberries inhibit the binding of bacteria to bladder tissue, thereby preventing infection.[1,2]	Blueberry Watermelon Smoothie: Blend 2 cups blueberries, 2 cups cubed seedless watermelon and ¼ cup ice until smooth and no ice pieces remain. Serve immediately.	Fresh Blueberries Carbohydrate: 21 g Fat: 0 g Protein: 1 g Sodium: 1 mg Vitamin A: 79.9 IU Vitamin C: 14.4 mg Vitamin E: 0.8 mg
Grapefruit	The citric acid and other organic acids in grapefruit help to alkalize the urine. Bacteria causing UTIs do not like alkaline environments, and this helps to cure infection. The vitamin C also helps to strengthen the immune system to fight infection.[3]	Citrus Honey Mint Salad: Combine peeled segments from 1 orange and 1 grapefruit. Mix ½ tablespoon honey, 1 tablespoon orange juice, 1 tablespoon grapefruit juice, and 1 teaspoon olive oil. Drizzle over citrus segments. Sprinkle with 1 tablespoon finely chopped mint.	Fresh Grapefruit Carbohydrate: 25 g Fat: 0 g Protein: 2 g Sodium: 0 mg Vitamin A: 2,645 IU Vitamin C: 71.8 mg Folate: 29.9 mcg
Watermelon	The consumption of watermelon stimulates the kidneys' eliminatory function and it helps to alkalize the urine. An alkaline environment helps to inhibit UTI-causing bacteria.[4]	Blueberry Watermelon Lime Salad: Combine 2 pounds cubed seedless watermelon, 1 heaped cup blueberries. Drizzle with the juice from two limes, and sprinkle with finely shredded fresh basil.	Fresh Watermelon Carbohydrate: 11 g Fat: 0 g Protein: 1 g Sodium: 2 mg Vitamin A: 865 IU Vitamin C: 12.3 mg Folate: 4.6 mcg
Grapes	Grapes contain antioxidants that help to strengthen the immune system to fight infection.[1] They also have a diuretic effect and aid in alkalizing the urine, thus helping in the cure of UTIs.[4]	Red Grape Raspberry Sorbet: Place frozen red seedless grapes and a few frozen raspberries into the food processor. Drizzle with a little lemon juice. Process until creamy.	Fresh Grapes Carbohydrate: 16 g Fat: 0 g Protein: 1 g Sodium: 2 mg Vitamin A: 92 IU Vitamin C: 3.7 mg Vitamin K: 13.4 mcg
Pumpkin Seeds	Squash seeds such as pumpkin seeds, also known as pepitas, contain cucurbitacin, an active ingredient that helps to reduce urinary tract and prostate inflammation.[3]	Roasted Pepitas: Heat oven to 325°F. Toss raw pepitas with a little olive oil. Spread a single layer on a baking sheet. Roast about 15 minutes until golden, stirring occasionally. Remove from oven. Immediately toss seeds with seasonings as desired.	Dried Green Pepitas Carbohydrate: 25 g Fat: 63 g Protein: 34 g Sodium: 25 mg Calcium: 59.3 mg Iron: 20.7 mg Zinc: 10.3 mg
Onions	The essential oil in onions, which contributes to their taste, is to some extent eliminated through the urine and acts as an antiseptic. Onions are also diuretic and help alkalize the urine.[3]	Baked Onions: Peel 6 onions, slice a thin layer off the top and bottom so they will stand flat. Place halves in a baking dish. Mix 1 cup vegetable broth, ¼ cup honey, 1 tablespoon olive oil, 1 teaspoon dried rosemary. Pour over onions. Bake at least 45 minutes until tender.	Cooked Onions Carbohydrate: 21 g Fat: 0 g Protein: 3 g Sodium: 6 mg Vitamin C: 10.9 mg Folate: 31.5 mcg Magnesium: 23.1 mg

DID YOU KNOW? A walk, even in winter, is beneficial to health and increases vitality.[5]

VARICOSE VEINS

A condition in which the veins become twisted and swollen and can be seen under the surface of the skin. These veins often look blue or purple. Varicose veins usually occur in the legs, but they can also form elsewhere in the body. Symptoms may include burning, throbbing or cramping pain and a feeling of heaviness in the limbs.

Foods	Health Benefits	How To Use	Composition (based on Cup)
Raspberries	Dark colored berries such as raspberries contain bioflavonoids which help to strengthen the walls of the veins and keep them healthy.[1]	Raspberry Yogurt: Blend 1 ½ cups soaked, drained cashews, 1 cup raspberries, 1 tablespoon lemon juice, up to ½ cup water, 2 soft pitted dates, pinch of salt, and ½ teaspoon psyllium husk powder. Refrigerate 15 minutes. Add more water if needed.	Fresh Raspberries Carbohydrate: 15 g Fat: 1 g Protein: 1 g Sodium: 1 mg Vitamin C: 32.2 mg Vitamin E: 1.1 mg Dietary Fiber: 8 g
Tangerines	Tangerines are high in vitamin C, which aids the body in producing collagen for strengthening the walls of the blood vessels.[2] Vitamin C may help to prevent varicose veins from getting worse.[1]	Tangerine Avocado Salad: Place spring greens on individual plates. Add mandarin and avocado slices. Sprinkle with roasted green pumpkin seeds. Drizzle with olive oil and lemon juice or Sunflower Seed Dressing.*	Fresh Tangerines Carbohydrate: 26 g Fat: 1 g Protein: 2 g Sodium: 4 mg Vitamin C: 52.1 mg Vitamin E: 0.4 mg Dietary Fiber: 4 g
Asparagus	Rutin, a bioflavonoid found in asparagus, may strengthen the walls of veins. It may help to relieve the aching, swelling and pain caused by varicose veins.[1]	Cream Sauce for Steamed Asparagus: Blend ½ cup cashews and 1 cup water until smooth. Add 1 cup water, ½ teaspoon salt, 1 teaspoon onion powder, 1 tablespoon vegan chicken flavor seasoning, 2 tablespoons cornstarch and blend. Place in saucepan and cook until thickened.	Cooked Asparagus Carbohydrate: 8 g Fat: 0 g Protein: 4 g Sodium: 26 mg Vitamin C: 13.8 mg Vitamin E: 2.6 mg Dietary Fiber: 4 g
Rice	Whole-grain brown rice is a good source of fiber, which is helpful in the treatment of varicose veins. Whole grains are also helpful for weight loss, helping reduce the risk of varicose veins.[3]	Yellow Rice: In a saucepan combine 1 cup uncooked brown rice, 2 ½ cups water, ½ teaspoon salt, 1 ½ teaspoons turmeric, 2 tablespoons honey, 1 tablespoon olive oil, and ½ cup raisins. Bring to a boil, reduce heat. Simmer for about 25 minutes until rice is fluffy and water has been absorbed.	Cooked Brown Rice Carbohydrate: 45 g Fat: 2 g Protein: 5 g Sodium: 10 mg Magnesium: 83.9 mg Zinc: 1.2 mg Dietary Fiber: 4 g
Garbanzos	Garbanzos contain the essential trace mineral zinc, which helps to keep veins healthy.[1] Zinc has antioxidant properties and it helps to protect cells from damage caused by free radicals.[4]	Simple Garbanzo Soup: Sauté 1 chopped onion, 1 large clove minced garlic, 1 diced red bell pepper, ½ teaspoon cumin. Add 2 cups vegetable broth, 2 cups tomato purée and 2 cups cooked garbanzos. Simmer for 10 minutes. Serve topped with fresh herbs.	Cooked Garbanzos Carbohydrate: 45 g Fat: 4 g Protein: 15 g Sodium: 11 mg Folate: 282 mcg Zinc: 2.5 mg Dietary Fiber: 12 g
Sunflower Seeds	Vitamin E found in sunflower seeds helps to keep veins healthy and may help to prevent the formation of varicose veins and keep them from getting worse.[1]	Sunflower Seed Pesto: Process 1 cup basil leaves, 1 cup arugula leaves and 3 cloves garlic until fine. Add ½ cup sunflower seeds, 1 tablespoon lemon juice, 1 teaspoon salt and ¼ cup olive oil. Process to desired consistency.	Sunflower Seeds Carbohydrate: 28 g Fat: 72 g Protein: 29 g Sodium: 13 mg Magnesium: 455 mg Zinc: 7 mg Dietary Fiber: 12 g

HEALTH TIP: Individuals with varicose veins need to drink at least 48 ounces of water daily.[5]

WEAK IMMUNE SYSTEM

A condition in which the immune system has been weakened, which prevents the body from being able to fight infections and disease adequately. Individuals who have a weak immune system find it easier to succumb to bacterial and viral infections, as well as parasites. Many of the causes of this condition are unknown, however the immune system is often weakened by under or malnourishment, stress, chemotherapy or infectious diseases.

Foods	Health Benefits	How To Use	Composition (based on Cup)
Mangos	Vitamin A is found in colorful foods such as mango. The carotenoids in these foods are converted into the antioxidant vitamin A, which helps to strengthen the immune system against infection.[1]	Mango Fruit Leather: Peel, cube and blend one or two mangos. Place parchment paper on a baking tray. Spread a thin layer of mango evenly on the parchment paper. Bake three or four hours at 175°F until dry to the touch.	Fresh Mangos Carbohydrate: 28 g Fat: 0 g Protein: 1 g Sodium: 3 mg Vitamin A: 1,262 IU Vitamin B6: 0.2 mg Vitamin C: 45.7 mg
Tangerines	Tangerines contain vitamin C, an antioxidant needed by immune system cells in order for the immune system to function normally. Vitamin C deficiency reduces resistance to certain pathogens.[2]	Tangerine Fruit Sauce: Blend 1 cup of orange or tangerine juice with 1½ tablespoons cornstarch. Heat in saucepan, stirring until thickened. Stir in 15 ounces tangerine segments and heat until warm. Enjoy on waffles, pancakes or in crepes.	Fresh Tangerines Carbohydrate: 26 g Fat: 1 g Protein: 2 g Sodium: 4 mg Vitamin A: 1,328 IU Vitamin C: 52.1 mg Vitamin E: 0.4 mg
Peanuts	Peanuts provide the body with vitamin E, a powerful antioxidant that assists the body in fighting off infection.[1] Vitamin E deficiency impairs immune function.[3]	Peanut Banana Ice Cream: Process 2 frozen, sliced bananas until creamy. Add 2 tablespoons sugar-free peanut butter, a dash of vanilla and a little salt to taste and process until mixed in. Scoop into small bowls and top with crushed peanuts.	Dry Roasted Peanuts Carbohydrate: 31 g Fat: 73 g Protein: 35g Sodium: 9 mg Vitamin E: 10.1 mg Vitamin B6: 0.4 mg Zinc: 4.8 mg
Potatoes	Vitamin B6, which can be found in potatoes, is essential to almost 200 biochemical reactions in the body, and therefore is of vital importance to the normal functioning of the immune system.[1]	Mediterranean Baked Potatoes: Sauté 1 diced onion, 2 cloves minced garlic, 1 diced bell pepper and 1 small diced zucchini until tender. Top hot baked potatoes with hummus and the sautéed vegetables. Sprinkle with fresh chopped parsley.	Baked Potatoes Carbohydrate: 63 g Fat: 0 g Protein: 7 g Sodium: 30 mg Vitamin C: 28.7 mg Vitamin B6: 0.9 mg Iron: 3.2 mg
Spinach	Consumption of the mineral zinc, one of the nutrients found in spinach, is essential for normal development and functioning of the cells in the immune system.[3]	Toasted Spinach Hummus Veggie Wrap: Spread center of wrap or tortilla with red pepper hummus. Layer with baby spinach, avocado slices, tomato slices, cooked white beans and sprouts. Fold up wrap tightly. Toast on sandwich griller until slightly browned. Cut in half and enjoy.	Cooked Spinach Carbohydrate: 7 g Fat: 0 g Protein: 5 g Sodium:126 mg Vitamin A: 18,867 IU Iron: 6.4 mg Zinc: 1.4 mg
White Beans	Legumes such as white beans provide the body with the mineral iron needed for a healthy immune system. Iron deficiency leads to impaired immune response.[3]	White Bean Soup: Sauté 1 diced onion, minced garlic, 1 cup sliced carrots in a little olive oil. Add 3 diced potatoes, 5 cups veggie stock and simmer until vegetables are tender. Add 2 cups cooked diced tomatoes, 1 cup tomato sauce, and 3 cups cooked white beans. Add salt to taste.	Cooked White Beans Carbohydrate: 45 g Fat: 1 g Protein: 17 g Sodium: 11 mg Vitamin B6: 0.2 mg Iron: 6.6 mg Zinc: 2.5 mg

DID YOU KNOW? Choosing to forgive helps to improve your physical health.[4]

WOUND HEALING

The process the body uses to repair the skin and other body tissue after having experienced trauma. Wound healing includes blood clotting, inflammation, the restoration of the structure and function of the diseased tissues, scarring and the healing of bones.

Foods	Health Benefits	How To Use	Composition (based on Cup)
Kiwifruit	Kiwifruit provides a good source of vitamin C, which is essential for collagen formation and assists with proper immune function.[1] Deficiency in vitamin C leads to impaired wound healing.[2]	Kiwifruit Pineapple Smoothie: Blend 2 peeled chopped kiwifruit, 1 sliced banana, 1 cup chopped pineapple and ¾ cup nondairy milk until smooth and creamy.	Fresh Kiwifruit Carbohydrate: 28g Fat: 0 g Protein: 2 g Sodium: 10 mg Vitamin A: 318 IU Vitamin C: 136.4 mg Magnesium: 54.7 mg
Apricots	Vitamin A, which can be found in apricots, is necessary for bone formation as well as epithelial tissue that makes up the skin.[1] It also plays a role in the production of collagen.[2]	Stewed Apricots and Apples: Place 12 dried apricots and 12 dried apple rings in saucepan with 1 ½ cups orange juice, 2 teaspoons honey and ½ cup water. Simmer 15 minutes until fruit is plump.	Dried Apricots Carbohydrate: 81 g Fat: 1 g Protein: 4 g Sodium: 13 mg Vitamin A: 4,686 IU Vitamin E: 6.5 mg Zinc: 0.5 mg
Butternut Squash	Butternut squash contains vitamin E, which is the major lipid soluble antioxidant in the skin.[1] Vitamin E helps to decrease inflammation and may decrease excess scar formation.[2]	Roasted Butternut: Toss butternut squash cubes with a little olive oil and garlic. Season with a little salt. Place on a baking sheet and roast in the oven at 400°F for about 30 minutes until tender and slightly brown.	Baked Butternut Squash Carbohydrate: 22 g Fat: 0 g Protein: 2 g Sodium: 8 mg Vitamin A: 22,869 IU Vitamin C: 31 mg Vitamin E: 2.6 mg
Quinoa	Quinoa provides the protein essential for every stage of wound healing. Adequate protein is needed for the formation of collagen, new blood vessels, and the production of new tissue.[3]	Quinoa Butternut Risotto: Sauté 1 diced onion and 2 cloves minced garlic in a little olive oil, add 3 cups shredded spinach, and cook until wilted. Stir in 1 cup roasted butternut cubes and 3 cups cooked quinoa. Add salt to taste.	Cooked Quinoa Carbohydrate: 39 g Fat: 4 g Protein: 8 g Sodium: 13 mg Vitamin A: 9.3 IU Arginine: 629 mg Zinc: 2 mg
Kidney Beans	Zinc found in kidney beans is needed in all stages of wound healing. Deficiency results in decreased immunity and a greater susceptibility to infection, impaired collagen production and tissue formation.[3]	Red Kidney Bean Dip: Sauté 1 diced onion and 3 cloves minced garlic in a little olive oil. Add 3 cups cooked kidney beans, 1 tablespoon tomato paste, ½ teaspoon ground cumin, ½ teaspoon ground coriander and juice from 1 lime. Remove from heat. Process. Leave slightly chunky.	Cooked Kidney Beans Carbohydrate: 40 g Fat: 1 g Protein: 15 g Sodium: 2 mg Vitamin C: 2.1 mg Arginine: 950 mg Zinc: 1.9 mg
Peanuts	Consumption of peanuts provides the body with arginine, a precursor for nitric oxide, which plays a vital role in the inflammatory process of the healing of wounds.[3]	Broccoli Pasta with Peanut Sauce: Whisk together 3 tablespoons sugar-free peanut butter, 2 tablespoons soy sauce ¾ tablespoon lime juice, 1 tablespoon hot water and 1 clove minced garlic. Stir into 4 cups hot cooked pasta. Stir in 2 cups freshly cooked broccoli florets.	Dry Roasted Peanuts Carbohydrate: 31 g Fat: 73 g Protein: 35g Sodium: 9 mg Arginine: 4,134 mg Magnesium: 257 mg Zinc: 4.8 mg

ENCOURAGEMENT: He healeth the broken in heart and bindeth up their wounds (Psalm 147:3).

Recipe Index By Ingredient

Bibliography

FOODS THAT OPTIMIZE HEALTH

1. Liu, R.H. "Health-Promoting Components of Fruits and Vegetables in the Diet." Advances in Nutrition: An International Review Journal 4 (2013): 384S-392S, Web. 6 June 2016.
2. Van Duyn, M.S. "Overview of the Health Benefits of Fruit and Vegetable Consumption for the Dietetics Professional." Journal of the American Dietary Association 100 (2000): 1511-1521, Web. June 6, 2016.
3. "Dietary Guidelines and My Plate." Choose My Plate. United States Department of Agriculture. Feb. 5, 2016. Web. June 6, 2016.
4. "The Vegetarian Food Pyramid." Loma Linda University School of Public Health, Department of Nutrition. Loma Linda University Libraries. March 2, 2016. Web. January 10, 2017.
5. "Nutrients and Health Benefits." Choose My Plate. United States Department of Agriculture. June 2, 2015. Web. June 6, 2016.
6. "Dietary Fiber: Essential for a Healthy Diet." Mayo Clinic. Mayo Foundation for Medical Education and Research. September 22, 2015. Web. June 6, 2016.
7. "Nuts and Your Health: Eating Nuts for Heart Health." Mayo Clinic. Mayo Foundation for Medical Education and Research. February 19, 2014. Web. June 6, 2016.
8. Karlson, Micaela "et al." "Seeds—Health Benefits, Barriers to Incorporation, and Strategies for Practitioners in Supporting Consumption Among Consumers." Nutrition Today 51:1 (2016) 50-59. Web. June 6, 2016.
9. Pamplona-Roger, George, "Oils and Margarine." Encyclopedia of Foods and Their Healing Power 1. (Madrid, Spain: Safeliz, 2002), 112-119.
10. White, E.G., Christ Object Lessons. (Hagerstown, MD: Review and Herald, 2002).
11. Diehl, Hans and Aileen Ludington, "From Sugar Highs to Sugar Blues," Health Power: Healthy by Choice, Not by Chance! (Hagerstown, MD: Review and Herald, 2011), 94-97.
12. Griffin, Vicki and Gina Griffin-Stearman. "Sugar," Lifestyle Matters Guilt-free Gourmet, vol. 3. (Lansing, MI: Lifestyle Matters, 2004). 135-140. January 10, 2017.

TEN GUIDELINES FOR GOOD HEALTH

1. White, E. G., The Ministry of Healing (Nampa, ID: Pacific Press Publishing, 2003).
2. White, E. G., Counsels on Health (Nampa, ID: Pacific Press, 2002).
3. White, E. G., Healthful Living (Payson, AZ: Leaves-of-Autumn Books. 1987).
4. White, E. G., Medical Ministry (Nampa, ID: Pacific Press. 2003).
5. White, E. G., Counsels on Stewardship (Hagerstown, MD: Review and Herald Publishing Association. 2000).

ACNE

1. Ferrell, Vance and Harold Cherne. "Acne," Natural Remedies Encyclopedia (Altamont, TN: Harvestime Books. 2008), 254-256.
2. Pamplona-Roger, George, "Foods for the Skin," Encyclopedia of Foods and Their Healing Power 2 (Madrid, Spain: Safeliz, 2002), 331.

ADHD

1. "Attention Deficit Hyperactivity Disorder." University of Maryland Medical Center. University of Maryland Medical Center. March 23, 2015. Web. August 15, 2016.
2. Konikowska, K., et al. "The Influence of Components of Diet on the Symptoms of ADHD in Children." National Institute of Hygiene 63:2 (2012): 127-134. PMC. Web. August 15, 2016.
3. "Diet and Attention Deficit Hyperactivity Disorder." Harvard Health Publications, Harvard Medical School. Harvard University. June 2009. Web. August 15, 2016.
4. Zhou, Fankun, et al. "Dietary, Nutrients Patterns and Blood Essential Elements in Chinese Children with ADHD." Nutrients 8:6 (2016): 352 PMC. Web. August 15, 2016.
5. White, E. G., The Faith I Live By (Hagerstown, MD: Review and Herald, 2000).

ALZHEIMER'S DISEASE

1. Di Fiore, Nancy. "Diet May Help Prevent Alzheimer's." Rush University Medical Center. Rush University, n.d. Web. June 9, 2016.
2. Pamplona-Roger, George, "Foods for the Nervous System," Encyclopedia of Foods and Their Healing Power 2 (Madrid, Spain: Safeliz, 2002), 34.
3. Shan, Liang and Hong-Fang Ji. "Associations Between Homocysteine, Folic Acid, Vitamin B12 and Alzheimer's Disease: Insights from Meta-Analyses." Journal of Alzheimer's Disease 46:3 (2015): 777-790. IOS Press Content Library. Web. June 9, 2016.
4. Lesniak, Wojciech, et al. "Concurrent Quantification of Tryptophan and Its Major Metabolites." Analytical Biochemistry 443:2 (2015): 222-231. PubMed. Web. June 9, 2016.
5. Ferrell, Vance and Harold Cherne, "Alzheimers' Disease," Natural Remedies Encyclopedia (Altamont, TN: Harvestime, 2008), 485-487.
6. Volpe, Stella. "Magnesium in Disease Prevention and Overall Health." Advances in Nutrition 4 (2013): 378S-383S. Advances in Nutrition. Web. June 13, 2016.
7. Petersen, Ronald. "Alzheimer's Disease: Can Exercise Prevent Memory Loss?" Mayo Clinic. Mayo Foundation for Medical Education and Research. October 22, 2014. Web. June 14, 2016.

ANEMIA

1. Ferrell, Vance, and Harold Cherne, "Anemia," Natural Remedies Encyclopedia (Altamont, TN: Harvestime, 2008), 440-442.
2. "Iron Deficiency Anemia." Mayo Clinic. Mayo Foundation for Medical Education and Research. January 24, 2014. Web. June 13, 2016.
3. Santoyo-Sanchez A., et al. "Dietary Recommendations in Patients with Deficiency Anemia." Revista Medica Del Hospital General De Mexico. 78:3 (2015) 144-150. Science Direct. Web June 13, 2016.
4. White, E. G., "Prayer Power," Prayer (Nampa, ID: Pacific Press, 2002) 83.

ANXIETY

1. Holland, Earle. "Omega-3 Reduces Anxiety and Inflammation in Healthy Students." Research News. Ohio State University. July 12, 2011. Web. June 14, 2016.
2. Vogelzangs, N. "Anxiety Disorders and Inflammation in a Large Adult Cohort." Translational Psychiatry 3 (2013) n.pag. Translational Psychiatry. Web. June 14, 2016.
3. Pamplona-Roger, George, "Foods for the Nervous System," Encyclopedia of Foods and Their Healing Power 2 (Madrid, Spain: Safeliz. 2002), 34.
4. Ehrlich, Steven. "Phosphorus." University of Maryland Medical Center. University of Maryland Medical Center. August 5, 2015. Web. June 14, 2016.
5. Hall-Flavin, Daniel. "Generalized Anxiety Disorder." Mayo Clinic. Mayo Foundation for Medical Education and Research. March 6, 2014. Web. June 14, 2016.
6. Bjelland, Ingvar. "Choline in Anxiety and Depression: The Hordaland Health Study1,2,3." The American Journal of Clinical Nutrition 90:4 (2009) 1056-1060. The American Journal of Clinical Nutrition. Web. June 14, 2016.
7. Russo, A. "Decreased Zinc and Increased Copper in Individuals with Anxiety." Nutrition and Metabolic Insights 4 (2011) 1-5. PMC. Web. June 14, 2016.
8. White, E. G., The Ministry of Healing (Nampa, ID: Pacific Press, 2003) 241.

ARTERIOSCLEROSIS

1. Ehrlich, Steven. "Vitamin C (Ascorbic Acid)." University of Maryland

1. Medical Center. University of Maryland Medical System. July 16, 2013. Web. June 20, 2016.
2. Erhlich, Steven. "Pomegranate." University of Maryland Medical Center. University of Maryland Medical System. February 2, 2016. Web. June 20, 2016.
3. "Dietary Guidelines to Treat and Prevent Atherosclerosis." Physicians Committee for Responsible Medicine. The Physicians Committee. n.d. Web. June 20, 2016.
4. Hruby, Adela, et al. "Magnesium Intake Is Inversely Associated With Coronary Artery Calcification." Journal of the American College of Cardiovascular Imaging 7:1 (2014): 59-69. JACC Cardiovasular Imaging. Web. June 20, 2016.
5. "Atherosclerosis (Holistic)." University of Michigan Health System. Regents of the University of Michigan. June 8, 2015. Web. June 20, 2016.
6. Ehrlich, Steven. "Atherosclerosis." University of Maryland Medical Center. University of Maryland Medical System. March 25, 2015. Web. June 20, 2016.

ARTHRITIS

1. De Lencastre Novaes, Letícia. "Stability, Purification and Applications of Bromelain: A Review." Biotechnology Progress 32:1 (2015) 5-13. Wiley Online Library. Web. June 15, 2016.
2. Dreyfuss, John. "The RA Diet: Anti-inflammatory and Nutritious." Cleveland Clinic Wellness. Cleveland Clinic. August 12, 2009. Web. June 15, 2016
3. "Nutrition Education Curriculum Section Eight: Nutrition and Arthritis." Physicians Committee for Responsible Medicine. The Physicians Committee. n.d. Web. June 15, 2016.
4. "Ginger." Arthritis Foundation. The Arthritis Foundation. n.d. Web. June 15, 2016.
5. "8 Food Ingredients That Can Cause Inflammation." Arthritis Foundation. The Arthritis Foundation. n.d. Web. June 15, 2016.

ASTHMA

1. Li, James. "Asthma: Can Foods I Eat Affect My Asthma Symptoms?" Mayo Clinic. Mayo Foundation for Medical Education and Research. March 19, 2015. Web. June 16, 2016.
2. Erlich, Steven. "Asthma." The University of Maryland Medical Center. The University of Maryland Medical Center. August 6, 2015. Web. June 16, 2016.
3. Mlcek, Jiri. "Quercetin and its Anti-Allergic Immune Response." Molecules 21:5 (2016) n.pag. Molecules. Web. June 16, 2016.
4. Gilliland, Frank. "Dietary Magnesium, Potassium, Sodium, and Children's Lung Function." American Journal of Epidemiology 155:2 (2002) 125-131. American Journal of Epidemiology. Web. June 16, 2016.
5. White, E. G., Prayer (Nampa, ID: Pacific Press Publishing. 2002) 83.

BRONCHITIS

1. Pamplona-Roger, George, "The Respiratory System," Encyclopedia of Foods and Their Healing Power 2 (Madrid, Spain. Safeliz, 2002), 139.
2. Drake, Victoria. "Immunity." Linus Pauling Institute. Oregon State University. August 2010. Web. June 20, 2016.
3. "Foods That Fight Inflammation." Harvard Health Publications, Harvard Medical School. Harvard University. July 2014. Web. June 20, 2016.
4. White, E. G., The Ministry of Healing (Nampa, ID: Pacific Press, 2003) 272.

CANCER

1. ACIR's Foods That Fight Cancer: Blueberries." American Institute for Cancer Research. American Institute for Cancer Research. December 4, 2012. Web. June 21, 2016.
2. "ACIR's Foods That Fight Cancer: Broccoli & Cruciferous Vegetables." American Institute for Cancer Research. American Institute for Cancer Research. May 17, 2013. Web. June 21, 2016.
3. "How Carotenoids Help Protect Against Cancer." Physicians Committee for Responsible Medicine. The Physicians Committee. n.d. Web. June 21, 2016.
4. "Foods for Cancer Prevention." Physicians Committee for Responsible Medicine. The Physicians Committee. n.d. Web. June 21, 2016.
5. "Garlic." Memorial Sloan Kettering Cancer Center. Memorial Sloan Kettering Cancer Center. May 20, 2016. Web. June 21, 2016.
6. "Can Turmeric Prevent or Treat Cancer?" Cancer Research UK. Cancer Research UK. August 6, 2015. Web. June 21, 2016.
7. Ravindran, Jayaraj, et al. "Curcumin and Cancer Cells: How Many Ways Can Curry Kill Tumor Cells Selectively?" American Association of Pharmaceutical Scientists Journal 11:3 (2009) 495-510. PMC. Web. June 21, 2016.
8. White, E. G., The Ministry of Healing (Nampa, ID: Pacific Press, 2003) 72.

CANDIDIASIS

1. Pamplona-Roger, George, "Foods for Infection." Encyclopedia of Foods and Their Healing Power 2 (Madrid, Spain: Safeliz, 2002), 350-351, 354.
2. "Candidiasis." University of Maryland Medical Center. University of Maryland Medical Center. December 19, 2015. Web. January 3, 2017.
3. Ferrell, Vance, and Harold Cherne, "Candidiasis," Natural Remedies Encyclopedia (Altamont, TN: Harvestime, 2008), 215-216.
4. Diehl, Hans, and Aileen Ludington, "Kiss of the Sun," Health Power (Hagerstown, MD: Review and Herald Publishing Association, 2011), 194-197.

CANKER SORES

1. Yasui, K, et al. "The Effect of Ascorbate on Minor Recurrent Aphthous Stomatitis." Acta Paediatrica 99 (2010): 442-442. CINAHL. Web. June 22, 2016.
2. Akintoye, Sunday, and Martin Greenberg. "Recurrent Aphthous Stomatitis." Dental Clinics of North America 58:2 (2014): 281-297. PMC. Web. June 22, 2016.
3. Kahn, Nabiha, et al. "Haematological Parameters and Recurrent Aphthous Stomatitis." Journal of the College of Physicians and Surgeons Pakistan 23:2 (2013): 124-127. PMC. Web. June 22, 2016.
4. Bao, Zhe-Xuan, et al. "Serum Zinc Levels in 386 Patients with Oral Mucosal Diseases: A Preliminary Study." Medicina Oral, Patología Oral y Cirugía Bucal 21:3 (2016): 335-340. PMC. Web. June 22, 2016.
5. Kozlak, Scott, et al. "Reduced Dietary Intake of Vitamin B12 and Folate in Patients with Recurrent Aphthous Stomatitis. Journal of Oral Pathology and Medicine 39:5 (2010): 420-423. PMC. Web. June 22, 2016.
6. Masri, Omar, et al. "Role of Vitamins in Gastrointestinal Diseases." World Journal of Gastroenterology 21:17 ((2015): 5191-5209. PMC. Web. June 22, 2016.
7. Ferrell, Vance, and Harold Cherne, "Canker Sores," Natural Remedies Encyclopedia (Altamont, TN: Harvestime, 2008), 249-250.

CARDIOVASCULAR DISEASE

1. Dohadwala, Mustali, and Joseph Vita. "Grapes and Cardiovascular Disease." The Journal of Nutrition 139:9 (2009): 1788S-1793S. PMC. Web. July 26, 2016.
2. Pamplona-Roger, George, "Foods for the Heart" Encyclopedia of Foods and Their Healing Power 2, (Madrid, Spain: Safeliz, 2002), 52-58.
3. "Heart Disease." Mayo Clinic. Mayo Foundation for Medical Education and Research. February 19, 2014. Web. July 26, 2016.
4. Threapleton, Diane, et al. "Dietary Fibre Intake and the Risk of Cardiovascular Disease: Systematic Review and Meta-analysis." BMJ 347 (2013): n.p. BMJ. Web. July 26, 2016.
5. Ferrell, Vance, and Harold Cherne, "Heart Problems," Natural Remedies Encyclopedia (Altamont, TN: Harvestime, 2008), 420-446.

CELIAC DISEASE

1. Wierdsma, Nicolette, et al. "Vitamin and Mineral Deficiencies Are Highly Prevalent in Newly Diagnosed Celiac Disease patients." Nutrients 5:10 (2013): 3975-3992. PMC. Web. September 13, 2016.
2. Tidy, Colin. "Vitamin A Deficiency." Patient: Trusted Medical Information and Support. EMIS Group. August 5, 2015. Web. September 13, 2016.
3. Hadithi, Muhammed, et al. "Effect of B Vitamin Supplementation on Plasma Homocysteine Levels in Celiac Disease." World Journal of Gastroenterology 15:8 (2009): 955-960. PMC. Web. September 13, 2016.
4. "Vitamin B6." University of Michigan Health System. Regents of the University of Michigan. June 4, 2015. Web. September 13, 2016.
5. "What People With Celiac Disease Need to Know About Osteoporosis." NIH Osteoporosis and Related Bone Diseases National Resource Center. National Institutes of Health. April 2016. Web. September 13, 2016.
6. Newson, Louise "Folate Deficiency." Patient: Trusted Medical Information and Support. EMIS Group. October 6, 2013. Web. September 13, 2016

CELLULITIS

1. Pamplona-Roger, George, "Foods for the Skin," *Encyclopedia of Foods and Their Healing Power 2* (Madrid, Spain: Safeliz, 2002), 332.
2. "Cellulitis." University of Maryland Medical Center. University of Maryland Medical Center. May 26, 2014. Web. December 7, 2016.
3. "101 Health and Wellness Tips for College Students." Rutgers. Rutgers The State University of New Jersey. n.d. Web. December 7, 2016.

CHRONIC FATIGUE SYNDROME

1. Riccio, Paolo, and Rocco Rossano. "Nutrition Facts in Multiple Sclerosis." ASN Neuro 7:1 (2015) n.p. PMC. Web. June 27, 2016.
2. Maric, Daniela, et al. "Multivitamin Mineral Supplementation in Patients with Chronic Fatigue Syndrome." Medical Science Monitor 20 (2014): 47-53 PMC. Web. June 27, 2016.
3. Costantini, Antonio, et al. "High Dose Thiamine Improves the Symptoms of Fibromyalgia." BMJ Case Reports (2013) n.p. . PMC. Web. June 27, 2016.
4. "Chronic Fatigue Syndrome." University of Maryland Medical Center. University of Maryland Medical Center. December 19, 2015. Web. June 27, 2016.
5. White, E. G., *Healthful Living* (Payson, AZ: Leaves-of-Autumn Books, 1987).

CIRRHOSIS

1. Pamplona-Roger, George, "Foods for the Liver and Gallbladder," *Encyclopedia of Foods and Their Healing Power 2* (Madrid, Spain: Safeliz, 2002), 171.
2. "Cirrhosis." University of Maryland Medical Center. University of Maryland Medical Center. August 22, 2015. Web. June 28, 2016.
3. Silva, Marco, et al. "Nutrition in Chronic Liver Disease." Portuguese Journal of Gastroenterology. 22:6 (2015) 268-276. Elsevier. Web. June 28, 2016.
4. Rossi, Roberta, et al. "Diagnosis and Treatment of Nutritional Deficiencies in Alcoholic Liver Disease: Overview of Available Evidence and Open Issues." Digestive and Liver Disease 47:10 (2015) 819-825. Digestive and Liver Disease. Web. June 28, 2016.
5. Osuntokun, O.T. and F.A. Olajubu. "Comparative Study of Phytochemical and Proximate Analysis of Seven Nigerian Medicinal Plants." Applied Science Research Journal 2:1 (2014) 10-26. Academia. Web. June 28, 2016.
6. Ferrell, Vance, and Harold Cherne, "Additional Healing Principles," *Natural Remedies Encyclopedia* (Altamont, TN: Harvestime, 2008). 26-28.

COMMON COLD

1. Kirkpatrick, Kristin. "Eat These Foods to Boost Your Immune System." Cleveland Clinic. January 15, 2015. Web. June 28, 2016.
2. "Vitamin C." Linus Pauling Institute Micronutrient Information Center. Oregon State University. January 14, 2014. Web. June 28, 2016.
3. "Selenium." University of Maryland Medical Center. University of Maryland Medical Center. October 19, 2015. Web. June 28, 2016.
4. Pamplona-Roger, George, "Foods for Infections," *Encyclopedia of Foods and Their Healing Power 2* (Madrid, Spain: Safeliz, 2002), 352.

CONSTIPATION

1. Xinias, I and A. Mavroudi. "Constipation in Childhood. An Update on Evaluation and Management." Hippokratia 19:1 (2015) 11-19. PMC. Web. June 29, 2016.
2. Chang, Chun-Chao, et al. "Kiwifruit Improves Bowel Function in Patients with Irritable Bowel Syndrome with Constipation." Asia Pacific Journal of Clinical Nutrition 19:4 (2010) 451-457. PMC. Web. June 29, 2016.
3. Lever, E, et al. "Systematic Review: The Effect of Prunes on Gastrointestinal Function." Alimentary Pharmacology and Therapeutics 40 (2014) 750-758. Wiley Online Library. Web. June 29, 2016.
4. Ferrell, Vance, and Harold Cherne, "Constipation," *Natural Remedies Encyclopedia* (Altamont, TN: Harvestime, 2008), 367-368.
5. 5. Lucas, G. "Dietary Fibre and Childhood Constipation." Sri Lanka Journal of Child Health 43:4 (2014) 191-192. Web. June 29, 2016.
6. "Constipation." Mayo Clinic. The Mayo Foundation for Medical Education and Research. April 31, 2013. Web. June 29, 2016.
7. Gutte, Krishna, et al. "Bioactive Components of Flaxseed and Its Health

Benefits." International Journal of Pharmaceutical Sciences Review and Research 31:1 (2014) 42-51. Research Gate. Web. June 29, 2016.

COPD

1. Keranis, E, et al. "Impact of Dietary Shift to Higher-Antioxidant Foods in COPD: A Randomized Trial." European Respiratory Journal 36:4 (2010) 774-780. European Respiratory Society. Web. June 29, 2016.
2. "The Slim Skinny Reference Guide." COPD Foundation. COPD Foundation. n.d. Web. June 29, 2016.
3. Berthon, Bronwyn, and Lisa Wood. "Nutrition and Respiratory Health." Nutrients 7:3 (2015) 1618-1643. PMC. Web. June 29, 2016.

CROHN'S DISEASE

1. "Chron's Disease." University of Maryland Medical Center. University of Maryland Medical Center. March 25, 2015. Web. June 22, 2016.
2. (2012): 164-172. CINAHL. Web. June 22, 2016.
3. "Chron's Disease." University of Maryland Medical Center. University of Maryland Medical Center. March 25, 2015. Web. June 22, 2016.
4. "Glutamine." University of Maryland Medical Center. University of Maryland Medical Center. August 5, 2015. Web. June 22, 2016.
5. White, E. G., *Counsels on Diet and Foods* (Takoma Park, MD: Review and Herald Publishing Association, 2001).

DEPRESSION

1. Kaner, Gülsah, et al. "Evaluation of Nutritional Status of Patients with Depression." Biomed Research International (2015): n.p. PMC. Web. June 30, 2016.
2. Du, Jing, et al. "The Role of Nutrients in Protecting Mitochondrial Function and Neurotransmitter Signaling: Implications for the Treatment of Depression, PTSD, and Suicidal Behaviors." Critical Reviews in Food Science and Nutrition (2016): n.p. PMC. Web. June 30, 2016.
3. Ferrell, Vance, and Harold Cherne, "Depression," *Natural Remedies Encyclopedia* (Altamont, TN: Harvestime, 2008), 494-495.

DIABETES

1. Craig, Winston. "Managing Diabetes with a Healthful Lifestyle." The Journal of Health and Healing 29:3 (2011): 6-9.
2. Ferrell, Vance, and Harold Cherne, "Diabetes," *Natural Remedies Encyclopedia* (Altamont, TN: Harvestime, 2008), 547-549.
3. Jamalan, Mostafa, et al. "Effect of Ascorbic Acid and Alpha-Tocopherol Supplementations on Serum Leptin, Tumor Necrosis Factor Alpha, and Serum amyloid A Levels in Individuals with Type 2 Diabetes Mellitus." Avicenna Journal of Phytomedicine 5:6 (2015): 531-539. PMC. Web. July 5, 2016.
4. Pamplona-Roger, George, "Foods for Metabolism," *Encyclopedia of Foods and Their Healing Power 2* (Madrid, Spain: Safeliz, 2002), 288-289.
5. Baldwin, Bernell. "Nutritional Guidelines for Diabetics." The Journal of Health and Healing 29:3 (2011): 10-11. Web. July 5, 2016.
6. Messina, Virginia. "Nutritional and Health Benefits of Dried Beans." The American Journal of Clinical Nutrition 100 (2014) 437S-442S. The American Journal of Clinical Nutrition. Web. July 5, 2016.

DIARRHEA

1. "Magnesium." National Institutes of Health. U.S. Department of Health and Human Services. February 11, 2016. Web. July 5, 2016.
2. Pamplona-Roger, George, "Foods for the Intestine," *Encyclopedia of Foods and Their Healing Power 2* (Madrid, Spain: Safeliz, 2002), 213-214.
3. "Diarrhea." University of Maryland Medical Center. University of Maryland Medical Center. April 1, 2016. Web. July 5, 2016.
4. White, E. G., *The Desire of Ages* (Coldwater, MI: Remnant Publications, 2013), 822.

DIVERTICULAR DISEASE

1. Pamplona-Roger, George, "Foods for the Intestine," *Encyclopedia of Foods and Their Healing Power 2* (Madrid, Spain: Safeliz, 2002), 217.
2. "Diverticular Disease (Diverticulosis and Diverticulitis)." Dr McDougall's Health and Medical Center. John A. McDougall. M.D. n.d. Web. December 21, 2016.
3. "Diverticular Disease." University of Maryland Medical Center. University of Maryland Medical Center. March 25, 2015. Web. December 21, 2016.

4. "Diverticular Disease and Diet." UCSF Medical Center. The Regents of the University of California. n.d. Web. December 21, 2016.

5. "Treatment for Diverticulosis and Diverticulitis." NIH. National Institutes of Health. May 2016. Web. December 21, 2016.

6. White, E. G., *Prayer* (Nampa, ID: Pacific Press Publishing Association, 2002), 58.

ECZEMA

1. "Eczema." University of Maryland Medical Center. University of Maryland Medical Center. September 29, 2015. Web. July 6, 2016.

2. "Vitamin A (Retinol)." University of Maryland Medical Center. University of Maryland Medical Center. August 5, 2015. Web. July 6, 2016.

3. Peroni, Diego, et al. "How Changes in Nutrition Have Influenced the Development of Allergic Diseases in Childhood." Italian Journal of Pediatrics 38:22 (2012) n.pag. PMC. U.S. National Library of Medicine. Web. July 6, 2016.

4. Jaffary, Fariba, et al. "Effects of Oral Vitamin E on Treatment of Atopic Dermatitis: A Randomized Controlled Trial." Journal of Research in Medical Sciences 20:11 (2015): 1053-1057. PMC. U.S. National Library of Medicine. Web. July 6, 2016.

5. Pamplona-Roger, George, "Foods for the Skin," *Encyclopedia of Foods and Their Healing Power 2* (Madrid, Spain: Safeliz, 2002), 334-335.

6. "Minerals and Skin Health." Linus Pauling Institute: Micronutrient Information Center. Oregon State University. January 2013 Web. July 6, 2016.

7. Ferrell, Vance, and Harold Cherne, "Eczema," *Natural Remedies Encyclopedia* (Altamont, TN: Harvestime, 2008), 270-272.

EPILEPSY

1. Gaby, Alan. "Natural Approaches to Epilepsy. Alternative Medicine Review 12:1 (2007): 9-24. Alternative Medicine Review. Web. January 4, 2017.

2. Pamplona-Roger, George, "Foods for the Nervous System," *Encyclopedia of Foods and Their Healing Power 2* (Madrid, Spain: Safeliz, 2002), 32.

3. White, E. G., *Christian Temperance and Bible Hygiene* (New York: Teach Services, 2005), 41.

EYE CONDITIONS

1. Pamplona-Roger, George, "Foods for the Eyes," *Encyclopedia of Foods and Their Healing Power 2* (Madrid, Spain: Safeliz, 2002), 23-24.

2. Hobbs, Ronald, and Paul Bernstein. "Nutrient Supplementation for Age-related Macular Degeneration, Cataract, and Dry Eye." Journal of Ophthalmic and Vision Research 9:4 (2014): 487-493. PMC. Web. July 12, 2016.

3. Mamatha, Bangera, et al. "Risk Factors for Nuclear and Cortical Cataracts: A Hospital Based Study." Journal of Ophthalmic and Vision Research 10:3 (2015) 243-249. PMC. Web. July 12, 2016.

4. Brignole-Baudouin, Francoise, et al. "A Multicenter, Double-Masked, Randomized, Controlled Trial Assessing the Effect of Oral Supplementation of Omega-3 and Omega-6 Fatty Acids on a Conjunctival Inflammatory Marker in Dry Eye Patients." Acta Ophthalmologica 89:7 (2011): e591- e597. Wiley Online Library. Web. July 12, 2016.

5. "Funny Eye Facts." Canadian Association of Optometrists. Canadian Association of Optometrists. n.d. Web. July 13, 2016.

FATIGUE

1. "3 Top Nutritional Deficiencies Fatigue Causes." Daily University Health News. University Health News. June 16, 2016. Web. July 7, 2016

2. "The Energy Diet." NHS Choices. National Health Service UK. February 21, 2015. Web. July 7, 2016.

3. "How to Beat Fatigue." Arthritis Foundation. Arthritis Foundation. n.d. Web. July 7, 2016.

FIBROMYALGIA

1. Abraham, Guy and Jorge Fletchas. "Management of Fibromyalgia: Rationale for the Use of Magnesium and Malic Acid." Journal of Nutritional and Environmental Medicine 3:1 (2009) 49-59. ResearchGate. Web. July 11, 2016.

2. Ferrell, Vance, and Harold Cherne, "Fibromyalgia," *Natural Remedies Encyclopedia* (Altamont, TN: Harvestime, 2008), 531-533.

3. "Fibromyalgia." University of Maryland Medical Center. University of Maryland Medical Center. April 1, 2016. Web. July 11, 2016.

4. Batista, E, et al. "Food Intake Assessment and Quality of Life in Women with Fibromyalgia." Revista Brasileira De Reumatologia 56:2 (2016): 105-110. ScienceDirect. Web. July 11, 2016.

5. Costantini, Antonio, et al. "High-Dose Thiamine Improves the Symptoms of Fibromyalgia." BMJ Case Reports (2013): n.p. PMC. Web. July 11, 2016.

GALLBLADDER CONDITIONS

1. Gaby, Alan. "Nutritional Approaches to the Prevention and Treatment of Gallstones." Alternative Medicine Review 14:3 (2009) 258-267. PMC. Web. July 13, 2016.

2. Pamplona-Roger, George, "Foods for the Liver and Gallbladder," *Encyclopedia of Foods and Their Healing Power 2* (Madrid, Spain: Safeliz, 2002), 173-174.

3. "Gallbladder Disease." University of Maryland Medical Center. University of Maryland Medical Center. April 1, 2016. Web. July 13, 2016.

4. Stinton, Laura, and Eldon Shaffer. "Epidemiology of Gallbladder Disease: Cholelithiasis and Cancer." Gut and Liver 6:2 (2012): 172-187. PMC. Web. July 13, 2016.

5. "Pribis, Peter and Barbara Shukitt-Hale. "Cognition: the new frontier for nuts and berries." The American Journal of Clinical Nutrition 100:1 (2014): 347S-32S. American Society for Nutrition. Web. July 14, 2016.

6. "Gallstones." Mayo Clinic. Mayo Foundation for Medical Education and Research. July 25, 2013. Web. July 14, 2016.

GASTRITIS

1. Aditi, Anupam and David Graham. "Vitamin C, Gastritis, and Gastric Disease: A Historical Review and Update." Digestive Diseases and Sciences. 57:10 (2012): 2504-2515. PMC. Web. September 13, 2016.

2. Pamplona-Roger, George, "Foods for the Stomach," *Encyclopedia of Foods and Their Healing Power 2* (Madrid, Spain: Safeliz, 2002), 184-185.

3. Clifford, Tom, et al. "The Potential Benefits of Red Beetroot Supplementation in Health and Disease." Nutrients 7:4 (2015): 2801-2822. PMC. Web. September 13, 2016.

4. "4 Causes of Gastritis That You Can Treat on Your Own." Health Reports. University Health News. June 14, 2016. Web. September 13, 2016.

5. Ferrell, Vance, and Harold Cherne, "Gastroenteritis." *Natural Remedies Encyclopedia*. (Altamont, TN: Harvestime, 2008), 352-353.

GERD

1. "Gastroesophageal reflux disease." University of Maryland Medical Center. University of Maryland Medical Center. September 29, 2015. Web. December 14, 2016.

2. El-Seraq, H. et al. "Dietary Intake and the Risk of Gastroesophageal Reflux Disease: A Cross Sectional Study in Volunteers." Gut 54:1 (2005): 11-17. PMC. Web. December 14, 2016.

3. Madell, Robin and Valencia Higuera. "Acid Reflux Diet and Nutrition Guide." Healthline. Healthline Media. August 18, 2016. Web. December 14, 2016.

4. Ferrell, Vance, and Harold Cherne, "Heartburn," *Natural Remedies Encyclopedia* (Altamont, TN: Harvestime, 2008), 346-347.

GOUT

1. Zhang, Yuqing, et al. "Cherry Consumption and Decreased Risk of Recurrent Gout Attacks." Arthritis and Rheumatism 64:12 (2012): 4001-4011. Wiley Online Library. Web. July 18, 2016.

2. "Gout." University of Maryland Medical Center. University of Maryland Medical Center. April 1, 2016. Web. July 18, 2016.

3. Ferrell, Vance, and Harold Cherne, "Gout," *Natural Remedies Encyclopedia* (Altamont, TN: Harvestime, 2008), 520-522.

4. "Turmeric." University of Maryland Medical Center. University of Maryland Medical Center. June 26, 2014. Web. July 18, 2016.

5. White, E.G., *The Ministry of Healing* (Nampa, ID: Pacific Press, 2003), 393.

GUM DISEASE

1. Lamoreux, Diana. "The Role of Nutrition in the Development, Maintenance, and Repair of the Periodontium: How Diet Impacts the Immune System." RDH. Penwell Corporation. June 12, 2015. Web. July 19, 2016.

2. "Periodontitis." Mayo Clinic. Mayo Foundation for Medical Education and Research. February 4, 2014. Web. July 20, 2016.

HAIR LOSS

1. Rushton, D. "Nutritional Factors and Hair Loss." Clinical and Experimental Dermatology 27:5 (2002): 396-404. Wiley Online Library. Web. July 20, 2016.
2. Pamplona-Roger, George, "Foods for the Skin," *Encyclopedia of Foods and Their Healing Power 2* (Madrid, Spain: Safeliz, 2002), 331.
3. Trost, L. et al. "The Diagnosis and Treatment of Iron Deficiency and its Potential Relationship to Hair Loss." Journal of the American Academy of Dermatology 54:5 (2006): 824-844. Elsevier. Web. July 20, 2016.
4. Beoy, Lim, et al. "Effects of Tocotrienol Supplementation on Hair Growth in Human Volunteers." Tropical Life Sciences Research 21:2 (2010): 91-99. PMC. Web. July 20, 2016.
5. Ferrell, Vance, and Harold Cherne, "The Water That Cleanses," *Natural Remedies Encyclopedia* (Altamont, TN: Harvestime, 2008), 64-67.

HEADACHES

1. "Migraine Diet: A Natural Approach to Migraines." Physicians Committee for Responsible Medicine. The Physicians Committee. n.d. Web. July 21, 2016.
2. Shaik, Munvar, and Siew Gan. "Vitamin Supplementation as Possible Prophylactic Treatment Against Migraine with Aura and Menstrual Migraine." Biomed Research International 2015 (2015): n.p. PMC. Web. July 21, 2016.
3. Sun-Edelstein, and Alexander Mauskop. "Alternative Headache Treatments: Nutraceuticals, Behavioral and Physical Treatments." Headache Currents (2011): n.p. American Headache Society. Web. July 21, 2016.
4. Cordero, Mario, et al. "Oxidative Stress Correlates with Headache Symptoms in Fibromyalgia: Coenzyme Q10 Effect on Clinical Improvement." PLOS|ONE 10 7:4 (2012) n.p. PMC. Web. July 21, 2016.
5. White, E. G., *The Ministry of Healing* (Nampa, ID: Pacific Press, 2003), 481.

HEARING LOSS

1. Choi, Yoon-Hyeong, et al. "Antioxidant Vitamins and Magnesium and the Risk of Hearing Loss in the US General Population." American Journal of Clinical Nutrition 99:1 (2014): 148-155. PMC. Web. July 25, 2016.
2. Khazaee, Mojtaba, et al. "Hearing Loss Protection Using Vitamins." The Scientific Journal of Rehabilitation Medicine 1:4 (2013): 42-46. Shahid Beheshti University of Medical Sciences. Web. July 25, 2016.
3. Curhan, S, et al. "Cartenoids, Vitamin A, Vitamin C, Vitamin E and Folate and Risk of Self-Reported Hearing Loss in Women." American Journal of Clinical Nutrition 102:5 (2015): 1167-1175. PMC. Web. July 25, 2016.
4. Houston, Denise, et al. "Age-related Hearing Loss, Vitamin B-12, and Folate in Elderly Women." The American Journal of Clinical Nutrition 69:3 (1999): 564-571. PMC. Web. July 25, 2016.
5. Kaya, Hakan, et al. "Vitamins A, C, and E and Selenium in the Treatment of Idiopathic Sudden Sensorinural Hearing Loss." European Archives of Oto-Rhino-Laryngology 272:5 (2015): 1119-1125. PMC. Web. July 25, 2016.

HEMORRHOIDS

1. Balch, Phyllis, *Prescription for Nutritional Healing*, 5th ed. (New York: Avery, 2010).
2. Pamplona-Roger, George, "Foods for the Intestine," *Encyclopedia of Foods and Their Healing Power 2* (Madrid, Spain: Safeliz, 2002), 206-218.
3. "Hemorrhoids." University of Maryland Medical Center. University of Maryland Medical Center. April 4, 2015. Web. July 27, 2016.
4. "Hemorrhoids." Mayo Clinic. Mayo Foundation for Medical and Educational Research. June 19, 2013. Web. July 27, 2016.
5. Lohsiriwat, Varut. "Hemorrhoids: From Basic Pathophysiology to Clinical Management." World Journal of Gastroenterology 18:17 (2012): 2009-2017. PMC. Web. July 27, 2016.

HEPATITIS

1. "Viral Hepatitis." U.S. Department of Veterans Affairs. U.S. Department of Veterans Affairs. n.d. Web. August 10, 2016.
2. Santana, R.C. et al. "Assessment of Indicators of Vitamin A Status in Non-cirrhotic Chronic Hepatitis C Patients." Brazilian Journal of Medical and Biological Research 49:1 (2016): n.p. PMC. Web. August 10, 2016.
3. "Viral Hepatitis." University of Maryland Medical Center. University of Maryland Medical Center. October 19, 2015. Web. August 10, 2016.
4. Flanagan, Judith, et al. "Role of Carnitine in Disease." Nutrition and Metabolism 7:30 (2010): n.p. PMC. Web. August 10, 2016.
5. Paracha, Usman, et al. "Oxidative Stress and Hepatitis C Virus." Virology Journal 10:251 (2013): n.p. BioMed Central Ltd. Web. August 10, 2016.
6. White, E. G., *Daughters of God* (Hagerstown, MD: Review and Herald, 1998), 185.

HIV/AIDS

1. "Diet and Nutrition." HIV InSite. University of California, San Francisco Center for HIV Information. August 3, 2011. Web. August 11, 2016.
2. "Vitamin C." National Institutes of Health Office of Dietary Supplements. U.S. Department of Health and Human Services. February 11, 2016. Web. August 11, 2016.
3. "Special Eating Needs for People Living with HIV/AIDS." Living Well With HIV/AIDS. Food and Agriculture Organization of the United Nations. n.d. Web. August 11, 2016.
4. "Selenium." National Institutes of Health Office of Dietary Supplements. U.S. Department of Health and Human Services. February 11, 2016. Web. August 11, 2016.
5. Mehta, Saurabh, and Wafaie Fawzi. "Micronutrient Supplementation as Adjunct Treatment for HIV-Infected Patients." Clinical Infectious Diseases 50:12 (2010): 1661-1663. Oxford University Press. Web. August 11, 2016.
6. "HIV/AIDS." Mayo Clinic. Mayo Foundation for Medical Education and Research. July 21, 2015. Web. August 11, 2016.
7. "Carnitine." National Institutes of Health Office of Dietary Supplements. U.S. Department of Health and Human Services. May 10, 2013. Web. August 11, 2016.
8. Diehl, Hans, and Aileen Ludington, *Health Power* (Hagerstown, MD: Review and Herald, 2011).

HYPERCHOLESTEROLEMIA

1. "11 Foods That Lower Cholesterol." Harvard Health Publications. Harvard University. August 11, 2015. Web. June 23, 2016.
2. Kris-Etherton, Penny. "Walnuts Decrease Risk of Cardiovascular Disease: A Summary of Efficacy and Biologic Mechanisms." The Journal of Nutrition 144 (204): 547S-554S. The Journal of Nutrition. Web. June 23, 2016.
3. "Cholesterol: Top Foods to Improve Your Numbers." Mayo Clinic. May Foundation for Medical Education and Research. June 12, 2015. Web. June 23, 2016.
4. Kristensen, Mette, et al. "Flaxseed Dietary Fibers Lower Cholesterol and Increase Fecal Fat Excretion, But Magnitude of Effect Depend on Food Type." Nutrition and Metabolism 9:8 (2012): n.p. BioMed Central. Web. June 23, 2016.
5. Kousalya, P, et al. "A Study on Nutritional and Phytochemicals of Five Edible Green Leafy Plants." Middle-East Journal of Scientific Research 23:12 (2015): 2828-2832. IDOSI. Web. June 23, 2016.
6. Bazzano, L, et al. "Non-soy Legume Consumption Lowers Cholesterol Levels: A Meta-analysis of Randomized Controlled Trials." Nutrition, Metabolism and Cardiovascular Diseases 21:2 (2011): 94-103. Science Direct. Web. June 23, 2016.
7. "Apples and More." University of Illinois Extension. University of Illinois. (2016) Web. June 23, 2016.

HYPERTENSION

1. Feyh, Andrew, et al. "Role of Dietary Components in Modulating Hypertension." Journal of Clinical and Experimental Cardiology 7:4 (2016): 433. PMC. Web. August 16, 2016.
2. Frisoli, Tiberio, et al. "Beyond Salt: Lifestyle Modifications and Blood Pressure." European Heart Journal 32:24 (2011): 3081-3087. Oxford University Press. Web. August 16, 2016.
3. Johns, David, et al. "Dietary Patterns, Cardiometabolic Risk Factors, and the Incidence of Cardiovascular Disease in Severe Obesity." Obesity 23:5 (2015): 1063-1070. Web. August 16, 2016.
4. Khalesi, Saman, et al. "Flaxseed Consumption May Reduce Blood Pressure: A Systematic Review and Meta-analysis of Controlled Trials." The Journal of Nutrition 145:4 (2015) 758-765. Web. August 16, 2016.

5. Clifford, Tom, et al. "The Potential Benefits of Red Beetroot Supplementation in Health and Disease." Nutrients 7:4 (2015): 2801-2822. PMC. Web. January 17, 2017.
6. White, E. G. *The Ministry of Healing* (Nampa, ID: Pacific Press, 2003).

HYPERTHYROIDISM

1. "Hyperthyroidism." University of Maryland Medical Center. University of Maryland Medical Center. March 20, 2014. Web. August 17, 2016.
2. Benvenga, Salvatore, et al. "Usefulness of L-Carnitine, A Naturally Occurring Peripheral Antagonist of Thyroid Hormone Action, in Iatrogenic Hyperthyroidism: A Randomized, Double-Blind, Placebo-Controlled Clinical Trial." The Journal of Clinical Endocrinology and Metabolism 86:8 (2011): n.p. Endocrine Society. Web. August 17, 2016.
3. "Hyperthyroidism." Mayo Clinic. Mayo Foundation for Medical Education and Research. October 28, 2015. Web. August 17, 2016.
4. Breese McCoy, Sara. "Coincidence of Remission of Postpartum Graves' Disease and Use of Omega-3 Fatty Acid Supplements." Thyroid Research 4 (2011): 16. PMC. Web. August 17, 2016.
5. "Hyperthyroidism Natural Treatment for Graves' Disease." Health Reports. University Health News. January 8, 2016. Web. August 17, 2016.
6. Pamplona-Roger, George, "Foods for Metabolism," *Encyclopedia of Foods and Their Healing Power 2* (Madrid, Spain: Safeliz, 2002), 331.
7. Lewis, Jessica. "Does Drinking Water Reduce Bloating?" Livestrong. com. Demand Media. June 15, 2015. Web. August 18, 2016.

HYPOTHYROIDISM

1. Ferrell, Vance, and Harold Cherne, "Hypothyroidism," Natural Remedies Encyclopedia (Altamont, TN: Harvestime, 2008), 549-552.
2. Pamplona-Roger, George, "Foods for Metabolism," *Encyclopedia of Foods and Their Healing Power 2* (Madrid, Spain: Safeliz, 2002), 292.
3. "Hypothyroidism." University of Maryland Medical Center. University of Maryland Medical Center. April 8, 2014. Web. August 17, 2016.
4. Ferrell, Vance, and Harold Cherne, "Flu," *Natural Remedies Encyclopedia*, (Altamont, TN: Harvestime, 2008), 226-227.

INFLUENZA

1. "Influenza." University of Maryland Medical Center. University of Maryland Medical Center. September 29, 2015. Web. August 18, 2016.
2. "Home Care Guide for Influenza." Department of Veterans Affairs. U. S. Department of Veterans Affairs. March 2006. Web. August 18, 2016.
3. "Vitamin C." Linus Pauling Institute Micronutrient Information Center. Oregon State University. January 14, 2014. Web. August 18, 2016.
4. "Eat These Foods to Boost Your Immune System." Health Essentials. Cleveland Clinic. January 15, 2015. Web. August 18, 2016.
5. Dudhatra, Ghanshyam, et al. "A Comprehensive Review of Pharmacotherapeutics of Herbal Bioenhancers." The Scientific World Journal 2012 (2012): n.p. PMC. Web. August 18, 2016.

INSOMNIA

1. "Eat to Dream: Penn Study Shows Dietary Nutrients Associated with Certain Sleep Patterns." Penn Medicine. Penn Medicine. February 6, 2013. Web. August 22, 2016.
2. "Insomnia." University of Maryland Medical Center. University of Maryland Medical Center. February 4, 2016. Web. August 22, 2016.
3. "Five Foods That Help You Sleep." Health Essentials. Cleveland Clinic. June 12, 2014. Web. August 22, 2016.
4. Portas, C, et al. "Serotonin and the Sleep/Wake Cycle: Special Emphasis on Microdialysis Studies." Progress in Neurobiology 60:1 (2000): 13-35. Science Direct. Web. August 2, 2016.
5. Abbasi, Behnood, et al. "The Effect of Magnesium Supplementation on Primary Insomnia in the elderly: A Double-Blind Placebo-Controlled Clinical Trial." Journal of Research in Medical Sciences 17:12 (2012): 1161-1169. PMC. Web. August 22, 2016.
6. "L-Tryptophan." University of Michigan Health System. Regents of the University of Michigan. May 24, 2015. Web. August 22, 2016.
7. Liu, Ann, et al. "Tart Cherry Juice Increases Sleep time in Older Adults with Insomnia." The FASEB Journal 28:1 (2014): supplement 830.9. The Federation of American Societies for Experimental Biology. Web. August 22, 2016.
8. Ferrell, Vance, and Harold Cherne, "Insomnia." *Natural Remedies Encyclopedia* (Altamont, TN: Harvestime, 2008), 448-450.

IRRITABLE BOWEL SYNDROME

1. "Irritable Bowel Syndrome." Cleveland Clinic. Cleveland Clinic. December 2, 2014. Web. August 18, 2016.
2. Pamplona-Roger, George, "Foods for the Intestine," Encyclopedia of *Foods and Their Healing Power 2* (Madrid, Spain: Safeliz, 2002), 212.
3. "Irritable Bowel Syndrome Diet." UPMC Life Changing Medicine. University of Pittsburg Medical Center. April 2011. Web. August 18, 2016.
4. Ferrell, Vance, and Harold Cherne, "Irritable Bowel Syndrome," *Natural Remedies Encyclopedia* (Altamont, TN: Harvestime, 2008), 372-373.

KIDNEY DISEASE

1. Pamplona-Roger, George, "Foods for the Urinary Tract," *Encyclopedia of Foods and Their Healing Power 2* (Madrid, Sprain: Safeliz, 2002), 242-247.
2. "Vitamins and Minerals in Kidney Disease." National Kidney Foundation. National Kidney Foundation. 2016. Web. August 22, 2016.
3. "Diet – Chronic Kidney Disease." Medline Plus. U.S. National Library of Medicine. September 22, 2015. Web. August 22, 2016.
4. White, E. G., *Counsels on Health* (Nampa, ID: Pacific Press, 2002), 565.

LUPUS

1. Klack, Karen, et al. "Diet and Nutritional Aspects in Systemic Lupus Erythematosus."Revista Brasileira de Reumatologia 52:3 (2012): 384-408. Scientific Electronic Library Online. Web. August 23. 2016.
2. "Omega-3 Fatty Acids: An Essential Contribution." Harvard T.H. Chan. Harvard University. n.d. Web. August 23, 2016.
3. Ferrell, Vance, and Harold Cherne, "Flu," *Natural Remedies Encyclopedia* (Altamont, TN: Harvestime, 2008), 226-227.

MIGRAINE

1. Shaik, Munvar Miya and Siew Hua Gan. "Vitamin Supplementation as Possible Prophylactic Treatment against Migraine with Aura and Menstrual Migraine." BioMed Research International (2015): n.p. PMC. Web. August 24, 2016.
2. "Migraine Diet: A Natural Approach to Migraines." Physicians Committee for Responsible Medicine. The Physicians Committee. n.d. Web. August 24, 2016.
3. "Magnesium." Migraine and Food. National Health Service UK (2011). Web. August 24,2016.
4. "L-Tryptophan." University of Michigan Health System. The Regents of the University of Michigan. May 24, 2015. Web. August 24, 2016.
5. Ferrell, Vance, and Harold Cherne, "Migraine," *Natural Remedies Encyclopedia* (Altamont, TN: Harvestime, 2008), 450-461.

MULTIPLE SCLEROSIS

1. Ferrell, Vance, and Harold Cherne, "Multiple Sclerosis," *Natural Remedies Encyclopedia* (Altamont, TN: Harvestime, 2008), 478-479.
2. Riccio, Paolo and Rocco Rossano. "Nutrition Facts in Multiple Sclerosis." ASN Neuro. 7:1 (2015): n.p. National Center for Biochemistry Information. Web. August 24, 2016.
3. Pamplona-Roger, George, "Foods for the Skin," *Encyclopedia of Foods and Their Healing Power 2* (Madrid, Spain: Safeliz, 2002), 39.
4. Hadgkiss, E., et al. "The Association of Diet with Quality of Life, Disability, and Relapse Rate in an International Sample of People with Multiple Sclerosis." Nutritional Neuroscience 18:3 (2015): 125-136. Taylor and Francis Group. Web. August 24, 2016.
5. White, E. G., *The Ministry of Healing* (Nampa, ID: Pacific Press, 2003), 25.

MUSCLE CRAMPS

1. Larson-Meyer, Enette, *Vegetarian Sports Nutrition* (Champaign, IL: Human Kinetics, 2007).
2. Ferrell, Vance, and Harold Cherne, "Muscle Cramps," *Natural Remedies Encyclopedia* (Altamont, TN: Harvestime, 2008), 27-29.
3. El-Hennawy, A, and S. Zaib. "A Selected Controlled Trial of Supplementary Vitamin E for Treatment of Muscle Cramps in Hemodialysis Patients." American Journal of Therapeutics 17:5 (2010): 455-459. PMC. Web. August 29, 2016.
4. Pamplona-Roger, George, "Foods for the Musculoskeletal System," *Encyclopedia of Foods and Their Healing Power 2* (Madrid, Spain: Safeliz, 2002), 318.
5. "Nocturnal Leg Cramps." Diseases and Conditions. Cleveland Clinic. October 30, 2014. Web. August 29, 2016.

6. "Magnesium in Diet." Medline Plus. U.S. National Library of Medicine. February 2, 2015. Web. August 29, 2016.

OBESITY

1. "Obesity." University of Maryland Medical Center. University of Maryland Medical Center. March 24, 2015. Web. August 25, 2016.
2. "Food and Diet." Obesity Prevention Source. Harvard T.H. Chan School of Public Health. n.d. Web. August 25, 2016.
3. Pamplona-Roger, George, "Foods for Metabolism," *Encyclopedia of Foods and Their Healing Power 2* (Madrid, Spain: Safeliz, 2002), 286-287.
4. Ferrell, Vance, and Harold Cherne, "Obesity," *Natural Remedies Encyclopedia* (Altamont, TN: Harvestime, 2008), 388-390.

OSTEOPEROSIS

1. Pizzorno, Lara. "Nothing Boring About Boron." Integrative Medicine: A Clinician's Journal 14:4 (2015): 35-48. PMC. Web. August 29, 2016.
2. "Osteoporosis." University of Maryland Medical Center. University of Maryland Medical Center. March 24, 2015. Web. August 29, 2016.
3. O'Keefe, James, et al. "Nutritional Strategies for Skeletal and Cardiovascular Health: Hard Bones, Soft Arteries, Rather Than Vice Versa." Open Heart 3:1 (2016): n.p. PMC. Web. August 29, 2016.
4. "Calcium and Vitamin D: Important at Every Age." NIH Osteoporosis and Related Bone Diseases National Resource Center. National Institute of Health. May 2015. Web. August 29, 2016.
5. Ishimi, Yoshiko. "Osteoporosis and Lifestyle." Journal of Nutritional Science and Vitaminology 61 (2015): S139-S141. Center for Academic Publications Japan. Web. August 29, 2016.
6. White, E. G., *The Faith I Live By* (Hagerstown, MD: Review and Herald, 2000), 172.

PARKINSON'S DISEASE

1. Seidl, Stacey, et al. "The Emerging Role of Nutrition in Parkinson's Disease." Frontiers in Aging Neuroscience 6:36 (2014): n.p. PMC. Web. August 30, 2016.
2. "Nutrition and Parkinson's Disease." The Parkinson's Institute. The Parkinson's Institute and Clinical Center. n.d. Web. August 30, 2016.
3. Traviss, Karol. "Nutrition and Parkinson's Disease: What Matters Most?" Parkinson's Disease Foundation. Parkinson's Disease Foundation, Inc. n.d. Web. August 30, 2016.
4. "Parkinson's disease." University of Maryland Medical Center. University of Maryland Medical Center. September 10, 2012. Web. August 30, 2016.
5. Pamplona-Roger, George, "Foods for the Nervous System," *Encyclopedia of Foods and Their Healing Power 2* (Madrid, Spain: Safeliz, 2002), 37.
6. "Folic Acid Could Suppress Parkinson's—New Study." University of Leicester. University of Leicester. Web. August 30, 2016.
7. Mohseni Mehran, S. and B. Golshani. "Simultaneous Determination of Levodopa and Carbidopa from Fava Bean, Green Peas and Green Beans by High Performance Liquid Gas Chromatography." Journal of Clinical and Diagnostic Research 7:6 (2013): 1004-1007. PMC. Web. August 30, 2016.
8. Ferrell, Vance, and Harold Cherne, "Parkinson's Disease," Natural Remedies Encyclopedia (Altamont, TN: Harvestime, 2008), 480-482.

PEPTIC ULCERS

1. Farzaei, M, et al. "Role of Dietary Polyphenols in the Management of PepticUulcer." World Journal of Gastroenterology 21:21 (2015): 6499-6517. PMC. Web. November 1, 2016.
2. Vomero, N and E. Colpo. "Nutritional Care in Peptic Ulcer." Brazilian Archives of Digestive Surgery 27.4 (2014): 298–302. PMC. Web. November 1, 2016.
3. Pamplona-Roger, George, "Foods for the Stomach," *Encyclopedia of Foods and Their Healing Power 2* (Madrid, Spain: Safeliz, 2002), 186-187.
4. "Vitamin B9 (Folic acid)." University of Maryland Medical Center. University of Maryland Medical Center. August 5, 2015. Web. November 1, 2016.

PREMENSTRUAL SYNDROME

1. Pamplona-Roger, George, "Foods for the Reproductive System," *Encyclopedia of Foods and Their Healing Power 2* (Madrid, Spain: Safeliz, 2002), 261.
2. "11 Diet Changes That Help You Fight PMS." Health Essentials. Cleveland Clinic.
3. "Calcium." Linus Pauling Institute Micronutrient Information Center. Oregon State University. August 4, 2015. Web. September 6, 2016.
4. Ferrell, Vance, and Harold Cherne, "Premenstrual Syndrome," *Natural Remedies Encyclopedia* (Altamont, TN: Harvestime, 2008), 643-644.
5. Chocano-Bedoya, P, et al. "Dietary Vitamin B Intake and Incident Premenstrual Syndrome." The American Journal of Clinical Nutrition 93:5 (2011): 1080-1086. PMC. Web. September 6, 2016.
6. "Using Foods Against Menstrual Pain." Physicians Committee for Responsible Medicine. The Physicians Committee. n.d. Web. September 6, 2016.

PSORIASIS

1. Solis, Marina, et al. "Nutritional Status and Food Intake of Patients with Systemic Psoriasis and Psoriatic Arthritis Associated." Einstein (São Paulo) 10:1 (2012) 44-52. Scientific Electronic Library Online Brazil. Web. September 8, 2016
2. Wolters, M. "Diet and Psoriasis: Experimental Data and Clinical Evidence." The British Journal of Dermatology 153:4 (2005): 706-714. Medscape. Web. September 8, 2016.
3. Barrea, Luigi, et al. "Environmental Risk Factors in Psoriasis: The Point of View of the Nutritionist." International Journal of Environmental Research and Public Health 13:7 (2016): 743. PMC. Web. September 8, 2016.
4. Pamplona-Roger, George, "Foods for the Skin," *Encyclopedia of Foods and Their Healing Power 2* (Madrid, Spain: Safeliz, 2002), 335.
5. "Diet and Psoriasis." National Psoriasis Foundation. National Psoriasis Foundation USA. n.d. Web. September 8, 2016.
6. "Psoriasis." University of Maryland Medical Center. University of Maryland Medical Center. December 18, 2012. Web. September 8, 2016.

RESTLESS LEGS SYNDROME

1. Patrick, Lyn. "Restless Legs Syndrome: Pathophysiology and the Role of Iron and Folate." Alternative Medicine Review 12:2 (2007): 101-112. Alternative Medicine Review. Web. December 19, 2016.
2. Sagheb, M, et al. "Efficacy of Vitamins C, E and Their Combination for Treatment of Restless Legs Syndrome in Hemodialysis Patients: A Randomized Double-Blind, Placebo-Controlled Trial." Sleep Medicine 13:5 (2012): 542-545. PMC. Web. December 19, 2016.
3. "Restless Legs Syndrome." Winchester Hospital. Lahey Health. n.d. Web. December 19, 2016.
4. "Magnesium." University of Maryland Medical Center. University of Maryland Medical Center. August 6, 2015. Web. December 19, 2016.
5. "Restless Legs Syndrome Fact Sheet." National Institute of Neurological Disorders and Stroke. NIH. n.d. Web. December 19, 2016.
6. "Causes of Restless Legs Syndrome." Neurology and Neurosurgery. Johns Hopkins Medicine. n.d. Web. December 19, 2016.
7. White, E. G., *Mind, Character, and Personality*, Volume 2 (Hagerstown, MD: Review and Herald, 2001), 596.

SHINGLES

1. "Managing Shingles Naturally." Daily University Health News. University Health News. February 16, 2016. Web. September 14, 2016.
2. "Vitamin A (Retinol)." University of Maryland Medical Center. University of Maryland Medical Center. August 5, 2015.
3. Thomas, S, et al. "Micronutrient Intake and the Risk of Herpes Zoster: A Case-Control Study." International Journal of Epidemiology 35:2 (2006): 307-314. PMC. Web. September 14, 2016.
4. "Lysine." University of Michigan Health System. Regents of the University of Michigan. June 1, 2015. Web. September 14, 2016.
5. "Shingles." National Nutrition. CA, National Nutrition. July 31, 2015. Web. September 14, 2016.

SINUSITIS

1. "Sinusitis." University of Maryland Medical Center. University of Maryland Medical Center. April 2, 2016. Web. September 22, 2016.
2. Wongvibulsin, Shannon. "A Guide to Natural Ways to Alleviate Allergy and Sinusitis Symptoms." UCLA Health. 2014. Web. September 22, 2016.
3. Dhanawat, Geetendra. "Rhinitis, sinusitis and ocular disease – 2100. New Approach to Treat Allergic Rhinitis with Vitamin E, Cod Liver Oil and Vitamin C with Use of Nasal Steroidal Spray." World Allergy Orga-

nization Journal 6: Suppl 1 (2013): 175. PMC. Web. September 22, 2016.

4. Ferrell, Vance, and Harold Cherne, "Sinus Trouble," *Natural Remedies Encyclopedia* (Altamont, TN: Harvestime, 2008), 295-296.

STRESS

1. Wongvibulsin, S. "Eat Right, Drink Well, Stress Less: Stress-Reducing Foods, Herbal Supplements and Teas." Explore Integrative Medicine. UCLA Health. 2014. Web. November 2, 2016.

2. "How to Eat Right to Reduce Stress." Physicians Committee for Responsible Medicine. The Physicians Committee. n.d. Web. November 2, 2016.

3. Pamplona-Roger, George, "Foods for the Nervous System," *Encyclopedia of Foods and Their Healing Power 2* (Madrid, Spain: Safeliz, 2002). 35.

4. "Stress." University of Maryland Medical Center. University of Maryland Medical Center. December 9, 2014. Web. November 2, 2016.

5. White, E. G., *Messages to Young People* (Hagerstown, MD: Review and Herald, 2002), 409.

STROKE

1. "Eating Well After a Stroke." Cleveland Clinic. The Cleveland Clinic Foundation. n.d. Web. December 6, 2016.

2. "Stroke." University of Maryland Medical Center. University of Maryland Medical Center. February 4, 2015. Web. December 6, 2016.

3. "Whole Grains." Heart and Stroke Foundation of Canada. Heart and Stroke Foundation of Canada. n.d. Web. December 6, 2016.

4. Corliss, Julie. "Folic Acid, a B Vitamin, Lowers Stroke Risk in People with High Blood Pressure." Harvard Health Publications. Harvard University. March 18, 2015. Web. December 6, 2016.

5. Ferrell, Vance, and Harold Cherne, "Stroke," *Natural Remedies Encyclopedia* (Altamont, TN: Harvestime, 2008), 432-433.

ULCERATIVE COLITIS

1. "Diet, Nutrition and Inflammatory Bowel Disease." Crohn's and Colitis Foundation of America. Crohn's and Colitis Foundation of America. n.d. Web. December 12, 2016.

2. Pamplona-Roger, George, "Foods for the Intestine," *Encyclopedia of Foods and Their Healing Power 2* (Madrid, Spain: Safeliz, 2002), 213-215.

3. Cunha, John. "Ulcerative Colitis Diet Plan." MedicineNet.com. MedicineNet Inc. July 6, 2016. Web. December 12, 2016.

4. Ferrell, Vance, and Harold Cherne, "Colitis," *Natural Remedies Encyclopedia* (Altamont, TN: Harvestime, 2008), 373-374.

UNDERWEIGHT

1. Collins, Sonya. "Healthy Ways to Gain Weight." WebMD. WebMD. September 23, 2015. Web. December 13, 2016.

2. Pamplona-Roger, George, "Foods for Metabolism," *Encyclopedia of Foods and Their Healing Power 2* (Madrid, Spain: Safeliz, 2002), 284.

3. Zeratsky, Katherine. "What's a Good Way to Gain Weight If You're Underweight?" Mayo Clinic. Mayo Foundation for Medical Education and Research. n.d. Web. December 13, 2016.

4. White, E. G., *Counsels on Health* (Nampa, ID: Pacific Press, 2002), 533.

URINARY TRACT INFECTION

1. "Urinary Tract Infection in Women." University of Maryland Medical Center. University of Maryland Medical Center. July 6, 2014. Web. December 13, 2016.

2. "Urinary Tract Infection." University of Maryland Medical Center University of Maryland Medical Center. September 17, 2012. Web. December 13, 2016.

3. Pamplona-Roger, George, "Foods for Infection," *Encyclopedia of Foods and Their Healing Power 2* (Madrid, Spain: Safeliz, 2002), 349.

4. Pamplona-Roger, George, "Foods for the Urinary Tract," *Encyclopedia of Foods and Their Healing Power 2* (Madrid, Spain: Safeliz, 2002), 243.

5. Ferrell, Vance, and Harold Cherne, "The Air You Breathe," *Natural Remedies Encyclopedia* (Altamont, TN: Harvestime, 2008), 31-36.

VARICOSE VEINS

1. "Varicose Veins." University of Maryland Medical Center. University of Maryland Medical Center. January 5, 2015. Web. December 15, 2016.

2. "Vitamin C (Ascorbic Acid)." University of Maryland Medical Center. University of Maryland Medical Center. July 16, 2013. Web. December 15, 2016.

3. "Varicose Veins." Mayo Clinic. Mayo Foundation for Medical Education and Research. January 22, 2016. Web. December 15, 2016.

4. "Zinc." University of Maryland Medical Center. University of Maryland Medical Center. July 16, 2016. Web. December 15, 2016.

5. Ferrell, Vance, and Harold Cherne, "Varicose Veins," *Natural Remedies Encyclopedia* (Altamont, TN: Harvestime, 2008), 438-439.

WEAK IMMUNE SYSTEM

1. "Eat These Foods to Boost Your Immune System." Health Essentials. Cleveland Clinic. January 15, 2015. Web. December 20, 2016.

2. Ströhle A, and A. Hahn. "Vitamin C and Immune Function." Medizinische Monatsschrift für Pharmazeuten 32:2 (2009): 49-54. PMC. Web. December 20, 2016.

3. "Immunity." Linus Pauling Institute Micronutrient Information Center. Oregon State University. July 2016. Web. December 20, 2016.

4. "Forgiveness: Your Health Depends on It." Healthy Aging. The Johns Hopkins University. n.d. Web. December 20, 2016.

WOUND HEALING

1. MacKay, Douglas, and Alan Miller. "Nutritional support for wound healing." Alternative Medicine Review. (2003): 359+. Academic OneFile. December 19, 2016.

2. Guo, Shujuan, and Luisa DiPietro. "Factors Affecting Wound Healing." Journal of Dental Research 89:3 (2010): 219-229. PMC. December 19, 2016.

3. Quain, Angela, and Nancy Khardori. "Nutrition in Wound Care Management: A Comprehensive Overview." Wounds 27:12 (2015): 327-335. HMP Communications LLC. December 19, 2016.

BOOKS YOU CAN TRUST!

The History of Freedom

Are you ready to dig deeper into God's word? Are you ready to discover for yourself the truth about the last days?

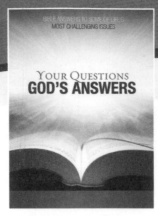

Your Questions God's Answers

God's answers from the Bible. Is there hope? What will be the signs of the end of the world, and many others.

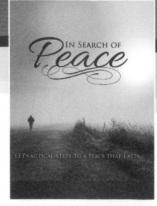

In Search of Peace

An all time best-seller, printed in over 100 languages. Find the answer to problems people are facing like how to achieve freedom from worry, guilt, and fear.

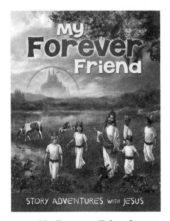

My Forever Friend

Each story from the life of Christ features beautiful artwork and text that will engage your child.

Old Testament Bible Story Adventures

The Bible is full of great stories. Your children will love to read about the faith and courage of God's followers.

New Testament Bible Story Adventures

Jesus is God, but He became a person to that all of us could learn a better way to live. Your children will discover peace and security as they read about Jesus and His love for them.

Give Them Something Better

Beautiful, Delicious, Nutritious, Fresh. That is what every meal should be and can be with this wonderful new resource.

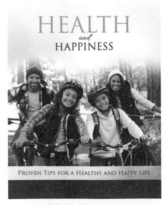

Health and Happiness

This classic how-to book will be both textbook and teacher for the class you always wanted. Learn how to enjoy living longer and find rest for the mind and healing for the body.

Habits that Heal: Habits from America's Longest Living People

A group of people in Loma Linda, California, are known as one of the world's healthiest longest living people. Discover the secret to their long, healthy lives.

FAMILY HOME CHRISTIAN BOOKS

To order visit: www.FamilyHomeChristianBooks.com
or call now: (800) 4-A-NEW-LIFE (800) 426-3954